# How to Stop Bullying in Classrooms and Schools

This book should be in th[...]se who work with kids in schools. If every tea[...]utilized just some of the strategies outlined in this book, we would truly see safer classrooms and less bullying in our schools!

Sabina Low, Wichita State University

. . . an excellent resource for helping educators, especially classroom teachers, learn about the importance of bullying remediation. This well-organized book provides an easy-to-read review of the extent of the problem, the strategies that a classroom teacher may follow to address it, and the ways to develop effective solutions.

Farzana Sultana, University of South Carolina

The premise of this guidebook for teacher educators, school professionals, and in-service and pre-service teachers is that bullying occurs because of breakdowns in relationships. The focus of the 10-point empirically researched anti-bullying program it presents is based on building and repairing relationships. Explaining how to use social architecture to erase bullying from classrooms, *How to Stop Bullying in Classrooms and Schools*:

- Translates research into easily understandable language
- Provides a step-by-step plan *and* the tools (classroom exercises, activities, practical strategies) to insure success in building classrooms where acceptance, inclusion, and respect reign
- Examines the teacher's role, classroom management, bystander intervention, friendship, peer support, empathy, incompatible activities, stopping incidents, and adult support from a relationship perspective

Part 1 builds a foundation of knowledge by describing the five Ws of bullying: who, what, when, where, and why. Facts including the definition, prevalence, myths, characteristics, and consequences are explained. Part 2 provides a thorough look at ways social architecture can be implemented in the classroom. If every teacher in every classroom learned to apply this book's principles and suggestions for encouraging positive peer relationships, minimizing opportunities for bullying, and decreasing rewards, bullying would no longer plague our schools and educators could give 100% of their attention to academics.

**Phyllis Kaufman Goodstein**, a Licensed Master of Social Work (LMSW), has counseled elementary and middle school students.

# How to Stop Bullying in Classrooms and Schools

## Using Social Architecture to Prevent, Lessen, and End Bullying

*PHYLLIS KAUFMAN GOODSTEIN, LMSW*

Routledge
Taylor & Francis Group

NEW YORK AND LONDON

First published 2013
by Routledge
711 Third Avenue, New York, NY 10017

Simultaneously published in the UK
by Routledge
2 Park Square, Milton Park, Abingdon, Oxon OX14 4RN

*Routledge is an imprint of the Taylor & Francis Group, an informa business*

*Library of Congress Cataloging in Publication Data*
Goodstein, Phyllis Kaufman.
    How to stop bullying in classrooms and schools: using
    social architecture to prevent, lessen, and end bullying/
    Phyllis Kaufman Goodstein.
        p. cm.
    Includes bibliographical references and index.
    1. Bullying in schools—Prevention.    2. Bullying—Prevention.
    3. Classroom management.    I. Title.
    LB3013.3.G66 2012
    371.78—dc23
    2012021170

ISBN: 978-0-415-63026-9 (hbk)
ISBN: 978-0-415-63027-6 (pbk)
ISBN: 978-0-203-09793-9 (ebk)

Typeset in Bembo and Gill Sans
by Florence Production Ltd, Stoodleigh, Devon

SUSTAINABLE
FORESTRY
INITIATIVE

Certified Sourcing
www.sfiprogram.org
SFI-00555
The SFI label applies to the text stock.

Printed and bound in the United States of America by
Walsworth Publishing Company, Marceline, MO.

*This book is dedicated to Arnie, Eric, and Steven*

*for all their love and support.*

# Contents

# Preface

Bullying has always been a tolerable part of human history. Society believed "boys will be boys" and "it's a rite of passage" until tragedy shattered these myths.

In 1982, three Norwegian youths between the ages of 10 and 14 bullycided (committed suicide because of bullying). In 1984 and 1985, 16 suicides were attributed to bullying in Japan. Similar deaths were recorded in the United Kingdom, Australia, Canada, and countries worldwide. Then, in 1999, 12 students and one teacher were killed in the bullying-motivated Columbine High School massacre. "We're going to kick-start a revolution" (Gibbs, Roche, Goldstein, Harrington, & Woodbury, 1999, para. 8) 18-year-old shooter Eric Harris said in a video made prior to the attack. They did. Bullets speak louder than words.

A domino effect was seen throughout the 1980s and 1990s as one country after another responded to the untimely ending of young lives with bullying research. The findings showed that bullying is not a harmless activity; rather, it can have damaging consequences. Educators responded with an assortment of prevention projects. The results have been discouraging:

- A meta-analysis of school bullying intervention studies found "The majority of outcomes evidenced no meaningful change, positive or negative" (Merrell, Gueldner, Ross, & Isava, 2008, p. 26).
- "Most studies suggest that bullying is not decreasing" (Hamarus & Kaikkonen, 2008, p. 333).
- "We have 67 bullying prevention programs none of which are working in the U.S.," said bullying researcher, expert, and professor, Dorothy L. Espelage (Espelage, 2010).

It appears that the existing bullying programs are "more likely to influence knowledge, attitudes, and self-perceptions rather than actual bullying behaviors" (Merrell et al., 2008, p. 26).

Ineffective programs make some educational institutions free-for-all playgrounds of aggression. We need to find effective solutions because of (a) the frequency and repetition of bullying, (b) the damaging and many times long lasting ramifications of this abuse, (c) the negative impact bullying has on education, and (d) the fact that antisocial behavior may lead to patterns of violence that continue over time.

Bullying can be challenged. We have seen successes in some programs, albeit small, but saving one child from the pain bullying inflicts makes the efforts worthwhile. Researchers need to isolate the elements that contributed to favorable outcomes and build on them. This author suggests that the successful parts of interventions addressed social relationships. Relationships are pivotal factors in bullying because the breakdown of relationships causes disrespect, intolerance, exclusion, and antisocial behavior.

Research confirms that bullying is "a relationship problem" (Craig & Pepler, 2003, p. 577). The distinguished Canadian researcher and professor, Debra J. Pepler, was the first person to apply the metaphors "social scaffolding" and "social architecture" to bullying (Pepler, 2006). Social scaffolding is used to teach relationship skills while social architecture occurs when adults organize children so they will have positive peer interactions while eliminating factors that can contribute to harmful experiences. Pepler created a three point plan incorporating these concepts (PREVNet, 2007a):

1. Separate those who bully from those who are bullied. While separated, teach each relationship skills. (Scaffolding)
2. Move children who are bullied from the fringes of the social ecology into the mainstream. (Social architecture)
3. Develop respectful, inclusive, and supportive climates. (Social architecture)

This approach says schools should teach more than "reading, 'riting, and 'rithmetic" (PREVNet, 2007a, p. 7). They should also focus on the three social Rs: *relationships*, *respect*, and *responsibility*. Adults have a responsibility to protect children from abuse and to teach youngsters how to assume their responsibilities to follow the three Ss: stand up, speak out, and stop bullying.

Social architecture and social scaffolding are not stand alone interventions. They complement other strategies and should be used alongside them. However, if every teacher in every classroom religiously adhered to social architecture and social scaffolding, bullying in schools would be eliminated or minimized. If relationship building skills, and inclusive, tolerant, and respectful values are taught, reinforced, and internalized, prosocial behaviors would spill over into hallways, lunchrooms, playgrounds, buses, and communities.

It is easier to prevent a problem than wrestle with a full-blown monster. "The most effective intervention program is one that never has to be implemented, thanks to the effectiveness of proactive prevention" (Roberts & Coursol, 1996, Assessment of the Magnitude section, para. 1). That is the beauty of social architecture. It does not wait for trouble. The intervention is proactive—it sets up the classroom environment before a crisis, stomping on the match before it is struck. Social architecture and social scaffolding keep youngsters safe and protect the learning environment.

This book provides a comprehensive course, teaching readers how to reorganize relationships so they promote inclusive, respectful, and bully free classrooms and schools. It takes the effective and relationship-related parts of present day interventions, adds new and unique information, and weaves them into Pepler's plan. The writing capitalizes on Pepler's work and suggestions and applies them to education, by giving educators a toolbox of free or low cost, easily accessible, and practical empirically researched strategies, exercises, successfully used teacher techniques, recommendations, and resources.

Part 1 builds a foundation of knowledge by describing the five Ws—the who, what, when, where, and why of bullying. Facts including the definition, prevalence, myths, characteristics, and consequences are explained.

Part 2 provides a thorough look at ways social architecture can be implemented in the classroom. It begins by showing how relationships affect bullying, then defines social architecture, and explains the critical role and influence of teachers. Classroom management strategies follow. The role of bystanders is emphasized. Friendship, peer support programs, empathy, and activities incompatible with bullying are next. Stopping and responding to bullying episodes are explained in detail. Parental support is also included. Websites for teachers, parents, and children, lesson plans, PowerPoint presentations, literature, short videos, anti-bullying commercials, and online games put ready-to-use information into the hands of educators.

This book is limited to social architecture in elementary and middle schools because that is where the majority of bullying occurs, although educators on any level will benefit from the information. It touches on the equally important social scaffolding; however, the teaching of relationship skills deserves a full length review by itself. It is important to note that social architecture is not a strategy solely for teachers; it should be a priority for schools, parents, the community, and society. The author does not undervalue these groups but only touches on them because the writing focuses on the classroom teacher.

The terms "bully" and "victim" are not used in this book unless they are part of a quotation. Instead of "bully," those who bully, those who aggress, those who abuse or offend are used. Instead of "victim," the person who was bullied, the person who was targeted, or the person who was abused are used. These phrases are used to separate the behavior from the child. In reality, there are no "bullies." Yes, there are misguided children who display bullying behavior. There are no "victims." Youngsters are bullied or targeted.

Using "bully" and "victim" unfairly labels and stigmatizes the recipient. It can cause children to take on the characteristics of the titles. Name tags also focus blame on the participants and ignore contextual factors behind bullying. Finally, calling youngsters "bullies" or "victims" is essentially name calling, which is bullying—the very behavior we want to extinguish.

"Abuse" is used interchangeably with "bullying" because we should recognize bullying for what it is: peer-to-peer abuse, adult-to-child abuse, child-to-adult abuse, and adult-to-adult abuse.

## Personal Acknowledgments

This book would not have been published if Naomi Silverman hadn't read and advocated for the manuscript. Thank you for your belief in it and your assistance throughout the publishing process. I also want to acknowledge Kevin Henderson, who was always available to help and did so in a prompt and professional manner.

A great big thanks, debt of gratitude, and lots of hugs to:

Andy Cueto for showing me how to use vector graphic software and for being such a great teacher.

Jessica Goldberg, who always responded to my educational questions and gave me prompt and sound information and advice.

Linda Greenzang, who always keeps her eyes out for bullying information and is an unending source of support.

Katlin O'Neill for her thoughtful responses to my educational queries, the hours she spent helping edit the manuscript, and her invaluable and respected feedback.

Debra Pitman, who found just the right words to encourage me to continue writing this book when I grew weary.

Sue and Mark Roland, who always suggest ideas to promote my bullying endeavors, offer to help and follow through, without me even asking.

Jacinth Watson for her above and beyond kindness and efforts on my behalf. You moved mountains!

The staff of the East Meadow Public Library for all their help and assistance.

George Bennet, Peggy Bismark, Gail and Jay Glantz, Irma Krassner, Pat Lanigan, Marilyn Mohsin, and Marina and Peter Urazov, because they are special.

My sister, Ellen Bennet, for all the love she showers upon me. You can't pick sisters but God gave me the very best.

My husband, Arnie, and sons, Eric and Steven, for their love and understanding as I sacrificed my time with them to research and write this book.

My parents, Laura and Bill Kaufman, who are always with me. Although they have passed I know they are looking down with smiles.

# Acknowledgments

The following publishers, websites, organizations, researchers, and authors granted permission to use their material in the book. Their kindness made it a more informative and valuable resource. I would like to thank:

BenBella Books for allowing me to use excerpts from *Please stop laughing at us* by Jodee Blanco. An example of formative consequences and Darla's story came from this book.

Jim Bryngelson from Courtesy and Respect Empower (CARE) for allowing me to use "The School Violence Continuum."

EducationWorld for allowing me to use the activity in Linda Starr's article "Bullying and diversity lesson: what's your name?" (www.educationworld.com/a_lesson/00-2/lp2061.shtml) (Simon says "Who are you?") and material from "Names can hurt you: de-myth-tifying the classroom bully". (www.educationworld.com/a_issues/issues102.shtml).

Free Spirit Publishing for allowing me to use the "Upstander Hero" and the accompanying wording from *Bystander power: now with anti-bullying action* by Phyllis Kaufman Goodstein, LMSW, and Elizabeth Verdick. Special thanks to Judy Galbraith for granting permission, Eric Braun for helping me with the process, co-author Elizabeth Verdick, and Lauren Ernst.

Friendly Schools and Families for allowing me to use examples from the "How to say 'no' to friends and still be friends" section that appears on the "I Know Bullying is Going On" page of their website (www.friendlyschools.com.au/students/bystander.php).

P.P. Huppie-Parsons, coordinator of the Violence Prevention Toolkit Project, Native Women's Association of Canada, for graciously sharing and describing the "Ball of String Fling." I adapted it to bullying (Yarn it!).

Jossey-Bass (a Wiley imprint) for allowing me to use Kenneth Shore's instructions for the toothpaste activity (Putting the Squeeze on Bullying) from the *Elementary teacher's discipline problem solver: a practical A–Z guide for managing classroom behavior problems*.

Alfie Kohn for allowing me to use his information on the dangers of competition. A more comprehensive argument against competition can be found in "The case against competition" by Alfie Kohn (www.alfiekohn.org/parenting/tcac.htm).

Debra J. Pepler and Wendy M. Craig for allowing me to use the "Developmental Continuum of Bullying: Power and Aggression" that appeared in *Making a difference in bullying*, Report #60.

Promoting Relationships and Eliminating Violence (PREVNet), Debra J. Pepler, and Wendy M. Craig for allowing me to use excerpts from *Bullying in schools: guidelines for intervention and prevention*.

Scholastic, Inc. for allowing me to use the "Musical Chairs" activity from *Help for "They won't let me play with them!"* by William Kridler from scholastic.com. Copyright © Scholastic Inc. Reprinted by permission. (Inclusive Twist to Musical Chairs.)

The Developmental Studies Center for allowing me to use *We do NOT do that here* by Kenni Smith, which originally appeared on the Developmental Studies Center™ website (www.devstu.org) on September 22, 2010. Copyright © Developmental Studies Center. Eric Schaps, referenced in the blog, is founder of the Developmental Studies Center.

The *Virginia Journal of Education* for allowing me to use excerpts from "Kindness curbs kids' name-calling" by Rebekah Saxon (Stopping the Inappropriate Use of "Retard" and "Gay").

Sharon Tracy and Quabbin Mediation (info@quabbinmediation.org) for allowing me to publish responses that can be used in various bystander situations. The responses are a part of the Training Active Bystanders (TAB) program.

# Part 1

# THE 5 WS—WHO, WHAT, WHEN, WHERE, AND WHY

# Chapter 1

# Why Should Teachers Learn About Bullying?

Teachers should learn about bullying because it has a lengthy résumé of short and long term physical, psychological, social, and academic consequences that not only affect the bullied, but those who bully, bystanders, teachers, and society. To date, there is no vaccination against the damage caused by this form of human degradation.

Teachers should learn about bullying because young minds will not focus on schoolwork if they are afraid of being bullied. Grades increase when bullying decreases (Luiselli, Putnam, Handler, & Feinberg, 2005).

Teachers should learn about bullying because many are not aware of how much bullying occurs. In one study, 71% of teachers said 15% or less of students was frequently bullied. Students said the prevalence of bullying was 28% (Bradshaw, Sawyer, & O'Brennan, 2007). In other investigations, teachers intervened in only 4% of playground and 18% of classroom bullying incidents (Atlas & Pepler, 1998; Craig & Pepler, 1997).

Teachers should learn about bullying because they have a responsibility to stop the abuse. As many as 98% of teachers questioned in a National Education Association (NEA) survey said it was "their job" to intervene when witnessing bullying (Bradshaw, Waasdorp, O'Brennan, & Gulemetova, 2011). Yet, many do not know what to look for or what to do. Respondents said they had a need for additional training in intervening with the different forms of bullying: physical (51%), verbal (49%), relational (57%), cyberbullying (74%), and sexting (71%) (Bradshaw et al., 2011). *The lack of knowledge keeps many educators at bay and they cannot be blamed.* The college curriculum for education majors does not include Bullying 101, so teachers receive little or no training on this issue. Inservice courses help but are often short and sporadic. The bullying education of teachers has been called "woefully inadequate" (P.K. Smith, 2011, p. 421).

Teachers should learn about bullying because beliefs motivate behavior. Educators who believed bullying was a normal activity were less likely to intervene (Kochenderfer-Ladd & Pelletier, 2008).

Teachers should learn about bullying because "Bullies are raised in the home, but their victims are too frequently created in the classroom" (Starr, 2009, para.1) (www.educationworld.com/a_issues/issues102.shtml).

Teachers should learn about bullying because it is the most common form of school violence and an educator's response, or lack of, facilitates or ends this dangerous activity. Ignoring or dismissing bullying may be (mis)interpreted by students as an endorsement of abuse. On the other hand, if teachers send a loud and clear message (by words, actions, and examples) that bullying will not be tolerated and enforce it, bullying will disappear. Educators have leverage and *can* make a difference. Teachers should not underestimate their potential to be powerful agents of change.

Teachers should learn about bullying because it can be the portal into a world of violence:

> Violence does not begin with gang warfare, rape, murder, and suicide. That is when society becomes afraid of violence. Instead it begins as put downs, insults, threats, harassment, and bullying, where inappropriate lessons of how to deal with others are learned and where frustration, resentment, and anger build.
>
> (Hazler, 2000, Violence Continuum section, para. 6)

Teachers should learn about bullying because some educators leave the profession because of the stress associated with school violence and discipline problems (Gonzalez, Brown, & Slate, 2008; Smith & Smith, 2006). A U.S. governmental report found that "34 percent of teachers agreed or strongly agreed that student misbehavior interfered with their teaching" (Dinkes, Kemp, Baum, & Synder, 2009, p. 44). Thirty percent of teachers participating in the NEA survey said they were bullied by students (Bradshaw et al., 2011). Stop bullying of students and bullying of teachers will follow suit.

Teachers should learn about bullying because they also bully. In one investigation, "45% of teachers admitted to having bullied a student" (Twemlow, Fonagy, Sacco, & Brethour, 2006, p. 194).

Teachers should learn about bullying because educators "can be sued personally for money damages if you witness instances of bullying and various types of harassment (based on race, national origin, gender, sexual orientation, or disability) and fail to take action to address it or report it" (Simpson, 2011, p. 1).

Teachers should learn about bullying because it is a learned behavior. Babies do not come out of the uterus bullying. If children are taught how to bully they can be taught replacement behaviors.

Teachers should learn about bullying because allowing exclusion, intolerance, disrespect, and cruelty creates a cultural norm of bullying.

Teachers should learn about bullying because complacency gives bullying air to breathe. Bullying thrives in schools where adults have a "kids will be kids" attitude (Holt, Keyes, & Koenig, 2011). Youngsters are abused every school day because bullying is tolerated. Instead, bullying should be seen as smoke pouring out of a building. It means there is a problem and immediate help is needed.

Teachers should learn about bullying because this violation of human rights is like cancer; it will keep growing and spreading unless confronted with aggressive treatment. Educators can be the chemotherapy that removes the malignant, life squeezing growth from their schools.

Teachers should learn about bullying because ignorance allows abuse to control their classrooms. Awareness and education puts educators in charge. Knowledge arms teachers with the skills and resources needed to change antisocial behavior. Obtaining a bullying education should be given the same importance as teaching reading, writing, and arithmetic.

# Chapter 2

# The Definition

## What is Bullying?

There is no universally accepted definition of bullying but most experts agree on the following three criteria:

1. *Repetition*—Bullying is most often characterized by repetition. The frequency has a cumulative effect, wearing away the recipient's sense of safety. In some instances, a single incident can be considered bullying.
2. *Intentionality*—Bullying is not accidental. It is done purposely with the aim of hurting, humiliating, demeaning, or intimidating the person being bullied.
3. *Power imbalance*—The individual who bullies possesses a real or perceived advantage that makes it difficult for the bullied person to defend him- or herself. The power differential can be age, size, social status, race, culture, finance, intelligence, numbers, strength, or verbal ability. The person bullying gains power with time, while the power of the person being bullied decreases.

These elements can be combined into a working definition of bullying:

Bullying occurs when one or more people *intentionally* and *repeatedly* try to hurt another person(s). The person or group who bullies has some type of *advantage* over the person who is targeted.

## What Bullying is Not

Bullying is always aggressive, but not all acts of aggression are bullying.

- Two friends fighting (assuming they have equality) is not bullying because there is parity.
- Horseplay, rough play, play fights, accidents, or playful teasing lack the intent to hurt and are not usually repeated.
- Impulsive actions are instinctive, single events where the person aggressing acts without thinking, thus there is no desire to harm.
- If people do not possess the cognitive ability to realize they are hurting others it is not bullying, even if all criteria are met.

## Types of Bullying

The many faces of bullying can be divided into four categories: physical, verbal, relational, and cyberbullying. Different types of bullying are found within each group, with varying levels of intensity.

Abuse can be face-to-face, private, public, or anonymous and can be done physically, verbally, with the written word or communication devices, by ignoring or excluding, through gestures, or by manipulating others. Bullying does not have to be an action. It can be the threat or fear of what might happen.

Bullying can also be classified as "direct" or "indirect." Direct bullying is overt, obvious, and done "in a person's face." Physical and verbal bullying are examples. Indirect bullying is covert, inconspicuous, and done "behind a person's back." Relational and cyberbullying fit into this group.

### Physical Bullying

Physical bullying is the most recognized form of bullying. It is the easiest type to spot and can leave visible evidence in the form of cuts and bruises. Youngsters tell us that physical bullying occurs in about one third of all bullying episodes (Coloroso, 2003). While both genders physically abuse, males use this form of bullying more often than females. It is also more common with younger children.

---

### Box 2.1: Chip Away Bullying

The damage done during physical bullying may leave visible evidence (e.g., blood, scrapes) or can leave invisible injuries when the toll is in the form of hurt feelings that are hidden deep within the body. If children were aware of the harm, the bullying might be tempered or averted. The following activity can help students realize that the consequences of bullying are real and painful, whether seen or unseen.

1.    Open a bag of potato chips.
2.    Pour the contents onto a paper plate, noting that the chips are whole.
3.    Tape eyes, ears, a nose, and mouth onto the bag to humanize it. Name this "person" (e.g., Joe).
4.    Return the potato chips to the bag. Tape it shut.
5.    The class examines Joe. Is Joe intact? (Yes.) Is Joe ripped? (No.) Are there any marks on Joe? (No.).
6.    Tell students to name types of physical bullying. The teacher slaps Joe with each example.
7.    Perform a visual inspection. Is Joe intact? (Yes.) Is Joe ripped? (No.) Are there any marks on Joe? (No.) Joe appears to be the same before and after bullying. Stress that there are no *obvious* signs of damage.
8.    Open Joe and pour the contents of the bag onto the plate. Little pieces of chips will flow from Joe. The damage was not detected because Joe's outer wrapping concealed the crushed chips, the same way human skin hides wounds beneath its surface.

Examples of physical bullying include hitting, kicking, shoving, choking, slapping, grabbing, pinching, biting, spitting, poking, touching, scratching, tripping, hair pulling, strangling, flashing private parts, forcing physical contact, sexual grabbing, knocking down books, throwing objects, restraining, blocking paths, threatening, obscene gestures, staring down, rolling eyes, putting signs on a person's back, games of salugi, pulling up clothes, pulling down pants, putting heads in toilet bowls and flushing (swirlies), locking someone in a room or locker, stalking, stealing, or damaging property.

## Verbal Bullying

As children's verbal skills increase they discover that words can be used to brighten a person's day or become weapons of destruction. As much as 70% of bullying is verbal, making it the most frequent form of abuse, and it is used by both sexes (Coloroso, 2003). Words can be whispered, spoken in a second and leave no marks, making this type of bullying difficult to identify. Children hesitate to report verbal bullying because it is hard to back up their claims. Justice is not guaranteed, even with proof, because interpretation is subjective.

Verbal bullying includes cruel comments about a person's appearance, intelligence, interests, clothes, culture, race, religion, family, speech, disability, or sexual orientation. It also includes yelling, mimicking, mocking, cursing, hurtful jokes, threatening, laughing, harassing phone calls, and whispering behind someone's back.

Adults often discount verbal bashing thinking words are harmless, but research confirms that "Sticks and stones will break my bones but names will never harm me" is a damaging myth. A middle school student said "There is another kind of violence, and that is violence by talking. It can leave you hurting more than a cut with a knife.

---

**Box 2.2: Putting the Squeeze on Bullying**

Shore describes an exercise that can curb verbal bullying.

> She [the teacher] takes out toothpaste and construction paper and tells the class that the toothpaste represents hurtful words and the construction paper the student being teased. She has a student come to the front of the class and squeeze the toothpaste onto the paper. Then she asks her to put the toothpaste back in the tube. When she is unable to do this, the teacher makes the point that just as toothpaste, once out of the tube, cannot be put back, hurtful words, once out of your mouth, cannot be taken back.
>
> (2003, p. 278)

---

It can leave you bruised inside" (National Association of Attorneys General, 2000, introductory page, para. 2).

## Relational Bullying

Relational bullying becomes a new option in the bullying arsenal during late childhood and adolescence. Second in frequency behind verbal bullying, it occurs when someone covertly manipulates the social structure in attempts to destroy a person's relationship, acceptance, or status in the group. Relational bullying is often done anonymously by someone who gets others to do their bullying and makes it appear as if there was no intention to injure. This kind of abuse relies upon social intelligence and a social network to facilitate the aggression. Girls relationally bully more than boys.

Relational aggression is achieved by spreading lies and rumors meant to ruin reputations and ultimately friendships. It includes setting an individual up to look badly, ganging up on a person, exclusion, slander, ignoring, breaking confidences, scapegoating, criticizing a person's appearance or personality, prank calls, sarcasm, pressuring others not to befriend someone, withholding friendships, and sabotaging relationships. Phrases associated with relational bullying include "You can't play with us," "Did you know that . . .," "Guess what <person> told me," and "If you are friends with her, I won't be friends with you."

Social aggression warrants the same vigilance and consequences as direct forms of bullying. Children tell researchers that psychological injuries are just as painful, if not more so, than a barrage of punches. This view is supported by the fact that school shootings and bullycides are more often connected to the social emotional forms of bullying.

Part of the reason relational bullying is so damaging is because children are breaking away from their families and developing relationships with their peer groups. What contemporaries do and say affects identities and self-esteem.

---

**Box 2.3:  Goose the Gossip**

How can children respond when they do not want to be part of gossip?

- *Speak out*—Say "Gossip is mean and hurtful. I'm not going to spread lies."
- *Be silent*—Silence sends a loud message of disapproval.
- *Do not repeat rumors*—Gossip is like a chain with many links. Refusal to repeat rumors breaks the chain.
- *Respond with positive comments*—"Steven is funny. He always makes me laugh, even when I'm sad." "Eric is a great friend. He's always there when I need him."
- *Switch topics*—Switching topics might serve as a distraction.
- *Walk away*—People cannot hear or contribute to gossip if they are not present.

---

## Cyberbullying

The twenty-first century brought new technologies and with it came an insidious type of bullying that goes under the names of cyberbullying, electronic bullying, or internet bullying.

It uses telecommunication devices such as computers, cell phones, and pagers to hurt, humiliate, or intimidate others. The cyber pool of potential targets is large: 93% of 12- to 17-year-olds go online and 75% of teens have cell phones (Lenhart, Purcell, Smith, & Zickuhr, 2010). Thirty-two percent of teen internet users report cyberbullying (Lenhart, 2007).

Cyberbullying occurs when harassing, mean, or pornographic comments, or humiliating pictures are posted on the internet through instant messages, emails, chat rooms, social media (e.g., Facebook, MySpace), and video-sharing websites (e.g., YouTube), blogs, discussion groups, message boards, gaming sites, and polling places. People who cyberbully impersonate others, trick people into sharing passwords, exclude, cyberstalk, create cruel polls, and spread personal information and confidences without permission. Happy slapping (slapping) and hopping (assaults) involve physically hurting someone while an accomplice makes a video of the scene and downloads it to the web. Nasty messages and embarrassing photographs can be forwarded from one cell phone or computer to another. The intent is to hurt and defame the person being bullied. Teenagers can list 68 unique ways to cyberbully (Aftab, n.d.).

Involvement in traditional bullying is predictive of participation in cyberbullying and vice versa (Beran & Qing, 2007; Heirman & Walrave, 2008). The more time spent on a computer, the greater the chance of being cyberbullied.

Youngsters say that cyberbullying is equal to or worse than real life bullying. Research documents the harmful effects of cyber abuse (Associated Press-MTV, 2011; Hinduja & Patchin, 2010; Smith & Slonje, 2010; Tokunaga, 2010; Wang, Nansel, & Iannotti, 2011; Willard, 2007; Ybarra, Diener-West, & Leaf, 2007).

## Box 2.4: Hidden Danger

Put shredded paper into a small box and wrap the package with attractive gift wrap. Ask the class if they want a present—the contents of the box. Most students will say "Yes!" Before opening the box, tell the class to think of the box as their computer and the present inside as a stranger they might meet online. Open the box. The children will be disappointed.

Just as students could not see behind the wrapping paper, internet users cannot see behind computer screens. They do not know who they are chatting with, regardless of how "attractive" the person sounds. The chatter might be honest or could be someone who cyberbullies. Youngsters should not reveal any personal information and never arrange offline meetings with strangers.

## Similarities and Differences between Bullying and Cyberbullying

The motivation behind traditional bullying is the intent to control, intimidate, and hurt the person being targeted. Cyberbullying shares these similarities but has many differences from its offline colleagues.

Harmful acts are repeated with traditional bullying, with the hurt and humiliation compounded by each ensuing episode. Cyberbullying does not have to reoccur because cyber messages can be long lasting. Once sent, words or pictures can remain on a cell phone or website, or in emails, blogs, or message boards forever. Damage is done each time the hurtful material is seen. Every view can be considered repetition. Contrast this to insults scrawled on a desk or wall that can be wiped clean.

Offline bullying is only witnessed by those present; cyberbullying can be seen by a worldwide audience in a very short period of time.

In one sense, a power imbalance is not necessary with cyberbullying. The anonymity of the internet prevents the recipient from knowing who is orchestrating the attack. Thus, disadvantaged people sure to lose in face-to-face matches may now be braver and more daring because their identities are masked by computer monitors. Power is derived from anonymity, and the ability to spread rumors to a global audience, and harass someone anywhere, at any time, seven days a week, 365 days a year. However, power can be equalized by pressing the "off" button. While this advice sounds simple, it is not always realistic because the internet and cell phones are central to the lives of cyber generation children. Youths socialize, live, work, gather information, and check updates (e.g., sports scores, stock market). They also learn, get help and advice, and play on these devices.

Nothing is permanently deleted from a computer and everything can be traced, but one must have the knowledge to do so or will need the services of an expert, the police, or a lawyer. However, because evidence is left on computers discovering the culprit's identity may be easier than with offline bullying.

While all kinds of bullying are cruel, cyberbullying can be harsher because visual and verbal clues are not available. These signs help the person who bullies gauge the damage done, which can moderate the nastiness of the attack. Viciousness also increases when people think they can avoid accountability.

Most bullying is against someone known, for example a peer in the class, school, or neighborhood. However, abuse on the internet marks strangers to a greater extent. Cyberbullying is also more often done one-to-one, as in emails, texts, and instant messages, although others join the "fun" in chat rooms and on websites.

While most forms of bullying are immediate, there is a time lapse with cyberbullying while the message is transmitted. Another difference is that cyberbullying is done with the written word and pictures while other forms of bullying rely on physical and verbal actions.

In traditional bullying, people who are bullied receive a reprieve in the safety of their homes. Cyberbullying breaks down the front door and strips away the only refuge an overwhelmed child may have. There is no peace because cyberbullying can occur any hour of the day or night (David-Ferdon & Hertz, 2009; Heirman & Walrave, 2008; Hinduja & Patchin, 2009; Kowalski & Limber, 2007; Kowalski, Limber, & Agatston, 2008; Smith & Slonje, 2010; Tokunaga, 2010; Willard, 2007).

Cyberbullying can be difficult for teachers to police because it often occurs outside the school. The problem can be attacked through education—teach students and parents about the dangers of cyberbullying and share safety guidelines. Children can develop and sign internet safety pledges (e.g., http://origin.www.netsmartz.org/Resources/Pledges) agreeing not to cyberbully. Most importantly, cyberbullying can be arrested if we tackle it as we would offline bullying by teaching respect, acceptance, inclusion, tolerance, and kindness.

## Teasing

Some school districts ban teasing, citing it as a harmful action. Opponents argue that teasing has many benefits and its elimination is a mistake. Both parties may be correct; the disagreement can be due to a misuse of terminology.

"Teasing" understandably gets a bad image from its "bullying" partner when the terms are used interchangeably. When separated and explored, we can see teasing in a positive light.

Teasing is good natured play where *both* parties have fun with one another. Only one side is amused during bullying. Teasing can express affection, build relationships, and strengthen bonds, while bullying rips people apart. Teasing helps, while bullying is a calculated act that hurts.

Teasing is not meant to harm the receiver, while the definition of bullying includes a clause that indicates intent to injure. Teasing can lead to bullying behavior but teasers stop if asked or when they realize the other person is hurt. Those who bully will continue to inflict pain and derive pleasure from it.

The line between teasing and bullying is crossed when teasing becomes hurtful. How can teachers and students distinguish between teasing and bullying?

- *Definition*—Learn the definitions of both words, noting the differences.
- *Context*—Are qualities that are out of the person's control, such as race, religion, appearance, disability, or sexual orientation, being attacked? Or is it more lighthearted fun about less serious topics?
- *Intent*—Is the speaker's intent to have fun or to harm?
- *Body language*—Is non verbal communication friendly or hostile?
    - *Tone of voice*—angry, demeaning, sarcastic or warm, kind, silly, laughter?
    - *Facial expression*—frowning, sneering, clenched jaw or relaxed, winking, smiling?
    - *Eyes*—rolling, staring, glaring or a playful wink, animated?
    - *Hands*—clenched fists, hands on hips, or relaxed?
- *Harm*—Is someone being hurt? (This is based on the recipient's perspective.)
- *Relationship*—Are the children involved enemies or friends? Is there a power imbalance?

---

## Box 2.5: Stopping the Inappropriate Use of "Retard" and "Gay"

The terms "retard" and "gay" are commonly heard in classrooms and hallways. Saxon shares two strategies that can successfully eliminate the harmful use of these words:

> The first is to name the behavior that the name-calling fits. For instance, recently, a student referred to his science teacher as "retarded." I simply said, "Your use of the term retarded here is hurtful to people who have handicaps or have friends and family members with handicaps. Your science teacher is not mentally retarded. Please use a term that means what you are trying to say without putting down a group of people . . ."
>
> The second strategy is to clarify the meaning of the term being used. For example, when a student refers to a book as "gay" and it is clear that he or she really means "distasteful," a good response is "I'm confused. Are you saying that the book is a homosexual?" Typically, the student responds, "No, I mean that the book is boring." The close to this exchange can be as simple as, "Please use vocabulary words that mean what you are trying to say."
>
> (2005, p. 12)

Teachers should never accept the "I was only teasing" excuse for cruel behavior. If it hurts someone, it is not teasing.

---

## Differences Between Conflict and Bullying

Those who argue that bullying is a conflict that children should handle themselves would benefit from learning the definitions of both words. Conflicts occur when there is a disagreement between two *equal* parties. Both sides have equal ability to discuss, negotiate, and arrive at an amicable solution. In these instances, children should solve problems themselves. However, bullying is an abusive behavior *devoid of equality*. The person who bullies possesses a lot of power, while the recipient has little, if any. The power gap increases with each ensuing episode of bullying. In these cases, adult intervention is *necessary*.

Conflict is usually a one time, unplanned, and spontaneous event that happens because of a difference of opinion between friends. Bullying is an ongoing, planned attack that most often occurs between acquaintances or strangers. During conflict, both parties may become upset, accept responsibility, and cooperatively work toward an agreeable resolution. The arguing usually stops if someone becomes distressed. In contrast, those who bully want to hurt and dominate, and thrive on the power it gives them. They take no responsibility, blame the people they bully and look for solutions that benefit themselves, with no regard for anyone else. Friends often resume their relationship after a conflict ends and do not suffer long term damage. The wounds from bullying can last a lifetime.

*Table 2.1* Differences between conflict and bullying

| Normal conflict | Bullying |
| --- | --- |
| Accidental | Intent to hurt |
| Occasional | Repeated |
| Both parties have equal power | Imbalance in power |
| Does not seek to control or dominate | Seeks control and domination |
| May receive support | Majority of times the bullied are not supported |
| Will stop if the other person is hurt | Will continue if the other person is hurt |
| Feels badly if the other person gets hurt | Enjoys inflicting and witnessing pain |
| Both parties are upset | Bullied person is upset; person who bullies is happy |
| No one is angry if the bullied stands up for self | Aggressor is angry if bullied person stands up for self |
| Usually one-on-one | Can be one-on-one or group |
| Usually friends | Not usually friends |
| All parties accept responsibility | Person who bullies does not accept responsibility |
| No audience | Audience |
| Can occur anywhere | Locations with minimal or no adult supervision |
| All parties seek amicable solutions | People who bully want their own way |
| Friends after the conflict | Most times not friends after the bullying ends |
| Usually no long term damage | Can cause long term damage |
| Unplanned | Person who bullies plans attack |

## Box 2.6: Scarface

Mike Maxwell used the following exercise with students.

> He would draw a smiley face . . . on a piece of paper large enough for all to see and then invite children in the class to come and tease this "person". With each negative verbal statement received, the paper face would be torn. After several such examples, children would be asked why the face was torn and they readily recognized that this represented the harm . . . caused. Mike would then ask children to try to make it up to the "smiley face" and children would spontaneously offer apologies and/or positive statements and for each Mike would tape back one of the previous tears. Once each tear was "repaired", Mike would show the face to the class and ask what was left. The children recognized readily that these were scars. The smiley face [was] then placed at the front of the classroom as a reminder to all.
>
> (Hymel, Av-Gay, & Darwich, 2009, p. 31)

If bullied students ask for help, they should *not* be told to "work it out" with the person bullying them. The power imbalance prevents them from doing so. If they had the ability to solve the problem they would not have been bullied and would not be asking for assistance. Praise these youngsters for having the courage to come forward, validate their feelings, intervene, and help in any way possible. Assistance levels the playing field.

# Chapter 3

# The Facts

## Prevalence

Bullying is a frighteningly common occurrence in children's lives and has hit epidemic proportions: 77% of all students will experience bullying some time during their years at school (Hoover, Oliver, & Hazler, 1992).

Fifteen to 25% of American school aged youngsters are bullied with some frequency and 15 to 20% say they bully others with some frequency (Centers for Disease Control and Prevention, 2010; Josephson Institute, 2011; Nansel et al., 2001; Robers et al., 2010; Strauss, 2010). The range of percentages can be attributed to researchers using different definitions, time periods, frequencies, or methodologies.

Let's put those numbers in perspective. Fifty-six million students were projected to be enrolled in kindergarten through 12th grade in 2010, according to the United States Census Bureau (U.S. Department of Commerce, 2010). Using the above statistics, *between 8 and 14 million students experience frequent bullying and 8 to 11 million children admit to bullying others with some regularity! Forty-three million pupils will be bullied during their years at school!*

## Rates and Duration

Bullying occurs twice per hour in the classroom and every seven minutes on the school playground (Atlas & Pepler, 1998; Craig & Pepler, 1997).

The abuse can continue for years once a pattern is established:

- Data from survey results released by bullying pioneer and expert Dan Olweus in 2010 showed that 16% of participating U.S. students (524,054 in grades 3 through

12) was bullied for about a year. Twenty-three percent of girls and 30% of boys said they were abused for several years (as cited in Strauss, 2010).

● Findings from an eight year longitudinal study also found persistency in bullying and being bullied:

    – Nearly all boys who were bullied at age 16 received the same treatment at age eight. Forty-eight percent of the girls who were abused at 16 were targeted eight years earlier.

    – About half the males who bullied at age 16 were aggressing at age eight. One fourth of females who hurt others at age 16 mistreated others eight years prior (Sourander, Helstela, Helenius, & Piha, 2000).

The greater the frequency, the more stable bullying becomes. "Over time being the target of harassment starts to resemble a *social role* in the group: it has consequences for how the others view the victim and for the victim's possibility to connect with peers" (Salmivalli, 2010, p. 115).

## Where Does Bullying Occur?

Bullying occurs in and away from schools; however, the majority of bullying takes place in educational institutions (Nansel, Overpeck, Haynie, Ruan, & Scheidt, 2003; Williams, Chambers, Logan, & Robinson, 1996). In a U.S. governmental investigation, 79% of students said they were bullied inside their school, 23% were abused outside on school grounds, 8% on the school bus, and 4% elsewhere (Dinkes et al., 2009).

Vaillancourt et al. (2010) found that bullying locations vary by context. For example, the playground was the most dangerous area on the elementary level, followed by the outdoor recess area, hallways, indoor recess, and classrooms. In middle school, hallways were the most perilous location, followed by the lunchroom, outdoor recess areas, classrooms, indoor recess, and the front of the school.

The bathroom, locker room, bus, front and back of the school, gym, parking lot, coat room, and cubby areas are other hazardous bullying zones.

The common denominator in almost all of these locations is inadequate or no supervision and unstructured time. Under these conditions, opportunistic children have free reign. For example, recess, playgrounds, and hallways head the list of trouble spots because there are few adults supervising large numbers of children who are constantly moving around wide expanses with few or no organized activities.

## Development of Bullying

Traditional bullying begins during pre- and elementary school, peaks in middle school, and declines in high school. Lawyer, child advocate, cyberbullying, and cybersafety expert, Parry Aftab, found that "Cyberbullying starts in 3rd and peaks in 4th grade and again in 7th–8th grade" (Aftab, n.d., p. 1).

A spike in bullying is seen during the transition from elementary to middle school (Pellegrini et al., 2010). This happens because children vie for dominant positions in the social hierarchy of the new school. Youngsters hit, threaten, exclude, and use other forms of aggression to attain the highest social status possible.

This sets a dangerous precedent because children are learning the wrong way to structure relationships. If bullying successfully drives youngsters to the social summit, they learn that aggression is a way to get what they want.

## Gender

Boys bully more and are more frequently bullied (Froschl & Gropper, 1999; Nansel et al., 2001). While females generally pick on their own gender, males are more likely to mistreat both sexes. Boys will ignore bullying more than girls, who are more likely to intervene and get adult assistance.

Males bully in more direct and observable ways, such as physical and verbal bullying, while females favor covert forms such as relational bullying (Nansel et al., 2001). Girls may be more aggressive than statistics indicate because indirect abuse is difficult to detect. Furthermore, some past research did not include relational bullying in their definition of bullying, thereby skewing conclusions.

Each gender's choice of bullying methods can be traced back to what their group values. Males congregate in large loose groups, are competitive, have non verbal bonding, and hold the physical domain in high regard. Females treasure closer, more intimate relationships where they share confidences and feelings with a small number of girls. They have more dyadic relationships, emotional supportiveness, and social skills. Thus, social isolation can effectively crush young girls, while being the object of physical attacks can wound boys. It is as if children intuitively attack the most vulnerable area to inflict the greatest pain.

## Specific Populations

Youngsters with any kind of difference have a greater risk of being maltreated. For example, 91% of lesbian, gay, bisexual, or transgendered middle school students are verbally bullied; 59% suffer physical harassment; and 39% are physically assaulted. Eighty-five percent of overweight, 76% of those who dress differently, and 63% of children with disabilities are bullied (Gay, Lesbian & Straight Education Network, 2009). Members of minority groups and those who do not blend in are other highly bullied populations.

Then again, youngsters are bullied for being short or tall, smart or challenged, silly or serious, popular or unpopular, nice or mean. Their pants can be too big or tight;

Table 3.1 Male and female bullying and bystander behaviors

| Male | Female |
| --- | --- |
| Engage in more physical bullying | Engage in more relational bullying |
| Bullying is often done in overt ways | Bullying is often done in covert ways |
| Bully boys and girls | Bully girls more often |
| More accepting of bullying | Less accepting of bullying |
| More likely to bully and be bullied | Less likely to bully and be bullied |
| More likely to ignore bullying | More likely to intervene |
| Less likely to tell an adult | More likely to tell an adult |
| Less likely to comfort a bullied person | More likely to comfort a bullied person |
| Less likely to talk about being bullied | More likely to talk about being bullied |
| More likely to be in the bully, assistant, or reinforcer roles | More likely to be in the defender and outsider roles |
| More likely to be a "bully victim" | Less likely to be a "bully victim" |

their hair can be out of style or an unpopular color; their ears can stick out or be too small; or they may wear glasses or braces. They can be new to a school, blamed for a perceived slight, or be in the wrong place at the wrong time. No one is exempt from being placed on the hit list.

# Social Reasons for Bullying

Accusations are scattered in many directions when the causes of bullying are discussed. In reality, there are multiple reasons and they vary with each individual. Understanding factors that contribute to abusive behavior can help teachers use social architecture in the most beneficial way.

## Social Hierarchy and Dominance Theory

Friendships and peer groups form when youngsters gravitate toward those who are similar to them. Hierarchies then develop because some children have more influence while others have less.

Everyone wants to be on top of the social mountain but not everyone can fit at the peak. Twenty percent reign at the crest (Haber, 2006). This elite group is composed of athletes, cheerleaders, the good looking, wealthy, "preppies," the charismatic, and those considered "cool." Twenty percent find themselves stranded at the base (Haber, 2006). The "geeks," "nerds," "druggies," "punks," "special needs," "Goths," "rejects," "weirdoes," "bad," controversial, bullied, and those with alternative lifestyles comprise the bottom layer. The remaining 60% are sandwiched in the middle (Haber, 2006).

Those at the apex have a disproportionate amount of power over the social climate of a class or school. They also have access to favored resources. Depending on the age, resources could be toys, play spaces, a spot at the "popular" table, an invitation to a party, attention, status, or a relationship with a "hot" member of the opposite sex.

Price tags are placed on group membership. Conformity is the rule. Anyone who veers from the norms, whether it is in appearance, attitude, or behavior, or does not support and follow the rulers will be socially demoted within the group or, even worse, expelled. If aggressing against others is the group norm everyone is expected to participate. Youngsters who would not ordinarily bully acquiesce to the pressures and participate.

Bullying is also used to preserve dominance. Individual members and groups oppress anyone below them because they are considered threats to the maintenance of their elevated status. Those with low status bully to increase their power, fend off, or redirect attacks.

## Power and Status

Those who aggress have a strong need for power and status. How do they attain dominance? In a qualitative study, Hamarus and Kaikkonen explained that "the perception of difference . . . is at the core of bullying" (2008, p. 336). Someone who bullies defines some difference—something that has negative connotations within the youth culture and does not fit with its ideals. It could be behavior (e.g., annoying), personality (e.g., immature), beauty (e.g., unattractive), clothing (e.g., unfashionable), illness, or race (e.g., minority). The labeled difference means the individual is unlike the others, meaning that he or she should not be in the same community. This perception of "otherness" and "strangeness" leads to an "us" and "them" view. Those who do not have the difference gain status and power, while those who do endure social punishment that begins with isolation. Even students who do not appear to be bullying contribute because they refuse to associate with anyone who has a "reputation." Fear of being bullied keeps them from objecting. "Reputations" are formed when these children are made fun of, called names, or named in stories. Communities become unified and more powerful when they silence, isolate, oppress, and abuse those with differences.

In this way, those who bully create a social order where they can exercise power, control, and dominance. They decide who is "in" and who is "out," and children's social lives dangle from their every whim.

Why do they want this power? One teacher offered an explanation. "When students do not have something in their lives that makes them feel good, I think they turn to more negative ways to feel that sense of power, like bullying, drugs, and/or gangs" (Seeley, Tombari, Bennett, & Dunkle, 2011, p. 5).

## Lack of Friendships

Youngsters who bully survey the rich roster of students enrolled in schools and zero in on friendless children. It is easier to successfully abuse people who do not have friends coming to their defense. Rejected and poorly accepted classmates are also prime targets because these selections minimize any loss of status among peers.

## Social Learning Theory

Humans learn from each other through observation, modeling, and imitation, according to Albert Bandura's social learning theory. Bandura believes aggression is not inborn; rather, antisocial behavior is learned at home, and in school, the community, and greater society.

We see social learning theory in the home when children watch their parents use aggression to solve conflicts or deal with frustration. These youngsters may internalize violence as a normal and effective way to act. Aggression portrayed in the media can reinforce this belief.

When children grab blocks from classmates they are not the only ones learning that force can get toys, so do peers who witness the event. What lessons do children learn when teachers allow bullying to continue, or even worse, abuse their students? They learn that bullying is an acceptable and approved activity.

## Homophily Hypothesis

Belonging to a peer group takes on great importance during late childhood and early adolescence. The homophily hypothesis says those with similar characteristics find each other. Children with the same behaviors (e.g., prosocial, antisocial), goals, beliefs, demographics (e.g., age, gender, ethnicity), and interests affiliate with one another.

With respect to bullying, youngsters who aggress become friendly with others who perform antisocial acts. Abuse increases when bullying counterparts fraternize because they teach, engage in, and reinforce each other's behavior. People in the same group also become more similar with time (Espelage & Swearer, 2003; Espelage, Green, & Wasserman, 2008).

## Social Contagion

The term "contagious" is most often associated with germs transmitted from person to person. However, emotions and behavior can be transferred as well. In *Handbook of social psychology: group psychology and the phenomena of interaction* social contagion is defined as "The spread of affect or behaviour from one crowd participant to another; one person serves as the stimulus for the imitative actions of another" (as cited in Marsden, 1998, The Contagion Phenomenon section, para. 8). For example, if someone yawns, nearby people do the same. Normally reserved people can become part of rowdy crowds at sporting events.

Bullying can be contagious, too. Social contagion occurs when individuals who are susceptible to social influences imitate the bullying behavior of others.

## Conformity

If the group or class norm is bullying, most children will fall in line and copy the behavior. They conform to protect status, elevate social standing, or to prevent themselves from becoming the next target. Youngsters also fall to peer pressure.

## Attraction Theory

Children are attracted to others who possess qualities that reflect independence (e.g., aggression, disobedience) when they break away from parents. As such, youngsters are drawn to dominant and aggressive peers.

## Socio-ecological Systems Theory

The socio-ecological systems theory developed by Uri Bronfenbrenner in 1979 says that people do not live in isolation. Instead, they are part of a greater world and are affected by, and affect, its environmental and social factors. If we apply this theory to bullying, abusive behavior is prevented, developed, supported, discouraged, or stopped as a result of relationships and interactions between individuals and their families, peers, teachers, schools, communities, and cultures.

Several layers in Bronfenbrenner's model can impact the bullying experiences of the individual: the microsystem, mesosystem, exosystem, and macrosystem.

- *Individual*—The individual is at the center of the system. Factors such as a lack of empathy, a need to dominate, impulsiveness, low frustration levels, negativity toward school, pro violent attitudes, and psychiatric problems can lead to bullying.
- *Microsystem*—The microsystem is the individual's immediate environment. It includes people or places with whom or where the individual has direct contact— parents, family, peers, teachers, day care centers, classrooms, schools, and neighborhoods.

  - *Family*—Authoritarian homes, punitive discipline, physical and mental abuse, exposure to aggression, disengaged families, little warmth, no empathy, lack of supervision, family problems, and sibling bullying are positively correlated with aggressive behavior.
  - *Teachers*—If teachers lack knowledge, have poor classroom management skills, and allow hierarchical classrooms, bullying will flourish. Norms that sustain bullying develop when educators are apathetic, ignore bullying, have ineffective or no interventions, and have pro bullying attitudes.
  - *Schools*—Bullying is supported when schools look the other way, have no anti-bullying policies or fail to enforce guidelines, lack supervision, use punitive discipline, and have low academic standards and poor school climates.
  - *Peers*—Bullying is endorsed when peers support abuse, have pro violent attitudes, and reward those who aggress with high social status.

- *Mesosystem*—The mesosystem forms a connection between people or places in the microsystem. For example, the relationship between the parent and teacher can affect the child. Factors associated with a parent's job can also play a role in bullying. Long hours at work mean less supervision. Low pay may cause financial pressures. Children can find themselves on the receiving end of frustrations.

- *Exosystem*—Individuals may not directly interact with structures in the exosystem but are influenced by them. For example, school board policies and staff training can discourage abusive behavior. Violence in the neighborhood can encourage antisocial acts. Community groups and the media can have anti-bullying campaigns that sensitize the public and raise awareness, or can treat bullying as if it does not exist.
- *Macrosystem*—The macrosystem includes factors that affect people: belief systems, ideology, cultural values, customs, laws, economy, ethnicity, and poverty. For example, "kids will be kids" is a cultural norm that gives consent to bullying. Some societies have social class stratification where the ruling class has power and treats lower classes like trash. Certain ethnic groups demand subservience or have "macho" attitudes. Nations can ignore violence or enact laws that deter harmful behavior.

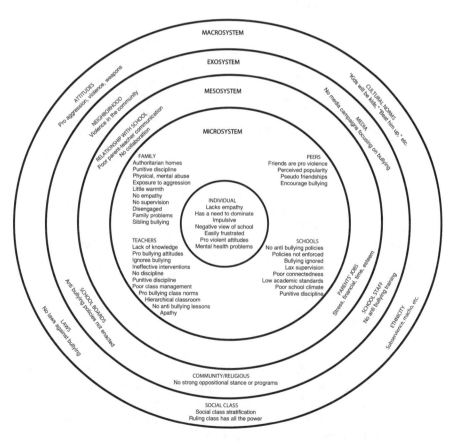

*Figure 3.1* A socio-ecological look at factors that can contribute to bullying

## *Rewards*

Human behavior is motivated. People who continually bully receive some type of "reward" or payoff. It could be that the need to control and dominate is met; power is increased; social status is raised; a reaction is achieved; or a material prize is received. The behavior is sustained when "success" is not countered with penalties.

Students who witness abuse by classmates are more likely to imitate a behavior when it is rewarded, void of negative consequences, or not admonished by peers or adults.

## *Bullying is Allowed*

When teachers and bystanders watch, ignore, or fail to act, they are giving the culprits permission to bully. Their silence is a "GO" sign. Students learn the rules of the road: Bullying is permitted, maintain speed. Those who abuse continue because they are not ticketed.

## Myths

Myths are dangerous because false information can promote antisocial behavior.

● **Bullying is a normal part of life. Accept it!**

It is true that bullying is an unfortunate part of life but there is nothing normal about harassing, humiliating, or hurting people. In fact, it is abnormal behavior and not condoned in civilized societies. If adults performed the exact bullying acts seen in schools they would be imprisoned for crimes called assault, battery, extortion, false imprisonment, larceny, robbery, hate crimes, sexual harassment, stalking, identity theft, or murder. (See Box 4.1: Yesterday It Was Called Bullying. . . .)

● **"Kids will be kids."**

"Kids will be kids" is doing what children do naturally—running, playing, talking, listening to music, and attending school. It is *not* natural to hurt others. When youngsters bully it is because they themselves were abused, were taught it is acceptable behavior, saw it modeled, or were not stopped from hurting others.

Saying "Kids will be kids" is a dismissive statement that says it is okay to systematically abuse power and hurt people. It's not! Toddlers walk on furniture, throw food, and grab other children's toys. Do parents and teachers allow them to continue because "Kids will be kids"? No. They tell their children what is right and wrong and guide them toward more appropriate conduct. Adults have to teach youngsters not to bully just as they instruct them on the proper ways to act.

- **The only person who has a problem with bullying is the person who is abused.**

"A single student who bullies can have far-reaching effects in the school and create a climate of fear and intimidation not only in his or her victims but in fellow students as well" (Bosworth, Espelage, & Simon, 1999, p. 341).

Bystanders are afraid of becoming the next to face the "firing squad," feel guilty for not intervening, and are angry they are put into situations that stir uncomfortable feelings. Children who bully encounter a myriad of problems (e.g., relationship, criminal) that follow them through life. Education is shortchanged as teachers try to quell bullying.

When we total these groups up, we find that 19%, *almost one fifth*, of the U.S. population is directly touched by bullying. In round numbers, that is 59 million people. In reality, almost every American is directly or indirectly affected because services needed to address the consequences of bullying are often picked up by taxpayers.

- **Bullied children need to stand up and fight back.**

Students who bully are almost guaranteed victory because they hold some type of advantage over the youngsters they target. That is why telling bullied children to stand up and fight back is dangerous.

Sporting promoters would not put a lightweight (135 pound limit) into the ring with a heavyweight boxer (200 or more pounds) because the 135 pounder would be grossly overmatched and at risk of injury. Does it make sense to tell a vulnerable child who probably has no experience of fighting to duel a seasoned professional who attacks at every opportunity?

What happened when targets greeted bullying with physical responses?

- The situation worsened 49% of the time (Davis & Nixon, 2010a).
- Bullied children who responded aggressively were 13 times less likely to defuse the bullying than those who employed problem solving strategies (Wilton, Craig, & Pepler, 2000).
- Children who fought back were more likely to experience long term bullying (Kochenderfer & Ladd, 1997).

The recommendation to fight back promotes violence as a legitimate means of handling problems. Climates of aggression are what schools are striving to prevent.

Another reason why bullied children should not physically fight back is because they might not know if their opponent is carrying a weapon. Even if those who bully don't have a deadly object that day, the possibility of them having a weapon another time is real. In a governmental investigation, 17% of students reported carrying a weapon at least one day within the past 30 days, with 6% bringing the weapon to school (Robers et al., 2010).

In addition, schools with zero tolerance policies give anyone who bullies *and* the student(s) who get bullied (if they physically defend themselves) detention, suspension, or expulsion. Thus, children who are abused suffer double jeopardy—a beating from bullying and punishment from the school.

- **It is wise to let children handle their own conflicts.**

As mentioned earlier, bullying is *not* a conflict.

Are those who are raped told to work the problem out with their rapists? Is it wise to tell molested children to mediate with those who violated them? No, because these are abusive situations where one person with greater power wanted to control and dominate another person who had less power. It is not rescuing when adults help; it is equalizing the power imbalance.

Furthermore, because of the inequity "the chances of the child being able to escape this situation [bullying] are fairly small, unless special efforts are made to effect changes" (Olweus, 1993a, p. 28).

Adults also need to remember that children are works in progress. They do not have the same thought and reasoning processes, knowledge, judgment, and life experiences that come with age. If teachers say "figure it out" some students will combat bullying in positive ways. However, some ignorantly select negative avenues and carry weapons, join gangs, or skip school. Others will ease the pain with alcohol or drugs, or choose to end the torment with bullycides or school shootings.

- **Those who bully will grow out of it.**

Unfortunately, many who bully do not outgrow their antisocial behavior. Two studies queried university students about their bullying histories. In these independently conducted investigations, 54% (Chapell et al., 2006) and 96% (Curwen, McNichol, & Sharpe, 2011) of subjects who bullied in post secondary schools also bullied during elementary and high school.

- **Bullying will always exist; there is nothing anyone can do to stop bullying.**

Americans once believed slavery was an institution. Before 1920, women did not have the right to vote. There was a day when people believed a man could do whatever he wanted to his wife, including beating and raping her. These events were once acceptable parts of everyday life until people realized the error in their thinking. Today, those oppressive behaviors are referred to as discrimination, inequality, rape, and domestic violence. Change came about because concerned citizens publicized the injustices and damage, and campaigned for reform. They educated the public and kept fighting until protection was provided, corrections were made, and laws were in place. Sometimes it took years, other times generations, and some are ongoing processes.

If these encroachments of human rights were abolished bullying can be too. People once believed bullying was harmless; we now know it is injurious. Knowledge is a crucial first step. If educators and parents teach respect and inclusion, and utilize anti-bullying strategies; if activists continue to champion the cause; if legislators enact laws and prosecute violators; and if society says "NO!" to bullying, then change will occur.

## Characteristics of Children Who Are Bullied and Those Who Bully

### Description of Those Who Are Bullied

The majority of bullied children are called "passive victims." The remainder is referred to as "bully victims" because they both bully and are bullied.

"Passive victims" fit the popular profile of bullied youngsters. They may be shy, quiet, introverted, insecure, cautious, sensitive, anxious, submissive, or lack assertiveness. Typically, they have low self-esteem and are not popular. This group often has difficulty making friends, displays poor social skills, and is nervous in new situations. "Passive victims" usually have better relationships with adults than peers. These characteristics negatively impact friendships, which in turn results in a lack of social support, loneliness, isolation, and sadness.

"Passive victims" shy away from conflict and rarely retaliate or defend themselves. Boys are usually smaller and weaker than their contemporaries. They may have poor coordination and weak athletic skills. Many times, girls are not as attractive as their classmates. Crying, withdrawal, or becoming quiet are typical responses for younger "passive victims." Older youngsters try to avoid or escape the abuse. Many submit to demands by handing over money and valuable possessions.

Mothers of male "passive victims" are usually overprotective, controlling, and meddling and boys are usually closer to them, while fathers are distant, critical, and neglectful. Mothers of bullied daughters share hostile, rejecting, and controlling relationships. Fathers can be uncaring and controlling (Berger, 2007; Card & Hodges, 2008; R.D. Duncan, 2011; Olweus, 1993a; Powell & Ladd, 2010; Ross, 2003; Sullivan, Cleary, & Sullivan, 2004).

### Description of Those Who Bully

Children who bully want to control and dominate others; they systematically use aggression to take advantage of weaker peers. Their aggression is goal oriented—for power, social, or material gain (Unnever, 2005). They can be impulsive, easily frustrated, and hot headed, and have a strong sense of entitlement. Males who bully are usually stronger than their peers (Olweus, 1993a) and have difficulty conforming to rules.

Some researchers argue that those who abuse have high self-esteem (Vaillancourt, Hymel, & McDougall, 2007), while others take the opposing point of view (O'Moore,

2000). Social skills are another area of controversy. Larke and Beran (2006) and Crick and Dodge (1999) found that those who bully have poor social skills, while Sutton, Smith, and Swettenham (1999) argue that those who aggress possess high levels of social intelligence because they can organize and manipulate peers into assisting, avoid detection, and figure out the most opportunistic time, place, method, and person to target for each attack. Both sides may be correct because social intelligence is required for the indirect forms of aggression such as relational bullying but is not as important with direct types such as physical bullying.

Those who aggress lack empathy, derive pleasure from the pain they cause, and do not assume responsibility for their behavior. The inability to feel the pain they create is the very reason those who bully hurt others without conscience. Their actions might be tempered if they experienced the anguish.

Some who abuse are rejected, while others have popularity (Pellegrini, Bartini, & Brooks, 1999; Vaillancourt et al., 2007). One study found "Aggression significantly decreased the likelihood of being admired by classmates" (Faris & Felmlee, 2011a, p. 13), while another found the ability to make friends was "positively related to bullying" (Nansel et al., 2001, p. 2097). Those who bully can also have "pseudo friendships" where relationships are not genuine but born out of fear. They are befriended as insurance policies against being targeted. If children who bully have popularity, it is seen in the younger grades. Popularity wanes with age. Those who bully then associate with others who share their pro violent views.

Research reports that 12.5% of those who bully have oppositional/conduct disorder, 29.2% have attention deficit disorders, and 12.5% have depression (Kumpulainen, Rasanen, & Puura, 2001). ADHD is also positively correlated with bullying (Bacchini, Affuso, & Trotta, 2008).

Those who bully often come from authoritarian homes (R.D. Duncan, 2011; Fuller, 2008). They are more likely to have parents who demand obedience, rule with an iron hand, are unresponsive, and use punitive forms of discipline. Punishment is inconsistent and not always logical—a beating or an emotional outburst for a minor infraction while a major transgression does not receive a second glance.

Parents also show little warmth, affection, or empathy. Adult supervision is scarce, with few limits and abundant freedom. Most times, parents do not know the whereabouts of their children, what they do, or who they befriend. Structure, rules, and boundaries are absent. There are also family problems (e.g., conflicts, abuse, divorce, financial stressors, single parents) in their homes (Cook, Williams, Guerra, & Kim, 2010; R.D. Duncan, 2011; Oliver & Oaks, 1994).

Put downs, sarcasm, belittling, rejection, and physical attacks are the norm. Nathaniel Floyd, a psychologist and bullying researcher and writer, said "In every bully, there is the shadow of the little kid who was once abused himself" (as cited in Greenbaum, Turner, & Stephens, 1988, p. 30). Floyd's statement is backed up by Bauer et al.'s (2006) study that discovered 97% of children who bullied had been abused.

There are no consequences for bullying behaviors that go past the front door because aggression is seen as appropriate; in fact, it is often applauded. Thus, children raised in these environments learn that battering is an acceptable and effective way to handle problems and get needs met.

## Description of "Bully Victims"

"Bully victims" switch between the bullying and bullied roles. They share many characteristics of those who abuse and those who are abused but their features are more closely aligned with those who bully.

"Bully victims" are stronger, more aggressive, and more active than "passive victims," and more likely to be male (Kumpulainen et al., 2001; Unnever, 2005). Their impulsiveness, immaturity, restlessness, anxiety, irritability, low frustration tolerance, hot tempers, poor concentration, weak social skills, and disruptiveness annoy others. They provoke confrontations and quickly retaliate for any wrongdoing done to them. As such, "bully victims" are socially ostracized and disdained, by both youngsters and adults (Farmer et al., 2010; Juvonen, Graham, & Schuster, 2003; Unnever, 2005).

Children who bully and are bullied have home lives filled with abuse, violence, and hostility. "Bully victims" have more difficulty with parental relationships compared to those who bully, those who are bullied, and uninvolved peers. They report a lack of warmth, neglect, low family cohesion, poor monitoring, and inconsistent discipline (R.D. Duncan, 2011; Schwartz, Dodge, Pettit, & Bates, 1997). Compared to peers, "bully victims" have higher rates of internalizing and externalizing behaviors and psychiatric problems, which contribute to their inappropriate actions, lack of impulse control, and difficulty reading social cues (Cook et al., 2010; Haynie et al., 2001; Juvonen et al., 2003).

"Bully victims" can be dangerous because their behaviors are usually angry reactions to real or imagined injustices and not used as the road to respect or power (Scaglione & Scaglione, 2006). They may bully out of anger in retaliation for real or perceived maltreatment they have suffered. Many school shooters fall into this group.

The above characteristics are the qualities most often associated with bullying. Students who possess some of these characteristics may not participate; children who do not fit the criteria may be the worst abusers. Generally, the more characteristics a youngster has, the greater the chance of involvement in bullying.

# Chapter 4

# Consequences of Bullying

## Consequences for Those Who Are Bullied

Some minimize the dangers of bullying because just about everyone is bullied at one time or another and most are not scarred by the abuse. That is because the bullying is short term or separated by periods of time. It is a different case for the millions of children who are repeatedly exposed to aggression.

The American Medical Association "recognizes bullying as a complex and abusive behavior with potentially serious social and mental health consequences for children and adolescents" (Council on Scientific Affairs, 2002, p. 3). The organization warns that bullying can harm youngsters as much as child abuse (Ritter, 2002).

### Anxiety and Post-traumatic Stress Disorder

A direct relationship exists between bullying and anxiety (Gladstone, Parker, & Malhi, 2006; Humphrey, Storch, & Geffken, 2007). If bullying increases, anxiety raises; if bullying lessens, anxiety lowers. Bullied children are four times more likely to develop anxiety with the numbers climbing to 6.4 times for those who are "bully victims" (Kaltiala-Heino, Rimpela, Rantanen, & Rimpela, 2000).

Anticipatory fear develops because the repetition of bullying puts the recipient in a perpetual state of fear. The bullying will occur because it always does, but unanswered questions cause worry. When will the bullying occur? How will it be done? Who will bully? How much will it hurt? Where will it take place? How can I escape? It is akin to being bullied even when the person is not bullied. The apprehension can be as problematic as the bullying.

Bullying can cause Post-Traumatic Stress Disorder (PTSD), with the risks increasing with the duration of the abuse. In one study, 37% of children who were bullied said they experienced PTSD symptoms (Mynard, Joseph, & Alexander, 2000). In another, overt and relational bullying caused signs of PTSD in elementary school students (Storch & Esposito, 2003).

PTSD is a type of anxiety disorder that occurs when "(1) the person experienced, witnessed, or was confronted with an event or events that involved actual or threatened death or serious injury, or a threat to the physical integrity of self or others" and "(2) the person's response involved intense fear, helplessness, or horror" (American Psychiatric Association, 2000, p. 467). The event is continually revisited, with the person avoiding anything associated with the trauma. There are also signs of increased arousal. The criteria for PTSD are met if these symptoms last more than a month and impair the ability to function normally (American Psychiatric Association, 2000).

## Lowered Self-esteem

Bullying can destroy self-esteem. It is not an instantaneous event but a process that erodes confidence over time. In the beginning, feelings are hurt. "Why are people treating me this way?" recipients of bullying wonder. Embarrassment and shame are experienced. The actual act is not always the most painful part of bullying; it can be the humiliation of being demeaned in front of others, which is magnified if bystanders support the person doling out the punishment. Each episode whittles away beliefs of being a worthy person. Youngsters who are repeatedly bullied begin to feel inferior and start thinking they caused the bullying and deserve to be treated inhumanely. Why wouldn't they? The verbal and physical beatings, demeaning, humiliating and cruel treatment, rejection, ostracism, isolation, and feelings that they do not fit in (in their eyes) confirm thoughts that there is something wrong with them.

## Depression

Lowered self-esteem, thinking life will not change, feeling trapped and that everyone is against them, helplessness, powerlessness, and hopelessness are byproducts of repeated bullying. These feelings can lead to depression, so it is not surprising to find a positive correlation between bullying and depression. "Victimization is most strongly related to depression," Hawker and Boulton (2000, p. 441) concluded after reviewing 20 years of bullying studies. More recent research also confirms the relationship (Fekkes, Pijpers, & Verloove-Vanhorick, 2004; Fleming & Jacobsen, 2009; Klomek, Marrocco, Kleinman, Schonfeld, & Gould, 2007).

Van der Wal, de Wit, and Hirasing (2003) found that frequency, type, and gender play a role in depression. When the researchers examined females who were *indirectly* bullied, 35.1% of frequently bullied, 13.6% of sometimes bullied, and 3.6% of those not bullied reported depression. Of males who were indirectly bullied, 27.7% of frequently bullied, 8.1% of sometimes bullied, and 2.1% of those not bullied had depression. When the investigators looked at females who were *directly* bullied, 42.6% of frequently bullied, 16.3% of sometimes bullied, and 6.4% of those not bullied suffered from depression. Of males who were directly bullied, 22.4% of frequently bullied, 7.5% of sometimes bullied, and 3.1% of those not bullied said they had depression. "Bully victims" have the highest rates of depression (Kaltiala-Heino et al., 2000).

Teachers should be aware of the signs of depression:

- *Mood*—depression, feeling low, sadness, hopelessness, crying easily.
- *Interest*—loss of interest in activities previously enjoyed.
- *Sleep*—insomnia or excessive sleep.
- *Energy*—lack of energy, fatigue, feeling tired.
- *Appetite*—increased or decreased appetite.
- *Weight*—weight loss or gain.
- *Worthlessness*—feelings of worthlessness or guilt.
- *Thinking*—difficulty concentrating, making decisions, remembering.
- *Psychomotor*—restlessness, irritability, frustration, agitation, anger.
- *Suicidal ideation*—repeated thoughts of death, hurting oneself, suicide attempts.

A person can have some symptoms and not be depressed or not exhibit any and be depressed. If teachers see any indication of depression or intuitively feel that something is wrong they should immediately refer the student to the school's mental health professional.

## Suicide

Depression is the number one cause of suicide. Not everyone who has depression will commit suicide but having major depression increases the risk of suicide (U.S. Department of Health and Human Services, SAMHSA, n.d.).

There is a clear link between bullying, suicidal ideation, and suicide (Y.S. Kim, Leventhal, Koh, & Boyce, 2009; Klomek et al., 2007, 2008; Luukkonen, 2010; Skapinakis et al., 2011).

- Research conducted by Espelage found "more than 80 percent of chronic victims have contemplated suicide" (as cited in Munsil & Jolly, 2009, p. 1).
- After reviewing 31 empirical studies that investigated suicide and bullying among children, Klomek, Sourander, and Gould concluded "victims of bullying exhibit high levels of suicidal ideation, and are more likely to have attempted suicide compared with non victims" (2010, p. 283). The conclusions were the same for elementary, middle, and high school students.
- Yale University scientists reviewed 37 studies, examining bullying and suicide in children and adolescents from 13 countries. "Almost all of the studies found connections between being bullied and suicidal thoughts among children" (Yale University, 2008, para. 4).

- Educational psychologist Wendy Sinclair, who treats four to five targets of bullying monthly, said "Many victims of bullying are so traumatised and disempowered by the bullying that they often express, in therapy, a desire to die rather than suffer further humiliation and abuse" (as cited in Govender, 2008, para. 24).

## Lost Children

Bullycide reports from the United States and nations around the world indicate that hundreds of youngsters have been bullied to death, ending their lives after they were broken down by abusive peers.

The United Kingdom charity, Beatbullying, reviewed suicides of 10- to 14-year-olds reported in the media. Forty-four percent of the deaths listed bullying as a contributory cause. The number probably paints part of the picture. Only cases publicized in the media were included and deaths were counted if there was no doubt of the role bullying played (BeatBullying, 2010).

In another study, English written news publications in the United States and worldwide were searched using the terms "bullying," "hazing," "ragging," and "death." A history of bullying was alleged in more than three-quarters (76%) of the deaths (Srabstein, 2008).

An internet search conducted by the author discovered the names of 27 American students who took their lives in 2010 because of bullying. Fourteen of those died during a two month period from September 9, 2010 to November 8, 2010, which coincides with the beginning of the school year. Realistically, these numbers are the tip of the bullyberg. The search only counted children whose deaths made the internet and it does not include youngsters who kept their bullying histories a secret but committed suicide because of it. In fact, some parents learn about bullying after their child's death by going through diaries, papers, computers and cell phones, and by talking to peers. Although an internet search does not follow the rigors of a scientific study, the data point out that bullycide has a presence in the United States (see Table 4.1).

Are there psychological problems with those who bullycide? After conducting research with male subjects who were bullied, Olweus concluded:

> Many of them would probably function reasonably well if they were not exposed to repeated bullying and harassment over long periods of time. The elevated levels of anxiety and stress that we could register in the school years were thus more a reflection of situation-related strain than of a relatively permanent personality disturbance.
>
> (1993b, p. 330)

The children who bullycided were not weak. Many suffered weeks, months, and even years of abuse. To do so required great strength. Just as the wind, rain, and elements wear away solid rock mountains, these youngsters' lives were eroded bit by

Table 4.1 U.S. bullycides in 2010

| Name | Age | State | Date of death |
| --- | --- | --- | --- |
| Phoebe Prince | 15 | Massachusetts | January 14, 2010 |
| Ernest Fuller | 12 | Virginia | January 20, 2010 |
| Montanna Lance | 9 | Texas | January 21, 2010 |
| Elle Louisa Welland | 17 | Unknown | January 25, 2010 |
| Dakota Deremus | 16 | Kansas | February 1, 2010 |
| Kimberly Linczeski | 12 | Michigan | March 6, 2010 |
| Alexis Pilkington | 17 | New York | March 21, 2010 |
| Jon Carmichael | 13 | Texas | March 28, 2010 |
| Alexandria Moore | 15 | Alabama | May 12, 2010 |
| Richard "Ty" Field Smalley | 11 | Oklahoma | May 13, 2010 |
| Celina Okwuone | 11 | Florida | May 20, 2010 |
| Christian Taylor | 16 | Virginia | May 31, 2010 |
| Justin Auberg | 15 | Minnesota | July 9, 2010 |
| Billy Lucas | 15 | Indiana | September 9, 2010 |
| Cody Barker | 17 | Wisconsin | September 13, 2010 |
| Tyler Clementi | 18 | New Jersey | September 22, 2010 |
| Asher Brown | 13 | Texas | September 23, 2010 |
| Harrison Chase Brown | 15 | Colorado | September 25, 2010 |
| Seth Walsh | 13 | California | September 28, 2010 |
| Felix Sacco | 17 | Massachusetts | September 29, 2010 |
| Caleb Nolt | 14 | Indiana | September 30, 2010 |
| Zach Harrington | 19 | Oklahoma | October 5, 2010 |
| Jordan Ryan Binion | 17 | Washington | October 19, 2010 |
| Jamarcus Bell | 14 | Indiana | October 20, 2010 |
| Cassidy Andel | 16 | North Dakota | November 4, 2010 |
| Brandon Bitner | 14 | Pennsylvania | November 5, 2010 |
| Samantha Kelly | 14 | Michigan | November 8, 2010 |

bit. During that time they tried healthy ways to stop the bullying: ignoring, walking away, avoiding, reporting to teachers, and telling parents, but the abuse did not stop. When they saw that adults could not or would not stop the wrongdoing, when they exhausted all strategies, when they believed there would be no end to the brutality, when they could no longer live in agony, they could think of only one solution: suicide. The bullying did end. What these children did not realize is that suicide is a permanent solution to a temporary problem. What adults need to realize is that words, gestures, actions, and inactions can be just as lethal as knives, guns, and bombs.

## Suicide Warning Signs

People may display some warning signs and not be suicidal or exhibit none and plan to end their lives. However, approximately three-quarters of those who commit suicide show some warning signs (Caruso, n.d.):

- Loss of interest in activities that were once enjoyed.
- Exhibiting depression or sadness most of the time.
- Sudden mood changes from sadness to happiness or agitation to calmness.
- Displaying feelings of hopelessness, helplessness, worthlessness, guilt, or shame.
- Changes in personality, behavior, appearance, or habits.
- Withdrawing from friends, family, and society.
- Changes in sleeping or eating habits.
- Anxiety, agitation.
- Rage or uncontrolled anger.
- Experiencing rejection, failure, or humiliation.
- Difficulty concentrating.
- Deterioration in schoolwork, or academic pressures.
- Increased absenteeism.
- Being the target of bullying, harassment, or crime.
- Social isolation, or relationship problems.
- Recklessness, impulsiveness, or risky behavior.
- Alcohol or drug use.
- Feeling trapped, and not seeing any solutions.
- Expressing an interest in suicide and death.
- Talking, writing, or drawing about wanting to hurt or kill oneself.
- Making statements such as "I can't do this anymore" or "The world would be better without me."
- Giving away or throwing out personal belongings and valuables.
- Signs of planning a suicide—making a date, time, place, or method, or rehearsing the act.

National Suicide Prevention Lifeline wallet cards with suicide warning signs and the Lifeline phone number can be downloaded free of charge. The organization has a variety of free resources (www.suicidepreventionlifeline.org).

## Protective Factors for Suicide

Protective factors reduce the potential of suicidal behavior by helping the person cope with stressful situations:

- Feeling part of a network of supportive friends.
- School connectedness.
- Parent, family, and community connectedness.
- Availability of school counselors.
- Treatment of mental health disorders.
- Willingness to ask for help.
- Good self-esteem.
- Believing one can cope with problems.

- Feeling a responsibility to others.
- Good social, conflict resolution, and problem solving skills.
- Impulse control.
- Restricted access to weapons or medications.
- Religious beliefs opposing suicide.

Good anti-bullying intervention programs build up at least half of these protective factors. For example, students will develop connections to peers and the school and feel responsible to others, if there is a family atmosphere where everyone is respected and accepted, and friendships are encouraged. Increased self-esteem will be a natural outcome. If social, conflict resolution, problem solving, anger management, self-control, and friendship skills are taught and practiced, stress can be diffused or averted. Students will also gain confidence in their coping abilities.

## What Should a Teacher Do if Suicidal Thinking is Suspected?

Teachers are not trained to treat students who have suicidal ideations and should not attempt to do so. The slightest suspicion should be investigated because it is better to err on the side of safety. If educators see warning signs they should follow their school's written plan. In the absence of guidelines, *immediately escort* the child to mental health personnel in the school. Call 911 if qualified staff cannot be reached.

Students who appear to be suicidal should *never be left alone*. Keep them separated from firearms, knives, scissors, medications, or anything that can cause injury or death.

## Death

Death from bullying is not always self-inflicted. Ten-year-old Myles Neuts was grabbed by two older male students when he went to the school bathroom and was hoisted onto a coat hook. As the fifth grader slowly strangled to death, the boys called friends into the lavatory to watch "the dummy" hanging. It was the first time Myles was bullied. It ended his life (CBC News Online, 2005).

## Physical Ailments

Bullying causes stress. Stress breaks down the body's immune system, endangering physical health. Athlete's foot, back aches, bed wetting, dizziness, eating disorders, fatigue, headaches, irritable bowel syndrome, migraines, mouth sores, neck and shoulder pain, palpitations, panic attacks, sleep problems, skin problems, stomach aches, sweating, and ulcers are some physical manifestations of bullying. The risk of acquiring ailments rises with the frequency, duration, and severity of abuse (Due et al., 2005; Gini & Pozzoli, 2009; Williams et al., 1996). Children who are bullied also suffer cuts, scratches, bruises, and broken bones.

## Absences

Each day, 160,000 American students stay home from school because they are afraid of being bullied. That means 28 million days of education are lost each year because of abuse.

In a study of 30,000 Australian students, 25% of frequently bullied girls and 19% of frequently bullied boys skipped school because of bullying (Rigby, 2003).

## Lower GPAs and Higher Dropout Rates

Being bullied has been linked to poor academic functioning (Card & Hodges, 2008; Juvonen, Wang, & Espinoza, 2011; Nakamoto & Schwartz, 2010). Grades decline for a variety of reasons:

- *Self-preservation*—Personal safety takes precedence over academic performance.
- *Concentration problems*—It is difficult to concentrate when nervous about future attacks or tending wounds from past assaults.
- *Avoidance*—Avoiding class or school is seen as a bullying prevention strategy.
- *Tiredness*—The stress of being bullied and sleep disruptions can fatigue the body.
- *Fear of being targeted*—Some students will purposely let grades slide because they do not want to be bullied for being the "class brain."

When youngsters cut classes to stay out of harm's way they often find that those who bully hound them in hallways, staircases, cafeterias, bathrooms, schoolyards, and other areas of the school. What is the solution? One out of 12 students drops out of school to protect him- or herself (Greenbaum et al., 1988). That means 8% of the student population finds educational institutions so hostile that they withdraw from school to insure their safety.

While a decision to end school early brings short term safety, it can present long term problems. For example, one study suggests "the possibility that an educational level of less than 12 years may be used to identify persons at higher absolute risk of death from CHD [coronary heart disease]" (Fiscella & Franks, 2004, p. 471).

There can also be an impact on future economics. Those who drop out of high school average $23,608 a year income; a high school education garners $32,552; those who graduate with a Bachelor's degree can expect a $53,300 paycheck; a Masters diploma pays $65,364; and those with professional degrees earn $79,508 (U.S. Department of Labor, Bureau of Labor Statistics, 2010).

Future financial earnings can be affected even if repeatedly abused students continue their education. "Wages at age 23 are higher for those individuals who did not experience bullying at school, with the wage differential being the most pronounced between those who have never been bullied and those who were frequently bullied at school" (Brown & Taylor, 2008, p. 396).

## Friendships

Often, those who are bullied have few, if any, friends (Olweus, 1993a). Any companions they have may become casualties of bullying. Children will not befriend those who are abused because the mere association with someone who is bullied could move them to the front of the "people to bully" line. Relational bullying also limits friendships: "If you are friends with him you can't be friends with me."

# Interrelationship Between the Consequences

A spider web (Figure 4.1) was purposely chosen to represent the relationships between different forms of bullying and their damaging consequences because (a) prey are entangled and trapped in spider webs. In the same way, those who are bullied become stuck in the web of abuse spun by those who aggress. They are at the mercy of their

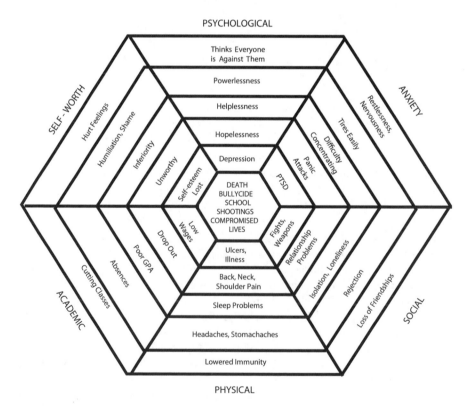

*Figure 4.1* Bullying web of harm

predators, who ultimately go for the kill (figuratively or literally); and (b) the threads on a web are interconnected as are the different consequences of bullying.

- *Physical*—Physical problems can lead to school absences (academic), which further distance isolated children from the mainstream (social) and cause struggles with schoolwork (academic). Poor grades can cause angst (anxiety) and feelings of inferiority (self-worth).
- *Anxiety*—Anxiety can lead to illness (physical and psychological) as the body breaks down from stress. Grades can decline because it is hard to concentrate when under the weather or worried (academic). If so, self-confidence (self-worth) may sink as low as report card marks. Peers are often turned off by anxious classmates (social).
- *Academic*—Children might get depressed (psychological) or become anxious (anxiety) because of poor academic performance. Their confidence (self-worth) may plunge, which could cause them to avoid social activities (social). If they drop out of school they will have an increased risk of being on the bottom of the wage scale. As such, their paychecks may not always cover expenses. Financial struggles can lead to distress (anxiety), illness (physical and psychological), humiliation, and shame (self-worth). Embarrassment may lead to isolation (social).
- *Social*—Rejection lowers confidence (self-worth) and can contribute to depression (psychological). Children with deficient social skills are often anxious (anxiety) in social situations. Ostracized children may be too upset to focus on school work (academic).
- *Self-worth*—A blow to self-worth can lead to depression (psychological). People with low self-esteem may have difficulty making friends because of an inability to present themselves in a positive light (social). The loss of belief in one's abilities can lead to a lack of effort in school (academic) and nervousness (anxiety). The stress can lead to illness (physical).
- *Psychological*—A decline in psychological health can lead to isolation and a loss of friends (social), poor school performance (academic), negative self-image (self-worth), and anxiety provoking thoughts (anxiety). The mind affects the body and the body affects the mind, so illnesses (physical) may occur.

The consequences of bullying can become a volatile mixture when stirred together. Those who are abused may internalize their feelings but locked emotions do not sit still and can emerge as physical or mental illness, or bullycide. Feelings could also be externalized and erupt in the form of yelling, fighting, or at the extreme end taking revenge, as seen with school shootings. Ultimately, bullying can put a stranglehold on the recipient's present and future life.

For example, Fosse (2006) found that half of the 160 young adults who went to a mental health professional for the first time were bullied during their youth. The worse the bullying experienced, the worse the psychiatric symptoms.

## How is Damage Determined?

Physical, psychological, social, or academic injury is affected by several variables.

- *Perception*—What is the recipient's interpretation of the event? It is less harmful if the act is seen as an innocent prank and more damaging if it is viewed as a personal attack designed to hurt, demean, or damage.
- *Type of bullying*—Verbal and relational bullying cause the most psychological pain. The distress also lingers longer with indirect abuse.
- *Frequency of bullying*—How often does the bullying occur? The cumulative consequences of ongoing abuse wither away confidence and health.
- *Duration of bullying*—Risks rise with the length of incidents.
- *Severity of bullying*—Poking will cause less injury than being thrown down a staircase. Exclusion by a single student is easier to deal with than silent treatment by an entire class.
- *Environment for bullying*—Public bullying increases humiliation because audiences are present. If bullying is experienced in the home, as with sibling and cyber-bullying, a safe refuge and a break from maltreatment are lost.
- *Number of contexts bullying occurs in*—If bullying is limited to one location, the child receives a reprieve in other venues. It allows time to treat wounds and regroup. The potential for harm increases as the number of bullying zones rises. Does the mistreatment only occur in school or does it also spill into the neighborhood or home?
- *Effectiveness of responses*—Successful responses empower and provide hope that bullying will end. Failed attempts increase feelings of helplessness and hopelessness.
- *Skills*—The chances of preventing, deflecting, or ending bullying increase with the number of skills a targeted person possesses.
- *Resources and support*—Knowledge, help, and support can lessen the sting, provide some immunity, or prevent or end bullying.

## Chicken or Egg?

Does bullying occur because youngsters lack social skills or do they lack abilities because they have been excluded and deprived of relationships? Do anxiety and depression cause bullying or are they a consequence of maltreatment? Would bullied children drop out of school if they were not abused, or do hostilities factor into their decision to withdraw?

Serious internalizing problems (e.g., anxiety, depression, loneliness, withdrawal) may play a part in bullying, but environmental factors appear to have a greater role because most problems develop *after* the abuse (Fekkes, Pijpers, Fredriks, Vogels, & Verloove-Vanhorick, 2006; Y.S. Kim, Leventhal, Koh, Hubbard, & Boyce, 2006). Consider the evidence:

- A study using identical twins as subjects found that twins who were bullied experienced significantly more internalizing symptoms than their non bullied co twin (Arseneault et al., 2008).
- Recipients of weekly school harassment said they felt "worse about themselves" (Rigby, 1997, How Children React section, para. 6) *after* bullying. The number of girls who felt "sad and miserable" (How Children React section, para. 6) after bullying rose with the frequency of abuse.
- Loneliness and avoidance began *after* kindergarten children were bullied (Kochenderfer & Ladd, 1996).

Those who are repeatedly bullied gradually *"take over the social environment's* (the dominant peers') *negative evaluations* of themselves as worthless and inadequate . . . These negative self-perceptions, which also imply an *increased vulnerability to depressive reactions,* tended to become internalized and 'cemented' within the individuals" (Olweus, 1993b, p. 331).

## Consequences for Those Who Bully

Conversations usually focus on those who are bullied when the harmful effects of bullying are discussed; however, those who abuse others often spin their own web of harm.

### Criminality and Violence

Bullying is a red flag, signaling the potential for a future of antisocial behavior. U.S. Secretary of Education Arne Duncan said "Just as you have gateway drugs, bullying . . . is a gateway behavior" (A. Duncan, 2010). Duncan's words are backed by research that substantiates the correlation between bullying and criminality (Farrington & Ttofi, 2011; Jiang, Walsh, & Augimeri, 2011; M.J. Kim, Catalano, Haggerty, & Abbott, 2011; Luukkonen, 2010; Olweus, 2011; Renda, Vassallo, & Edwards, 2011). For example, after performing a meta-analysis of investigations focusing on bullying and criminality, Ttofi, Farrington, Losel, and Loeber concluded *"School bullying is a strong and specific risk factor for later offending"* (2011, p. 80).

Ninety-two percent of incarcerated youth offenders between the ages of 16 and 21 who participated in a Kidscape qualitative survey admitted bullying at school. "They were told at school that bullying was wrong but, as nothing was ever done to stop their bullying behaviour, they had never had to face the consequences of their actions" (Elliott, 2002, Does Unchecked School Bullying Lead to Crime? section, para. 1). These adolescents and young adults continued assaulting, stealing, and hurting others thinking they could do so forever. The legal system proved them wrong. When they became of legal age, the rules changed; behaviors that were called "bullying" and tolerated during their school days were renamed "crimes." Aggressors were now handed "Go to jail" cards.

## Box 4.1: Yesterday It Was Called Bullying . . .

**Yesterday it was called bullying . . .**

| Action | Type of bullying done in school | Crime in adulthood |
|---|---|---|
| Threatens or tries to hit someone | Physical/verbal/relational/ cyberbullying | Assault |
| Purposely hits a person, with intent to harm | Physical bullying | Battery |
| Threatens or intimidates to get money or property | Physical/verbal/relational/ cyberbullying | Extortion |
| Confined or restrains someone | Physical bullying | False imprisonment |
| Takes property without permission, intent to keep property | Physical bullying | Larceny |
| Takes property through force, threat, or intimidation | Physical/verbal/relational/ cyberbullying | Robbery |
| Verbal lies that harm reputations | Verbal/relational/ cyberbullying | Slander |
| Targeted because of membership in a particular group | Physical/verbal/relational/ cyberbullying | Hate crimes |
| Unwanted verbal, physical, oral conduct of a sexual nature | Physical/verbal/relational/ cyberbullying | Sexual harassment |
| Attempted murder, murder | Physical bullying | Attempted murder, murder |

**. . . Today it is called a crime**

**Bullying is a crime that children are allowed to get away with.**

Compared to those who do not bully, youngsters who aggress are more likely to use tobacco, alcohol, and drugs; and have more traffic violations and drunk driving convictions. They exhibit higher rates of fighting, abusive behavior, shoplifting, robbery, vandalism, writing graffiti, weapon carrying, assault, rape, and murder (Farrington & Ttofi, 2011; Haynie et al., 2001; M.J. Kim et al., 2011; Luukkonen, 2010; Nansel et al., 2003; Olweus, 2011; Pepler, Craig, Connolly, & Henderson, 2002; Vieno, Gini, & Santinello 2011).

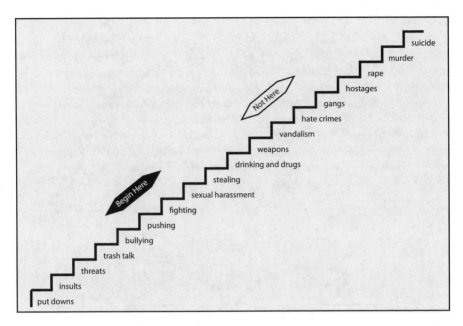

*Figure 4.2* The School Violence Continuum (created by Jim Bryngelson of Courtesy and Respect Empower (CARE))

If teachers do not stop acts of bullying, they are enabling illegal behavior. In this respect, educators become co-conspirators and fail these children. Instead of leaving schools with lessons in respect, tolerance, empathy, inclusion, and relationship skills, youngsters graduate with diplomas showing proficiency in bullying and then advance to Masters of Criminality.

The School Violence Continuum (Figure 4.2) illustrates the progression from low level violence to more serious forms. Readers can see that each succeeding act is more destructive and serious than the previous one. The message for everyone is that actions we think of as inconsequential, such as put downs, pushes, tripping, "accidentally" knocking into someone, damaging or destroying property, exclusion, rumors, pulling a ponytail, games of salugi, shooting rubber bands, threats, harassment, and trash talk, are not always benign. This is where violence is birthed. Although they appear to be harmless acts, seemingly innocent behaviors may be similar to microscopic cancer cells that proliferate to produce deadly results. It is crucial that teachers stop these actions when they first appear.

Society often wonders how violence can be eradicated. We need to look no further than the school playground, lunchroom, hallways, and classrooms. Stop aggression in schools and future violence will be prevented.

## Relationship Problems

Those who bully are besieged with person-to-person problems because they never learn how to have healthy relationships. They only know how to power their way through people. Their childhood "skills" travel with them throughout their lives. Bullying in school turns into sexual harassment, delinquency, gang involvement, and date violence in adolescence. Adulthood brings workplace harassment, marital abuse, child abuse, and elder abuse (Pepler & Craig, 2000).

Those who aggress bully their children who then repeat the antisocial behaviors with their offspring (Huesmann, Eron, Lefkowitz, & Walder, 1984). Bullying puts today's youth at risk *and* endangers unborn generations as well.

| Normative Aggression | Bullying | Sexual Harassment | Delinquency | Gang Involvement | Date Violence | Workplace Harassment | Marital Abuse | Child Abuse | Elder Abuse |
|---|---|---|---|---|---|---|---|---|---|
| CHILDHOOD | | ADOLESCENCE | | | | ADULTHOOD | | | |

*Figure 4.3* The Developmental Continuum of Bullying: power and aggression (Pepler & Craig, 2000, p. 5)

## Depression and Suicide

Those who bully have increased rates of depression, suicidal ideation, and suicide in comparison to peers (Y.S. Kim et al., 2009; Klomek et al., 2007, 2008).

One study found that 19.2% of girls who frequently *indirectly* bullied reported depression, compared to 14% who sometimes bullied indirectly, and 8.4% who never bullied indirectly. Of those girls who *directly* bullied frequently, 23.5% had depression symptoms, compared to 16% who sometimes bullied directly, and 9.7% who almost never bullied directly. For boys, 13.9% of those who frequently *indirectly* bullied had signs of depression, compared to 7.9% who sometimes bullied indirectly, and 4.3% of those who almost never bullied indirectly. Of the boys who *directly* bullied, 11.9% reported being depressed compared to 7.1% who sometimes bullied directly, and 4.3% of those who almost never bullied directly. Suicidal ideation increased with the frequency of bullying for both genders (Van der Wal et al., 2003).

## "Bully Victims"

Those who bully and are bullied are at an increased risk of problems. "Bully victims" have more physical symptoms, relationship problems, lower self-esteem, worse grades, less popularity, and more delinquent behaviors, when compared with those who bully, those who are bullied, and non participating peers (Arseneault et al., 2006; Haynie et al., 2001; Juvonen et al., 2003; Klomek et al., 2007).

"Bully victims" also have more psychiatric disorders. For example, among females in one study, 39.6% of "bully victims" reported two or more mental health problems, compared to 29.8% of those who only aggress, 15.6% of bullied youngsters, 9.5% of rarely involved children, and 5% of those who did not participate in bullying. For males, 18.6% of "bully victims" had multiple mental health problems, compared to 13.9% of those who only bullied, 9.1% of those who were bullied, 3.6% of youngsters who rarely participated, and 2.5% of those who abstained (Kaltiala-Heino et al., 2000).

---

## Box 4.2: Can Bullying Turn Children into Murderers?

Violent video games, the media, music, access to firearms, impaired mental health, poor parenting, religion, society, and teachers are blamed each time there is a school shooting. Surely, each attack has a complex set of reasons behind it, but has anyone listened to the triggermen?

"Your children who have ridiculed me, who have chosen not to accept me, who have treated me like I am not worth their time are dead," Columbine killer Eric Harris wrote in his suicide note (as cited in Vaughan & Clarke, 1999, para. 6). He blamed parents for the massacre saying they taught their children "to not accept what is different" (para. 17).

Evan Ramsey gunned down a student and principal at Bethel Regional High School in Alaska. He wrote "I feel rejected . . . I am sick and tired of being treated this way everyday" (Ramsey v. State, 2002, Opinion section, para. 7).

"I am not insane. I am angry," Pearl High School shooter Luke Woodham wrote. "I killed because people like me are mistreated every day" (Bowles, 1998, News section, page 9A).

Did anyone notice that the words of school shooters echo each other? This is *not* condoning murderous actions or excusing atrocities. It is pointing out the role that school bullying *may* have played.

What do researchers think?

- After reviewing and analyzing 15 incidents of school shootings between 1995 and 2001, Leary, Kowalski, Smith, and Phillips concluded that the main motivation in the majority of the shootings "seems to have been retribution, either for an ongoing pattern of ostracism and teasing or for an acute rejection" (2003, p. 212). Eighty percent of the cases reviewed "involved an ongoing pattern of teasing, bullying, or ostracism" (p. 210).
- "My research reveals that rejection and the accompanying humiliation was the dominant issue underlying every one of the rampage killings in the United States," wrote psychologist Elliot Aronson (2004, p. 356).

- In 1999, the U.S. Secret Service investigated school shootings that occurred from December, 1974 through May, 2000. They examined 37 incidents involving 41 attackers. The investigators found that "Almost three-quarters of the attackers felt persecuted, bullied, threatened, attacked, or injured by others prior to the incident" (Vossekuil, Fein, Reddy, Borum, & Modzeleski, 2002, p. 21). In recalling their interviews, investigators said some of the "attackers described being bullied in terms that suggested that these experiences approached torment. These attackers told of behaviors that, if they occurred in the workplace, likely would meet legal definitions of harassment and/or assault" (pp. 35–36). Investigators believed, "In some of these cases the experience of being bullied seemed to have a significant impact on the attacker and appeared to have been a factor in his decision to mount an attack at the school" (p. 21).
- Harris and Klebold's rampage was an "overtly political act in the name of oppressed students victimized by their peers" (Larkin, 2009, p. 1309), Ralph W. Larkin of the John Jay College of Criminal Justice wrote. "The Columbine shootings redefined such acts not merely as revenge but as a means of protest of bullying, intimidation, social isolation, and public rituals of humiliation" (p. 1309).

Those who write these youngsters off as "mental cases" will never give bullying motivated murders a death sentence. The majority of children diagnosed with mental illness do not point guns at fellow students and teachers.

"We are devastated by the final act of violence," Coloroso wrote (2003, p. xxi), "but rarely outraged by the events that led to the final act."

## Consequences for Bystanders

Bystanders struggle with an assortment of feelings. They are riddled with guilt and shame because fear and anxiety prevent them from intervening. They are confused because they do not know what to do. Bystanders feel for their abused peers and are angry at those who bully for the distress they cause. These emotions create feelings of helplessness and powerlessness.

Janson, Carney, Hazler, and Oh's research found that bystanders "experienced significant traumatic reactions as a result of witnessing common forms of repetitive abuse between their peers, reactions that were significant enough to call for direct attention by counselors" (2009, p. 323). The researchers also said the trauma was "substantially higher" than that of emergency personnel who responded to California earthquakes.

## Consequences for the School

Bullying causes a host of problems in schools. On the academic front, grades decline. With regard to staff, frustration and stress increase while morale drops. Some bullied students and fearful bystanders self-medicate with alcohol or drugs, join gangs, or carry weapons for protection. Those who bully may engage in unlawful activities. This brings an illegal element into the building. School reputations are negatively impacted.

Legally, schools are being held responsible for failing to safeguard students. For example, in 2007 a Florida jury awarded a 12-year-old boy four million dollars after he suffered permanent nerve damage because of a broken arm suffered at the hands of a peer who repeatedly bullied him (Jenkins, 2007).

Money that could be used on education is spent preventing and curbing bullying. R. Phillips, Linney, and Pack tell us that schools lose over one billion dollars of state funding each year because of bullying. Their calculations are based on:

160,000 students absent each day [because of bullying] × 180 school days in a school year =

28,800,000 student days lost . . .

28,800,000 × $40 [the national average schools receive from their states' daily attendance fund] =

$1,152,000,000.

(2008, p. 47)

---

## Box 4.3: Yarn It!

"Yarn it!" helps students realize the tension created by bullying.

1. Organize students into a circle.
2. While holding a ball of yarn the facilitator . . .

   a. wraps the end twice around his or her wrist;
   b. makes introductions (My name is < name >);
   c. states one way bullying has affected him or her.

3. The facilitator tosses the ball of yarn across the circle and asks the person who caught it to repeat the facilitator's actions. (See #2)
4. Repeat until everyone has a turn. The facilitator then says, "As you can see, we are all connected by the yarn, just as everyone in our classroom is joined together in one way or another. When someone harms another, it affects the person being abused, bystanders, and teachers, as well as the person who bullies. Those targeted are hurt by aggressive acts. Bystanders are upset when peers are attacked and fear they will be bullied next. Teachers have to stop teaching and attend to the bullying. Those who bully learn inappropriate ways to act. No one escapes the bullying web of harm."
5. The facilitator then says . . .

   a. If you have been or have seen someone physically bullied, take a step back.

b. If you have been or have seen someone verbally bullied, take a step back.

c. If you have been or have seen someone relationally bullied, take a step back.

d. If you have been or have heard about someone cyberbullied, take a step back.

e. If anyone has seen bullying occur in their classroom, take a step back.

f. If anyone has seen someone hurt by bullying, take a step back.

6. With each step backward, participants feel the increasing tension of the string as it is stretched tighter. "Do you feel the tension?" the facilitator asks. "It is similar to the tension students, school personnel, and the community feel when bullying occurs."

7. The facilitator then says . . .

a. If you have seen or heard a student tell someone to stop bullying, take a step forward.

b. If you have seen or heard of a student who helped someone who was bullied, take a step forward.

c. If you have seen or heard of a student who included all peers in his or her activities, take a step forward.

d. If you have seen or heard of a student who asked for adult assistance because of bullying, take a step forward.

e. If you have seen or heard of a student who stopped rumors, take a step forward.

f. If you have seen or heard of a student who performed an act of kindness, take a step forward.

8. The yarn's tension decreases with each step forward. "When students tell peers who bully to stop, when pupils help those who are hurt, when children include everyone in their activities, when adult assistance is sought, and when everyone practices acts of kindness," the facilitator says, "bullying in the classroom decreases and ends. Then, the tension disappears" (P.P. Huppie-Parsons, personal communication, October 6, 2009, adaptation).

## Consequences for Society

Bullying costs the U.S. economy billions of dollars each year. The healthcare, public assistance, police, judicial, and penal systems are tapped into when criminality and relationship-related problems (e.g., domestic violence, broken and dysfunctional homes, divorce) get out of control. Those involved in bullying drop out of school or do not enroll in higher education, thus limiting their earning power and taxable contributions. Lower education increases the chances of unemployment. Jobless people apply for unemployment benefits, healthcare, and public assistance.

Prevention also incurs expenses. "We estimate the present value of saving a 14-year-old high risk juvenile from a life of crime to range from $2.6 to $5.3 million," said Cohen and Piquero (2009, p. 25). A high risk child is one who is in danger of becoming a high school dropout, criminal, delinquent, or abuser of drugs (Cohen & Piquero, 2009). These behaviors are associated with bullying.

There are also intangible factors such as stress, fear, pain, and suffering.

Who covers the costs generated by bullying? Taxpayers pick up the tab in the form of increased taxes and higher premiums.

## Signs of Bullying

In the majority of cases, children who are bullied do not tell teachers about the abuse. This poses a problem as educators cannot intervene unless they know a problem exists. It forces teachers to become detectives, looking for non verbal, behavioral, and visual clues that signal bullying. Educators should investigate any suspicion, even if youngsters claim they are not being bullied.

### Physical Signs

● *More scratches, bruises, and injuries than normal*—Explanations that do not make sense or claims of self-inflicted injuries (falling) may be excuses to cover up bullying.
● *Frequent illnesses*—Stress breaks down the immune system, decreasing its resistance to illness.
● *Difficulty sleeping, nightmares*—Sleep is disrupted because of the physical and/or mental toll of bullying.
● *Stammering, stuttering, tics*—These may be physical manifestations of stress.
● *Tiredness*—Worry, stress, injuries, and lack of sleep can exhaust children who are bullied.
● *Physical differences*—Youngsters will be bullied for any perceived difference, such as being smaller, weaker, or not as pretty as classmates.

### Behavioral Signs

● *Sadness*—Unhappiness can be caused by friendlessness, humiliation, ostracism, or loneliness.
● *Anxiety*—Anticipatory fear keeps bullied kids in a constant state of anxiety.
● *Appearing depressed or suicidal*—Feelings of powerlessness, helplessness, and hopelessness can cause depression. Depression can lead to suicidal ideation.
● *Angry outbursts*—The degradation, pain, and injustice of bullying may create anger.
● *Starting to bully other children and siblings*—Takes frustrations out on others and tries to reclaim some of the lost power.

- *Quietness*—Children can be silent, if they are afraid of being mocked or if they are depressed.
- *Decreased self-confidence*—Humiliation, ridicule, and exclusion on a frequent basis will test even the strongest person's confidence.
- *Lack of eye contact*—The youngster does not want anyone to see the pain.

## Avoidant Signs

- *Cutting class, absenteeism*—People cannot be bullied if they are not present.
- *Frequently wanting to go to the nurse's office or home*—These places are safe sanctuaries.
- *Refusing to go to the bathroom*—Unsupervised restrooms are bullying hot spots.
- *Avoiding certain people, places*—This strategy is used to dodge those who bully.
- *Arriving late or leaving early*—Those who are abused keep their distance from the bullying crowd.
- *Volunteering for jobs to get out of recess*—Bullying flourishes during recess. Activities that steer students clear of abuse are sought.
- *Staying close to adults*—Adults can serve as deterrents or protectors.

## Academic Signs

- *Difficulty concentrating*—It is difficult to think when overwhelmed with fear and pain.
- *Loss of interest in schoolwork*—Safety is the top priority. Academics take a back seat.
- *Schoolwork is incomplete, sloppy, not up to par*—It is hard to focus on assignments when concerned about personal safety.
- *Missing homework*—An abused child may be too upset, hurt, or tired to complete assignments; or may lose papers during bullying episodes.
- *Decrease or increase in grades*—Marks usually decline but can rise when students use schoolwork to block painful thoughts of bullying.
- *Wariness about participating in group activities*—It is human instinct to avoid people who attack or have the potential to do so.
- *Refusing to participate in school events*—These activities are usually poorly supervised, increasing the risk of bullying.

## Social Signs

- *Being an object of harassment, ridicule, threats*—Incessant cruelty follows bullied children.
- *Having negative nicknames*—Friends do not give their buddies derogatory names. Names that hurt or put down are indicative of bullying.
- *Being the butt of jokes, being laughed at*—Everyone is made fun of at one time or another but bullied youngsters are constantly on the receiving end.

- *Being the last person picked for groups, teams*—Youngsters who are bullied are not wanted on teams or in groups. Placement is forced or by default when no one is left.
- *Loss of friends or not wanting to associate with old friends*—Friendships are often lost when kids are bullied because children are afraid to associate with bullied peers lest they can become the new targets. Not wanting to associate with friends might be because those "friends" now bully them.
- *Sitting alone*—The bullied are ostracized.
- *Shyness, sensitivity*—Shyness or sensitivity can be perceived as vulnerabilities, making the child a target.
- *Poor body language*—Non verbal communication can signal a lack of confidence or a weakness, making the person an appealing mark.
- *Deficiency in social skills*—Poor social skills can make a child stand out, raising the risk of being bullied. It also makes it difficult to defend oneself.
- *Lack of assertive skills*—Those with poor assertive skills have less success preventing, deflecting, or handling bullying.

## Miscellaneous Signs

- *Damaged property*—Books, clothes, and possessions can be damaged during bullying.
- *Missing property*—Bullied children may claim their schoolbooks, clothes, and valuables are "missing" or "lost" after being stolen or destroyed.
- *"Lost" money*—Those who are bullied may fear retaliation or are ashamed, so they say their money was "lost," when in reality it was stolen.
- *Stealing*—Students may steal money to pay for lunch or other expenses because their cash was stolen by someone who bullied them.
- *Carrying weapons for protection*—Sticks, knives, guns, or other weapons can be used for security and defense because there are no friends to help defend or deflect bullying.
- *Non aggressive children being accused of starting fights*—Red flags should go up when weak, shy, and non aggressive children who cannot defend themselves are found in the middle of fights and are always blamed for starting them. (Borba, 2012; Kidscape, 2010; Storey & Slaby, 2008; PREVNet, 2007b; U.S. Department of Health and Human Services, n.d.)

It is important to note that a child can display some signs and not be bullied or may not show any and be on the receiving end of someone's abuse. Generally, the more indicators exhibited, the greater the possibility that bullying exists.

Bullied children are more likely to report abuse under certain circumstances: if there are physical threats, physical bullying, injuries, or damaged possessions. The chances of telling also increase with frequency, a rise in the types or locations of bullying, and if episodes occur on the school bus (Petrosino, Guckenburg, DeVoe, & Hanson, 2010).

Table 4.2 Bullying sites on the internet

| General websites for teachers and parents | Bullying lesson plans | Bullying PowerPoint presentations |
|---|---|---|
| **Stop Bullying Now!** | **National Bullying Prevention Center (Pacer)** | "Bullying" |
| www.stopbullying.gov/ | www.pacer.org/bullying/sap/activities-ele.asp | www.slideshare.net/coolmum4u/bullying-3494068 |
| **Online Course—the ABCs of Bullying** | **Region of Waterloo (Canada)** | "Bully Free School" |
| http://pathwayscourses.samhsa.gov/bully/bully_intro_pg1.htm | http://chd.region.waterloo.on.ca/en/childfamilyhealth/bullyingprevention.asp | www.slideshare.net/robys/how-to-be-a-bully-free-school |
| **Pacer's National Bullying Prevention Center** | **National Crime Prevention Council** | "What is Bullying? 6th grade" |
| www.pacer.org/bullying/about/ | www.ncpc.org/topics/bullying/bullying-/teaching-kids-about-bullying | www2.gsu.edu/~wwwche/Brandy%20Bullying.ppt |
| **National Crime Prevention Council** | **Common Sense Media's Cyber Smart! Curriculum** | **Additional PowerPoint presentations are at:** |
| www.ncpc.org | http://cybersmartcurriculum.org/safetysecurity/lessons/ | www.slideshare.net |
| | | http://facs.pppst.com/bullying.html |
| **Bullying.org** | **Hotchalk's LessonPlanPages.com** | |
| www.bullying.org | www.lessonplanspage.com/SSODoSomethingAboutSchoolViolenceUnit Day1Bullying912.htm | |

| Cyberbullying | Websites for children | Bullying games and quizzes |
|---|---|---|
| **NetSmartz.org**<br>www.netsmartz.org/Educators | **Stop Bullying Now** (*Kids, teens, young adults*)<br>www.stopbullying.gov/kids/index.html | **"Round Up"**<br>www.bam.gov/sub_yourlife/yourlife_bullyroundup.html# |
| **Cyberbullying Research Center**<br>www.cyberbullying.us/resources.php | **Pacer Kids Against Bullying** (*Pacer Center*)<br>http://pacerkidsagainstbullying.org (Under 13)<br>http://pacerteensagainstbullying.org (Teens) | **"S-Team Heroes"**<br>www.teamheroes.ca/website/play.html |
| **Parry Aftab and wiredsafety.org**<br>www.stopcyberbullying.org | **Bullying.org**<br>www.bullying.org | **"Beat the Bully"**<br>http://pbskids.org/itsmylife/games/bullies_flash.html<br>www.wiredsafety.org |
| **Cyberbullying.org**<br>www.cyberbullying.org | **Netsmartz**<br>www.netsmartzkids.org (Kids)<br>www.nsteens.org (Tweens)<br>www.netsmartz.org/Teens (Teens) | |
| **Illinois Attorney General** (*Internet Safety Training Modules*)<br>www.illinoisattorneygeneral.gov/children/internet.html | **WiredKids.org** (*Kids, tweens, teens*)<br>www.wiredkids.org | |

*continued ...*

*Table 4.2 . . . continued*

**Pennsylvania Attorney General**
*(Internet Curriculum)*

www.attorneygeneral.gov/kidsparents.
aspx?id=1683

*Miscellaneous:*

**Stop Bullying Now! Resource Kit**

www.ask.hrsa.gov/detail_materials.cfm?ProdID=3109

**Eyes on Bullying**

www.eyesonbullying.org/toolkit.html

Note: The internet sites listed on this chart were put into categories for convenience. Many sites have overlapping information.

Table 4.3 Internet safety and cyberbullying information from around the world (tutorials, games, quizzes, animations, videos, downloads, case studies, and books)

| Name | Sponsor | URL | Teacher resources | Age, grade, level |
|---|---|---|---|---|
| **Hector's World** | NetSafe NetSmartz | www.hectorsworld.com/island/index. html | Yes | Ages 2–9 |
| **Material on basic internet safety, blogging, cell phones, cyberbullying, email, IMs, chatrooms, gaming, identity theft, revealing too much, social networking, spywear, spam, scams, and much more** | Workshop, a program of The National Center for Missing & Exploited Children | www.netsmartz.org/resources | Yes | Ages 5–adult |
| **Don't Be in the Dark** | Disney UK | www.disney.co.uk/DisneyOnline/ Safesurfing | Parent guide | Elementary |
| **Safe Surfing with Doug** | Disney UK | www.disney.co.uk/DisneyOnline/ Safesurfing/main.html | Parent guide | Elementary |
| **Learn With Professor Garfield** | Virginia Department of Education | www.learninglab.org | Yes | Elementary |
| **"Cyberbullying"** | | | | |
| **"Online Safety"** | | | | |
| **Faux Paw the Techno Cat** (several adventures) | iKeepSafe | www.ikeepsafe.org/educators/fauxpaw | Yes | Elementary |
| **Woogi World** | Woogi World, Inc. | www.woogiworld.com | Yes | Elementary |

continued ...

Table 4.3 ... *continued*

| Name | Sponsor | URL | Teacher resources | Age, grade, level |
|---|---|---|---|---|
| **Operation Safe Surf** | Pennsylvania Attorney General | www.attorneygeneral.gov/kid_site/elementary_school/index.htm | Yes | K–5 |
| | | www.attorneygeneral.gov/kid_site/middle_school/main_ms.swf | Yes | Middle School |
| **Welcome to the Web** | Teaching Ideas | www.teachingideas.co.uk/welcome/start.htm | Yes | Ages 7–11 |
| **Cyber Cafe** | Child Exploitation and Online Protection Centre, ThinkUKnow.co.uk | www.thinkuknow.co.uk/8_10/cybercafe | Yes | Ages 8–10 |
| **Safety Land** | AT & T | www.att.com/Common/images/safety/game.html | No | Grades 1–4 |
| **Zoe and Molly Online—Caught in the Net** | Canadian Centre for Child Protection | www.zoeandmolly.ca/app/en | Yes | Grade 3 |
| **Zoe and Molly Online** | | | Yes | Grade 4 |
| **Through the Wild Web Woods** | Council of Europe | www.wildwebwoods.org/popup_langSelection.php | No | Ages 7–10 |
| **Webonauts Internet Academy** | PBS Kids | www.pbskids.org/webonauts | Yes | Ages 8–10 |
| **KidSMART Captain Kara & Winston's SMART Adventure** | ChildNet International | www.kidsmart.org.uk www.childnet.com/kia/primary/smartadventure/default.aspx | Yes Yes | Grades 3–7, 8–11 Ages 6–11 |

| Title | Author/Organization | URL | | Level |
|---|---|---|---|---|
| My Secure Cyberspace Game | Carnegie Mellon University | www.carnegiecyberacademy.com | Yes | Grades 4–5 |
| Piracy Pirates | Media Awareness Network | www.media-awareness.ca/english/games/index.cfm | Yes | Ages 7–9 |
| Top Secret | | | Yes | Grades 6–8 |
| Privacy Playground: The First Adventure of the Three Cyber Pigs | | | Yes | Ages 8–10 |
| CyberSense and Nonsense: The Second Adventure of the Three Cyber Pigs | | | Yes | Ages 9–12 |
| Joel Cool or Joel Fool | | | Yes | Grades 6–8 |
| Stay Safe | BBC, CBBC | www.bbc.co.uk/cbbc/topics/stay-safe | No | Elementary |
| | | | No | Middle School |
| Investigate Cyberbullying | Chris Webster | www.cyberbullying.info | No | Ages 10–14 |
| CyberNetrix | Australian Government | www.cybersmart.gov.au/cybernetrix/index.html | Yes | Middle School |
| CyberQuoll | | www.cybersmart.gov.au/cyberquoll/html/menu.html | Yes | Upper Elementary |
| Everything You Need to Know About Wireless | CABLEVISION | www.powertolearn.com/internet_smarts/interactive_case_studies/index.shtml | No | Upper Elementary Middle School |

continued . . .

Table 4.3 ... continued

| Name | Sponsor | URL | Teacher resources | Age, grade, level |
|------|---------|-----|-------------------|-------------------|
| **Social Networking: Don't Give Yourself Away** | | | Yes | |
| **Digital Permanence: FOREVER is a Long Time** | | | Yes | |
| **Cyberbullying: Not Just Name-Calling** | | | Yes | |
| **Misinformation—Truth or Spoof** | | | Yes | |
| **Keeping Personal Info Private** | | | Yes | |
| **Let's Fight It Together** | Digizen.org, Childnet International | www.digizen.org/cyberbullying/fullFilm. aspx | Yes | Grades 4–12 |
| **Digital Literacy Tour** | Google and iKeepSafe | www.google.com/educators/ digitalliteracy.html | Yes | Grades 6–12 |
| **Own Your Space** | Microsoft | www.microsoft.com/download/en/ details.aspx?id=1522 | No | Grades 8–12 |
| **Life Online** | Girl Scouts and Windows | www.lmk.girlscouts.org | No | Teens |

Note: This chart introduces readers to some of the activities on the websites. Browsing the sites will unveil a wealth of information.

Part 2

# USING SOCIAL ARCHITECTURE TO PREVENT, LESSEN, AND END BULLYING

# Chapter 5

# Introduction to Social Architecture

## Bullying and Relationships

Bullying is relationship driven. Breakdowns in relationships are the keys that turn bullying to the start position. Strong relationships turn the engine off.

## The Bullying Triangle

The connection between bullying and relationships is illustrated with the bullying triangle.

Look at the specific relationships (Goodstein, 2008):

- *Bully–Bullied.* Bullying begins with people who seek power, control, and domination. They look for people they can easily oppress.
- *Bullied–Bully.* If the person who is attacked shows fear, submits to demands, or does not report incidents, bullying will most likely continue. If the individual does not act upset, responds assertively, makes a joke, or reports the episode, the chances of bullying ending increase.
- *Bully–Bystanders.* Those who bully love audiences because they want peers to see how "powerful" they are. If there are no bystanders, abuse will be curtailed. The longer bystanders stay, the longer bullying episodes continue.

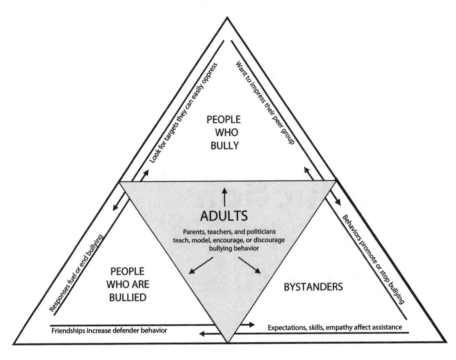

*Figure 5.1* The Bullying Triangle (Goodstein, 2008, adaptation)

- *Bystanders–Bully.* When bystanders watch, participate, laugh, cheer, gesture, or egg on bullying, they encourage the abuse. If bystanders say "stop bullying," help the person being attacked, leave, or get adult assistance, odds are the bullying will end.
- *Bystanders–Bullied.* Expectations, skills, empathy, friendships, and norms determine whether bystanders help bullied peers.
- *Bullied–Bystanders.* Friendships increase bystander intervention.

Adults are another important group in the bullying equation. To borrow a Reggie Jackson quotation, adults are "the straw that stirs the drink."

The first adults in children's lives are parents and guardians who teach and model prosocial skills or antisocial behavior. Educators become the next set of teachers and are pivotal players in bullying. Teacher conduct and classroom management can encourage or discourage abuse. Elected officials are a third group of adults who can affect bullying behavior. They can allow criminality to continue in schools or enact laws that protect children against abuse.

# What is Social Architecture?

Researchers have recognized the connection between relationships and bullying for years.

In 1993, Olweus advocated "*a restructuring of the social environment*" (1993b, p. 341). Bullying has been called "a relationship problem" (Craig & Pepler, 2003, p. 577). The socio-ecological perspective, the social hierarchy, dominancy, the homophily hypothesis, peer support, and bystander assistance have been the subjects of research, explored in scholarly journals, and applied to programs.

Debra J. Pepler, a distinguished Canadian research professor and bullying expert, was the first person to apply the metaphors "social scaffolding" and "social architecture" to bullying (Pepler, 2006). "Social scaffolding" considers "the supports required to provide children with the skills, capacities, and social cognitions to move out of the bullying and victimization roles" (PREVNet, 2007a, p. 13). Social architecture is "the opportunity to structure children's peer groups to promote positive peer experiences and to minimize or deconstruct negative peer experiences" (PREVNet, 2007a, p. 14). Pepler created a three point intervention plan around social scaffolding and social architecture:

1.  "Separate the child who is bullying from the victimized child and from the peers who reinforce the bullying behaviour" (PREVNet, 2007a, p. 15). While separated, teach all parties relationship skills. For example, help bullied children develop friendships, increase empathy in those who bully, and show bystanders safe and effective ways to intervene in bullying situations (PREVNet, 2007a). (Social scaffolding)
2.  "Embed victimized children within a positive per context" (PREVNet, 2007a, p. 15). For example, teachers can judiciously organize seating, groups, and teams based on the social dynamics of the class (PREVNet, 2007a). (Social architecture)
3.  "Promote a generally positive, respectful, accepting, and supportive climate within a social group" (PREVNet, 2007a, p. 15). For example, adults can help bystanders realize their roles and how they contribute to bullying, and can demonstrate ways to help (PREVNet, 2007a). (Social architecture)

The success of the program depends on adults providing organization, education, intervention, guidance, supervision, and support (PREVNet, 2007a).

# How to Implement Social Architecture in the Classroom

The author has created a 10 point program around Pepler's model of social architecture:

1. *The teacher's role*—Educators are role models and leaders in their classrooms. Their actions, or lack of, and their expectations teach pro bullying or anti-bullying lessons. As such, teachers need to be aware of their biases and prejudices, verbal, and non verbal communication. Educators need to learn all facets of bullying and examine the relationships in their classrooms. The relationships teachers form with children and the relationships teachers help students establish can stifle or fuel abuse.

2. *Education*—Teachers and children are the keys to anti-bullying efforts so they need to know the five Ws of bullying. The roles played must also be underscored, as well as effective responses.

3. *Classroom management*—Sound classroom management sets up a social ecology that helps children form healthy relationships while blotting out harmful encounters. It can be the difference between order and mayhem, safety or danger, learning or fooling around. Bullying is absent or minimized when there are connected classroom communities, rules, consequences, and documentation of bullying incidents. Instructional style, cooperative learning, the physical layout, and seating assignments also affect bullying.

4. *Bystanders/Upstanders*—Bystanders have the power to end bullying or keep it alive. This group, comprising the majority of students, need to learn how their actions can energize bullying, the importance and ways of telling, and skills that safely challenge abuse. Relationships and social dynamics sideline or prompt bystander action so they must also be addressed.

5. *Friendship*—Having even one good friend can mean the difference between becoming target practice or being overlooked. The teaching of friendship and social skills benefits all students.

6. *Peer support*—Peer support programs help youngsters develop relationships with those who are bullied and those who bully. Peers can comfort classmates, teach anti-bullying skills, raise confidence, and increase acceptance. Peer role models make an "It is not acceptable to bully" statement, thereby showing the student body that bullying is not the norm. They can also share bullying information with friends and younger children.

7. *Empathy*—Bullying would be extinct if those who bullied were able to feel the recipient's pain. Teachers can take advantage of exercises that raise empathy.

8. *Incompatible activities*—Actions that are incompatible with bullying can stop and prevent abuse and encourage healthy relationships.

9. *Stopping and responding to bullying incidents*—The way teachers stop bullying episodes and how they follow through affects future events. Their responses can deteriorate teacher–student relationships or build new ones and can determine if relationships between children involved in bullying continue to be damaged or are repaired.

10. *Adult support*—The power imbalance prevents children from ending bullying by themselves, in many instances, so they need adult assistance. Teachers, parents, and adult mentors can team up to provide education, help rebuild damaged relationships, and give support to those who are bullied, those who bully, and bystanders.

These ten points help alter relationships, the school culture, and norms.

The remainder of the book will more closely examine the 10 parts of social architecture, with a chapter dedicated to each. The only exception is number two, education. Bullying facts were discussed in the first part of this book and are dispersed throughout this volume.

# Chapter 6

# The Teacher's Role

## Why Should Teachers Spend Time on Social Architecture?

Socio-emotional and cognitive development are linked. Bullied children will not concentrate on coursework even if taught by the most exceptional teacher-of-the-year. An abused student's priority is survival—how to make it through the school day without being attacked or humiliated. Education is placed on the back burner. *Academic performance can be moved to the front of the class by keeping aggression out of the classroom.*

Social architecture is a proactive strategy that prevents abuse. Followers set the table beforehand, by minimizing opportunities for bullying, decreasing rewards, and encouraging positive peer relationships.

Teachers who use social architecture are prepared. Their strategies permeate the classroom, providing an omnipresent force field against abuse. As such, bullying episodes are rare, but if they occur educators are guided by carefully thought out interventions, not "on the spot" reactions.

Teachers must (a) examine the social relationships in their classrooms, (b) determine how they contribute to bullying, (c) anticipate problems, (d) develop strategies that promote positive relationships, and (e) put their anti-bullying blueprints into action.

It is true that precious time is taken away from teaching when planning and administering social architecture, but in the long run more time will be spent teaching because disruptions are lessened or eliminated. Social architecture complements academic performance. It does not take away from it.

## Box 6.1:  Time Travel

Make believe you are in a time machine that transports you back to your childhood, specifically a time you were bullied. Ask yourself the following questions:

- Was I hit, tripped, or pushed?
- Did someone steal or break any of my possessions?
- Was I on the receiving end of cruel comments or mean jokes?
- Did anyone threaten, make fun of, laugh at, or humiliate me?
- Was I purposely left out, ignored, or told that I could not play with someone?
- Did anyone break my confidence, spread lies, or take a friend away?
- Did I observe others being mistreated? Did I bully anyone?

If you were not bullied, think about a bullying episode you witnessed. Take a few minutes to recall the event. What happened? Did you feel sad, hurt, anxious, threatened, scared, terrified, worried, trapped, helpless, shaky, despairing, alienated, humiliated, ashamed, embarrassed, demeaned, devalued, worthless, used, angry, frustrated, confused, or indifferent? Try to feel these feelings. How did your peers, teachers, and adults react? Do you wish they would have behaved differently? How would you (or the person who was bullied) have liked to have been treated?

## Different Levels of Bullying

Classroom climates vary from class to class and school to school. In some classes bullying is outlawed; in others, bullying is the law. One study found that bullying in classrooms varied between zero and 54.5% (Atria, Strohmeier, & Spiel, 2007). Olweus's (1993a) research revealed similar findings: bullying can be four to five times greater in one school than in another.

What accounts for these differences? Schools with strong anti-bullying policies that *all* staff members enforce have less bullying. Within classrooms, teachers are "mission control." Educators' past histories, teaching styles, behaviors, beliefs, management skills, and relationships with students influence bullying levels. "*The attitudes of the teachers toward bully/victim problems and their behavior in bullying situations are of major significance for the extent of bully/victim problems in the school or the class*," Olweus wrote (1993a, p. 26). Ending bullying begins with classroom teachers.

## Teachers Are Role Models

Humans acquire information directly or indirectly by watching people's behaviors, actions, and reactions, and from the results of those factors. It is easy to understand why teachers are influential role models if we realize that educators are the adults with whom children spend the most time from age 5 through 18.

Educators consciously or unconsciously teach students healthy or unhealthy relationship skills when they model respect or disrespect, acceptance or intolerance, inclusion or exclusion, kindness or cruelty, and appropriate or inappropriate behavior. If an educator yells at a class for misbehaving, the children are taught that yelling is a way to gain control. If the instructor hits a pupil, the class learns that aggression solves problems. If the teacher shows impatience with a challenged student, bystanders assume insults should be used in difficult situations. The way a teacher acts or responds to one student affects *all* pupils because they are watching and learning.

Allowing, disregarding, or participating in bullying is equivalent to tacking a note onto the bulletin board saying "I support bullying." In those classrooms it is open season for hunting down underdogs. Those who aggress are given a license to bully.

The influence of teacher modeling is articulated in research:

- Teachers who discourage aggression have less bullying in their classrooms (Henry et al., 2000).
- Students of educators who clearly show a dislike of aggression reject aggressive classmates. Those who allow aggression have more pupils who exhibit aggressive behaviors (Chang, 2003).
- Youngsters bully the same way their teacher disciplines. A copycat effect occurs where children imitate their teachers' put downs, labeling, scolding, and even physical abuse (Yoneyama & Naito, 2003).
- "Teachers who are supportive, take an active interest in students, and treat them fairly, create an environment where bullying is less likely" (Barboza et al., 2009, p. 113). In fact, there is 24% less bullying in these classrooms.

*Everything* an educator does or does not do sets the class climate and lets students know what will and will not be allowed in the classroom. Actions, words, gestures, or lack of can be human shields protecting students against bullying or knives that cut into the psyches of youngsters. The lessons taught by modeling can mold behavior more than the most extraordinary class lesson or one-on-one talk. In some cases, teachers' modeling of prosocial behavior is the only exposure children have to appropriate ways of acting.

---

## Box 6.2: Self-evaluation

If teachers take an introspective look at themselves they may become aware of their own biases, difficulties, and limitations. Self-critiques help educators become more effective role models:

- Do I favor one sex, culture, or personality over another?
- Do I ever exclude or let students leave out classmates?
- Do I have trouble dealing with "difficult" students?
- Do I display aggressive behavior?
- Do I ignore bullying because it is easier for me?
- Do I consciously or unconsciously promote bullying?
- Am I afraid to confront a bullying situation because it reminds me of my past history of being bullied?
- Do I harshly punish children who bully because of my limitations?
- Do I have the necessary skills to handle bullying?
- Do I continually ask myself "What message am I sending to my students?"

## Actions To Be Aware of as a Role Model

### Respectful Actions and Talk

Children are mirrors who reflect behavior. Are your words and actions positive or negative? Do they encourage, teach, and support; or do they belittle and demean? Are they tinged with sarcasm?

It can be difficult to maintain composure and respond respectfully in the most trying situations. "Stop hitting her. You act like a first grader" will not change behavior. The youngster is now humiliated, possibly angry, and anxious about future feedback. It teaches bystanders that it is okay to belittle someone who has trouble with self-control. "What might be a better way to communicate your frustration?" or "Let's work together on what is upsetting you" are gentler, more effective responses.

### Tone of Voice

It is not what people say but how they say it. The same sentence conveyed in varying tones delivers different messages. Children pick up these undercurrents. Teachers should ask themselves "Is my tone just as warm with marginalized and challenging children and those who bully as it is with easy to handle students?" One way to increase awareness is by recording your voice and listening to how it sounds.

### Feelings and Emotions

It is important to get in touch with feelings because that is where words and actions originate. Unrecognized feelings control people; awareness allows humans to captain their own ships. If a teacher is angry it is important to locate the source because anger is generally a secondary response. Fear, frustration, humiliation, hurt, or resentment often precede it.

Teachers who respond angrily to someone who bullies should conduct an internal dialogue. "Why did I react in that manner? Was I frustrated because I could not figure out a way to connect with my student? Am I angry that the bullying took time away from teaching and my class will do poorly in the state exams? Do I resent the fact that the principal gave me difficult children this year while my colleagues received an easy ride?"

It is not wise to handle volatile bullying situations while angry because anger could affect rational thinking and judgment. However, teachers may have little choice as they do not decide the timing of confrontations. In those situations, counting to 10, deep breathing, a relaxation exercise, or momentary distraction with another thought can be used to calm down. If not, teachers should stop the bullying episode and wait for a better time to handle it. "We will talk about this later" allows time to regain composure.

## Gestures

Gestures are movements of the hands, arms, legs, face, or any part of the body. They communicate information. Smiling at a child who helps a bullied classmate, winking at a student who includes a peer in the group, and patting the back of a youngster who stood up to bullying expresses endorsement and praise. Putting an open palm up in a "stop" position, shaking an index finger, frowning, or stern looks put the receiver on notice that the educator is not pleased with the behavior. Non verbal communication can speak louder than words.

## Ignoring Bullying

When teachers close their eyes to bullying the day's lesson is that bullying is an acceptable activity and there is nothing wrong with hurting others.

## Taking Action or Refraining

A teacher's reaction to bullying reports affects future behavior. If educators ignore it, laugh, or do not take action, students will make a mockery out of "telling." If teachers intervene, effectively discipline, and teach, students will support anti-bullying initiatives.

## Encouraging or Discouraging Reporting

Are there discussions about the differences between telling and tattling? Is telling positively supported? Is the role of bystanders pointed out? Are there ways children can anonymously report? What assurances are there for an informant's safety? Is immediate action taken? Will interventions successfully stop bullying and prevent future incidents? Teachers are just as wrong as inactive bystanders if they do not consistently advocate reporting or fail to follow up on *all* bullying reports.

## Classroom Norms Against Aggression

Those who bully are less likely to be rejected and more likely to be popular in classes where bullying is normative. The reverse occurs when bullying is considered aberrant; those who aggress are low on the social scale. This occurs because children rebuff anyone who deviates from their group norm; that is, behavior is acceptable when it is similar to that of peers and not accepted when it differs. If bullying is not the norm those who bully will be rejected while those who are bullied will find greater acceptance (Sentse, Scholte, Salmivalli, & Voeten, 2007). Thus, it is critically important to have norms against aggression. The chances of anti-bullying norms developing in classrooms increase when teachers provide constant behavioral feedback (Henry et al., 2000).

## Make Anti-bullying a Presence in the Classroom

Children cannot help but notice if the classroom is saturated with anti-bullying messages. Curriculum connections to bullying, circle time with discussions about abuse, bully boxes, art projects, story time, reading, writing, charts, puppets, and posters about bullying keep it in the forefront. They also show pupils that the teacher takes bullying seriously and will not tolerate abuse in the classroom.

Activities that battle bullying can sensitize participants to the harmful consequences of bullying. It is also difficult to work on projects against bullying and aggress at the same time. Assign or challenge students to perform any of the following activities:

- Conduct a student survey on bullying.
- Sketch a map of bullying hot spots.
- Create anti-bullying awards.
- Design anti-bullying posters and place them around the classroom and school.
- Paint and hang an anti-bullying mural.
- Teach younger students about bullying.
- Participate in a peer support program.
- Fundraise and use the profits for anti-bullying t-shirts, bracelets, buttons, anti-bullying speakers, or presentations.
- Write a report about bullying and share it with the class or school.
- Produce a PowerPoint presentation or a video about bullying.
- Write an anti-bullying newsletter or handbook.
- Create anti-bullying messages for the morning announcements.
- Compose an anti-bullying show or song.
- Print and hand out wallet size cards on how to stop bullying.
- Join or start an anti-bullying club or committee.
- Organize an anti-bullying patrol.
- Plan and carry out an anti-bullying day.
- Develop an anti-bullying carnival.
- Set up an anti-bullying website.

## Labeling Students

Are students given specific names that negatively brand them? Separate the child from the behavior. Teachers *must* internalize the fact that no child, whether someone who bullies, is bullied, or a bystander, should ever be humiliated or demeaned no matter how challenging they are. The actions modeled by teachers today will be the behaviors of children tomorrow.

---

### Box 6.3: Inclusive Twist to Musical Chairs

Use this old favorite to raise issues of inclusion and exclusion. First, play the traditional way. When the game is over, explain that you'd like to try a different version—this time the object is to make sure no one is excluded. If everyone has a place to sit, the group wins. If anyone is without a place to sit, the group loses. When playing, eliminate a chair, but not a child, every time the music stops. Students will need to figure out creative ways to pile everyone on one chair.

Afterward, discuss the difference between the two experiences: How did it feel to sit on the sidelines? Have there been other times you've been on the sidelines while other children played? How did it feel? Can you think of other games you could redesign this way?

(Source: Kridler, n.d., Playing for Empathy section, para. 1)

---

# Chapter 7

# Classroom Management

## Anti-Bullying Efforts Begin on the First Day of School

A crusade to prevent bullying from rearing its ugly head should be a top priority and receive the same importance as the "not calling out" rule. If properly introduced, carried out, and reinforced, students will be supportive because (a) no one likes to be bullied, (b) witnessing mistreatment is uncomfortable, and (c) intolerance for bullying is a non negotiable expectation. When anti–bullying attitudes prevail, peer pressure makes offenders think twice because the social costs of bullying may be too expensive a price to pay.

Bullying is kept in check when teachers consistently and clearly convey their unyielding convictions that bullying will not be allowed. Teachers who communicate these expectations at the beginning of the school year have less bullying in their classrooms (Buhs & de Guzman, 2007). Expectations and enforcement of expectations produce results. On the whole, most children do not call out. Why? When they do teachers stop and explain that students must wait to be recognized before speaking. Youngsters do not get out of their seats. Why? When they do teachers stop and insist they return to their seats. Pupils do not stand on desks. Why? When they do teachers stop and explain that injuries can occur and furniture can be damaged. In the same vein, teachers should stop the class after *every* bullying incident, explain why it is wrong, and discuss more appropriate ways to behave.

The first day of school is not too early to start. *Do not wait* until a bullying incident occurs. Strike preemptively:

- On day one, clearly announce that there will be NO bullying in the classroom. It is unacceptable and abuse will NOT be tolerated.
- Explain the reasoning behind the statement: (a) Bullying is cruel and hurtful, (b) all students deserve to learn in safety, and (c) it is the students' and teacher's job to protect children.
- A bully free environment begins with education. Start with the definition and identify what bullying is and is not. This eliminates ignorance and misunderstandings. (Refer to the first section of this book.)
- Point out the different forms of bullying—physical, verbal, relational, and cyberbullying—and provide examples. Create a game by breaking the class into teams. Each has to act out possible bullying situations. The opposing team has to decide if the scene can be categorized as bullying.
- Show the "Bullying web of harm" (Figure 4.1) or an age appropriate version and explain the harmful consequences of bullying. Make a blank copy and ask students to fill in the ways they and their classmates have been harmed by bullying. Ask students "How did it feel?"
- Give "on the spot" lessons when bullying occurs. Stop the bullying; address the problem with those involved; and lead a classroom discussion. What bullying occurred? Why was it wrong? What roles did classmates play? What are more appropriate ways to handle the situation (for the person who bullied, was bullied, and bystanders)? The time and attention will be well spent; it helps create a bully free classroom culture.
- Increase the power of lessons by letting the bullied child become the teacher. Jaylen Arnold is a firsthand example of education in action. The 10-year-old boy has Tourette's Syndrome, Obsessive Compulsive Disorder, and Asperger's Syndrome. When Jaylen attended a public school he witnessed nastiness, fighting, and bullying, some of which were directed at him. The stress exacerbated Jaylen's disorders prompting a transfer back to his former school (Arnold, n.d., a).

  The story does not end there. This youngster did not want others to go through such a painful ordeal. Jaylen thought that teaching youngsters about Tourette's Syndrome would increase their understanding. He also wanted peers to know how much bullying hurts. To that end, Jaylen created a website (www.jaylenschallenge.org) and became a public speaker. The students who bullied Jaylen at the public school apologized after Jaylen spoke there. "All kids just need to know that their bullying changes kids and people forever" (Arnold, n.d.,b, p. 1). Jaylen's presentations are effective because he helps audiences see bullying through his eyes and feel his pain.

- Build relationships. How many times have teachers followed up "I don't like him" with "Have you ever spent any time with him?" and received a negative response? When youngsters have the opportunity (whether by choice, accident, or because an educator set up the situation) to spend time with the "disliked" person they often find that their negative perception of the peer does not match reality.

Relationships are born through interactions. Time together may replace ignorance with familiarity, knowledge, and understanding. Trust, respect, and friendships can develop. Cooperative learning, buddying up, and creating situations where classmates get to know one another plant seeds that can grow into friendships.

- Incorporate social emotional learning (SEL). Academia comes to mind when most people think about education. However, teaching should be holistic with educators also teaching about *relationships*, *respect*, and *responsibility*. While academics are and should be the priority, social emotional learning should not be neglected; in fact, it should be seen as a main objective of education. Had children learned how to regulate their emotions, empathize, establish positive relationships, resolve conflicts peacefully, make wise decisions, and realize their behavior has consequences, we would not see the terrorism of bullying controlling our schools.

  - SEL teaches *the person who bullies* self-awareness and self-management skills (being in touch with one's feelings, knowing strengths, controlling antisocial impulses, managing anger, non aggressive ways to react to social situations, calming techniques), social awareness (empathy, tolerance of differences), relationship skills (solving conflicts in non aggressive ways, getting along with all types of people, respecting differences, not bending to peer pressure), and responsible decision making (problem solving skills, correct ways to interpret social situations, respecting others, being aware of the consequences of actions, decreasing pro violent attitudes).
  - SEL teaches *the person who is bullied* self-awareness and self-management skills (being in touch with feelings, reducing internalizing and externalizing behaviors that may provoke bullying, decreasing reactions that reward and further aggression, recognizing strengths that could build self-esteem), social awareness (increasing social skills, respecting different perspectives, learning when it is appropriate to ask for assistance), relationship skills (improving communication, friendship, and relationship skills), and responsible decision making (learning safe and appropriate responses to bullying, problem solving skills, how to get help).
  - SEL teaches *bystanders* self-awareness and self-management skills (accurately gauging feelings, responding to bullying in assertive ways, assessing anti-bullying skill repertoires), social awareness (increasing empathy, making use of available resources), relationship skills (teaching ways to help bullied children defuse volatile bullying situations, resisting peer pressure, when and how to seek help), and responsible decision making (problem solving skills, how to respond to social pressure, the consequences of inaction, and not reporting) (Ragozzino & O'Brien, 2009).

A social emotional learning checklist for bullying is available from the Committee for Children, Steps to Respect (www.cfchildren.org/tabid/119/Default.aspx).

---

## Box 7.1: Sweet Beginnings

On the first day of school teacher Marissa Ochoa gives students treat bags filled with items that set the tone for the school year (Ochoa, n.d.). Educators can take Ochoa's creative idea one step further by designing an anti-bullying goody bag with a "We do not bully in our classroom" theme. Tape messages onto the items. For example:

Eraser—We will erase bullying from our classroom.
Bag of chips—We will chip in by creating anti-bullying rules.
Pencil—We will speak out against bullying because it is the "write" thing to do.
Sticker—We will stick together by including everyone in every activity.
Hershey Kiss—We will show kindness and love by defending bullied peers.
Smarties—It is smart to get adult help if we cannot handle bullying by ourselves.
Lifesavers—Friends can be lifesavers.

---

- Point out that no one is immune from abuse. A child who is free from bullying today can easily become tomorrow's target. *The only way to insure safety is to end bullying.*
- Keep talking about bullying. Do not stop at any point during the year. The more teachers talk about bullying, the greater the awareness.

## Building a Community

Building a community should be on top of every teacher's "Do Now" list. Communities are places where people work together, share common values and goals, and support one another. Relationships flourish when children are connected by the glue of a community. Members are less likely to bully and more likely to defend and protect peers.

Teachers can help youngsters develop classroom communities with good management techniques, instruction, and modeling. They also need to provide opportunities for community building, support children's efforts, and relinquish some control:

- During the summer, write a letter of introduction welcoming students into your class. Tell a little about yourself and the upcoming school year.
- Decorate the classroom with the basic necessities. Leave the remainder of the walls and spaces empty. This shows that it is "our" classroom and "we" will decorate it together.
- Organize desks so they face each other.
- Play "name learning" games during the first few days of school.

- Give students warm welcomes when they enter the classroom, throughout the year.
- Place pictures of the children around the classroom.
- Display class work.
- Let students create class rules.
- Encourage input on curriculum, discussions, and activities.
- Give choices.
- Ask for opinions.
- Use cooperative learning.
- Hold class meetings.
- Promote prosocial behavior. This can be achieved through modeling, discussions, activities, projects, or posters.
- Use community building language. Replace "I," "he," "she," and "you" with "we" and "us" (e.g., "We will help each other." "We will make this a better class for us."). Also, use terms associated with prosocial behavior—e.g., share, take turns, cooperate, help, please, sorry, listen, praise, greet, smile, negotiate, and respect.
- Play community building games, such as that in Box 7.2: Class *Profits* Together.
- Have a "No Exclusion" policy. Everyone is always welcome to join.
- Encourage children to include classmates who sit on the sidelines.
- Students who finish their work early should help peers.
- Create a directory of areas in which students excel. Use the children's expertise as resources (see Box 7.3: Who is Good in What in Our Class).
- List activities the class accomplished together that could not have been done individually.
- Assign classroom jobs and rotate the responsibilities.
- Celebrate birthdays, as long as it is within the beliefs of students.
- Create traditions and rituals.
- Embrace diversity.
- Show and expect respect. Every person is a valuable part of the class.
- Ban put downs, bullying, and other hurtful behaviors. Stop harmful behaviors immediately (Hittie, 2000; Jablon, n.d.; Kentucky Adult Education, n.d.; Servant, 2006).

---

## Box 7.2: Class *Profits* Together

Draw a jigsaw puzzle on a large sheet of paper that has enough pieces for each child in the class. Cut the puzzle into pieces and give one part to each student. Tell students to write their names in large print on the face of their piece and then collaboratively put the puzzle together.

> When finished, explain how the puzzle represents every pupil in their classroom. Each piece is a valuable part, just as each student in the class. The pieces are joined, making something bigger than each of the individual parts. It takes everyone working together, sharing, and helping to create a safe, bully free classroom.

An example of one community building activity is a note writing campaign. Each week students must write a positive note to a different classmate, complimenting him or her on an admired quality, behavior, or kindness displayed.

## Connectedness

Communities are built and strengthened with connectedness. Blum (2005) defined school connectedness as "The belief by students that adults in the school care about their learning and about them as individuals" and said "Strong scientific evidence demonstrates that increased student connection to school decreases absenteeism, fighting, bullying and vandalism while promoting educational motivation, classroom engagement, academic performance, school attendance and completion rates" (Blum, 2005, p. 1).

The degree of connectedness is affected by "1) academic engagement, 2) belonging, 3) discipline/fairness, 4) extracurricular activities, 5) lik[ing] school, 6) student voice, 7) peer relations, 8) safety, and 9) teacher support" (Libbey, 2004, p. 278). Think about school and class connectedness through the lens of bullying.

### Academic Engagement

Academic engagement involves a student's motivation to care, work hard, and achieve in school (Libbey, 2004).

*How bullying negatively affects academic engagement:*

- Children who are in a constant state of fear cannot concentrate on academics. It is human nature to avoid demeaning and dangerous situations so mistreated students skip classes, become truant, or drop out.

*How teachers can use social architecture to improve academic engagement:*

- Anti-bullying rules and consequences keep classrooms safe.
- Stop aggression immediately and provide effective interventions.

- Make respect, kindness, and inclusion an important goal.
- Children can save missed assignments, deliver, or hold schoolwork until an ill classmate returns to school.
- Tutoring can bridge the gap caused by poor attendance. A relationship may form if peers provide this extra help.
- Give students a voice in their learning (e.g., including them in curriculum planning).
- Give pupils choices.
- Enjoyable, practical, hands on lessons pique students' interests.
- Have high academic expectations.
- Relate lessons to the students' lives and worlds. Teachers can find out about their children's personalities, likes, hobbies, and concerns from discussions, schoolwork and surveys, and apply the information to coursework.
- Praise and value the effort, in addition to focusing on the final results. This motivates children to work harder.

## Belonging

Belonging is achieved when children feel they are part of their class and school. This feeling is achieved when they feel cared for, important, valued, and respected. Warm relationships with peers and teachers, and participation in school activities, increase a sense of belonging (Libbey, 2004).

*How bullying negatively affects belonging*:

- Repeatedly bullied students do not feel a part of their classes because they receive subhuman treatment—they are demeaned, denigrated, and ostracized. The situation is compounded if teachers ignore bullying or are abusive.

*How teachers can use social architecture to improve belonging*:

- Emphasize that every student is important to the classroom community. Class meetings can help accomplish this goal.
- Rotate classroom jobs to give each child a chance to contribute.
- If a pupil is having a difficulty, ask a classmate to help.
- Break up cliques.
- Buddy up vulnerable children.
- Help students get to know one another's talents.
- Call home when youngsters are absent. This lets children know they are missed.
- Cooperative learning provides a sense of belonging to a group.
- Large projects, with each child contributing one part, help pupils see they are a part of the class. For example, each child can complete one square on a quilt.

---

## Box 7.3: Who Is Good in What in Our Class

One teacher compiled a "Who Is Good in What in Our Class" directory. The book spotlighted the abilities of each student. When help was needed, for instance in math, a child who disclosed proficiency with numbers was consulted. "The resource directory encouraged mutual assistance and helped change the distribution of prestige and influence in the classroom" (Ginott, 1972, p. 265).

---

- Games that are more fun with a lot of participants, require minimal skills, and have no winners or losers promote inclusion (Doll, Zucker, & Brehm, 1999).
- Use cooperative activities. Limit competition.
- Stress inclusion and praise inclusive acts.
- Teach students to respect differences.
- Use terms such as "we" and "us," rather than "me" and "you."
- Incorporate empathy building into the curriculum and daily activities.
- Utilize peer support programs.
- Teachers should evaluate the role they might play in bullying and sensitize themselves to the feelings of bullied children. *It is easier to overlook bullying, but it is not the right or ethical decision to make.*

## Discipline/Fairness

Consequences should be fair, effective, and delivered equally to all offenders (Libbey, 2004).

*How bullying negatively affects discipline/fairness:*

- Bullying will continue if consequences are absent, ineffective, or unjust. Bystanders will not report abuse if punishments are punitive or harsh. Discipline that does not fit the crime is a prerequisite for anger and revenge.

*How teachers can use social architecture to improve discipline/fairness:*

- Include children in the formation of rules and discipline policies.
- An objective and thorough investigation of bullying episodes should be performed, with no child declared innocent or guilty before all facts are gathered and evaluated.
- Formative consequences and restorative practices are effective ways to shut down bullying. Punitive discipline burns connections.

- Eliminate zero tolerance policies.
- Teachers can turn mistakes and inappropriate actions into learning experiences. Instead of berating, build up. Instead of thrashing, teach.
- If adults dig below the surface they will discover hurting youngsters who have not learned the right way to express feelings. Working from this perspective yields more positive results.

## Extracurricular Activities

Extracurricular activities include participation in school sponsored non academic activities (Libbey, 2004).

*How bullying negatively affects extracurricular participation:*

- Supervision is scarce during extracurricular activities giving those who bully freedom to strike. Vulnerable children understandably shy away from potentially hazardous situations. As a result, they miss out on opportunities to develop new sports, non academic, social, and friendship skills.

*How teachers can use social architecture to improve extracurricular participation:*

- The same rules and consequences in effect during school hours should apply during extracurricular activities.
- Supervision during non academic events should be just as vigilant as in the classroom.
- Create "buddies" for extracurricular activities.
- Remind students that they are responsible for the safety of their classmates and themselves.
- Query students for a wish list of activities. Participation may be increased by having a roster of popular sport and non sport activities (e.g., book, art, chorus, band, chess, computer, public service, history, and English clubs).
- Create a club for children who are bullied. It can provide socialization and support.

## Liking School

Children who like school are eager to attend and enjoy their classes (Libbey, 2004).

*How bullying negatively affects liking of school:*

- School is seen as enemy territory for the bullied because exclusion, rejection, and beatings (verbal or physical) occur on a daily basis. They cannot catch their breath during quiet moments because they are besieged with anticipatory fear, wondering when the next projectile will hit. Bullying shrapnel rips into their hearts, causing pain and humiliation. Under these circumstances, no one would enjoy school.

*How teachers can use social architecture to improve students' liking of school:*

- Use team building activities, circle time/class discussions.
- Praise all accomplishments—academic, sports, musical, art, and volunteerism.
- Compliment efforts.
- Set small goals that can easily be accomplished.
- Make academic activities interesting, relevant, and participatory.
- Model kindness and compassion—students will follow their teacher's lead.
- Class work should be interesting, participatory, meaningful, relevant, and within children's comprehension.
- Peer support programs, bystander training, and inclusive activities help friendless children develop friendships, and increase connections to the school.
- Anti-bullying programs can lessen or end bullying.
- Increased supervision will decrease misbehavior.

## Student Voice

Students are given a voice when their opinions are valued, and when they are an important part of the decision-making team in academic and classroom issues (Libbey, 2004).

*How bullying negatively affects student voice:*

- Abused children are silenced by bullying.

*How teachers can use social architecture to improve student voice:*

- Ask students to suggest ways to improve their classroom and school.
- Encourage student participation in curriculum planning, grading, and class activities.
- Form a student anti-bullying committee. The message is "heard" when sent by classmates.
- Let children develop the class rules.
- Let students create, run, and participate in all anti-bullying projects.
- Immediately apply effective consequences when a student puts down, laughs at, or hurts peers.

## Peer Relations

Good peer relations are seen when children are liked by contemporaries and have friends (Libbey, 2004).

*How bullying negatively affects peer relations*:

● Most targeted youngsters are ostracized and friendless.

*How teachers can use social architecture to improve peer relations*:

● Teach friendship and prosocial skills.
● Encourage friendships with a variety of social groups.
● Many times, children apply labels without taking the time to get to know the person in question. Teachers can provide opportunities for interaction when they use cooperative learning, circle time/class meetings, or peer support programs.
● Use games where large numbers of players are required.
● Break up cliques.
● Promote inclusion. Ban exclusion.
● Bring left out children into activities and discussions. Even better, encourage students to watch for excluded peers and bring them into the group.
● Point out the abilities of youngsters who are bullied.
● Replace competitive activities with cooperative projects.

## Safety

Safety is gauged by how safe a child feels during the school day (Libbey, 2004).

*How bullying negatively affects safety*:

● Children who are bullied do not feel safe, especially during unstructured and loosely supervised times.

*How teachers can use social architecture to improve safety*:

● Create anti-bullying rules.
● Immediately stop bullying and issue effective consequences.
● Make supervision a priority.
● Separate those who bully from those who are bullied.
● Promote relationship building.
● Let bullied students know you are a supportive ally.
● Develop good classroom management.
● Build a culture of bystander intervention.

## Teacher Support

When children receive teacher support they feel close to, cared for, supported, liked, and valued by their educator (Libbey, 2004).

*How bullying negatively affects teacher support*:

● Targeted children do not feel supported when teachers ignore or participate in bullying, do not effectively intervene, or are told to handle the abuse by themselves.

*How teachers can use social architecture to improve teacher support*:

● Warmly welcome students each morning.
● Spend a few minutes talking to children before class begins. Show interest in them (e.g., "How was last night's basketball game?").
● Have one-on-one student–teacher lunches.
● Give greeting and birthday cards.
● Be positive and respectful to *every* child in the classroom.
● Build relationships with *each* student.
● Mentor a youngster.
● Praise children.
● Establish anti-bullying rules, consequences, and effective interventions.
● Help those who are targeted to recognize and build their strengths.
● Show those who bully how to use their leadership in positive ways.
● Let students know you will help, support, and protect them.
● Teach strategies to prevent or stop bullying.
● Be a matchmaker for bullied students.
● Help those who hurt others see the impact of their actions.
● Increase class empathy.

## Rules

Rules promote healthy relationships and respect, which are two goals of social architecture. They also create "a classroom climate that is inhospitable to bullying" (Crothers & Kolbert, 2008, p. 134) by helping youngsters get along and work together.

When the entire class jointly creates rules they take ownership and tell those who bully that maltreatment is not wanted in their classroom. This subtle pressure might be enough to deter abuse. Pluralistic ignorance, in which pupils with anti-bullying beliefs falsely think their peers have differing views when in fact they are similar, is negated because of discussions. In these ways, rules remove power from those who bully and place it into the hands of the caring majority. The discussions also show everyone the harmful effects of bullying and increase adherence. Teachers may also use the guidelines as a backdrop when discussing bullying with the class or when confronting a rule breaker.

Educators can facilitate the process. Third grade teacher Karen Rogers asks for suggestions, writes them on the board, and discusses each idea. She asks students to recall a time that particular rule was broken and asks what happened. For example "We will include all students in every activity" will generate stories of times when children were left out and how badly they felt. Conversations like these help pupils understand the reasons for the rule and why it would be a good addition to their list (as cited in Castle & Rogers, 1993). If the class does not suggest examples ask "What would happen if there was no rule like this?"

Rules should be written in the positive, telling youngsters what to do, instead of what not to do. "Do not leave anyone out" should be replaced with "Include all students in every activity." Four anti-bullying rules and examples follow:

1. *We will treat everyone with respect and kindness.* Include everyone in activities, respect and support differences, help those in need, think before speaking or acting, put yourself in other people's shoes, and treat others as you want to be treated.
2. *We will include all students in every activity.* Ask others to join your group, sit at your lunch table, and join in during recess. Put less popular students on your teams, invite them to your house, and include everyone in parties.
3. *We will help those who are bullied.* Say "Stop bullying," walk away with the person being bullied, ask an adult for help, comfort, and befriend those hurt by bullying.
4. *We will tell an adult if we cannot stop bullying.* Find the appropriate adult. For example, the bus driver should be told if bullying occurs on the bus. A hall monitor or nearby teacher should be informed if abuse occurs in the hallway.

Youngsters become confused and test boundaries when educators fail to uphold rules, so an important written or unwritten rule is "The teacher will act immediately if rules are violated and will protect all students."

Educators can redirect the class when rules are not followed by restating the regulations and applauding those who subscribe to them. Using "We will include all children in every activity," a teacher might say "Jordyn, you showed how caring you were by allowing Eytan to join your game."

Praise has many positive benefits. It gives children who follow the rules a well deserved pat on the back, motivates students to follow the rules, lets youngsters know their educator will notice when they observe the rules, shows the teacher values the guidelines, raises self-esteem, and reinforces the guidelines.

Periodic "booster" sessions will give the rules a front row seat in the class.

## Stressing the Importance of Rules

Teachers should place written copies of the rules in prominent places. Post rules on the door to let students know their classroom is a bully free zone. Rules should also be placed in visible spots inside the room, serving as constant reminders. Children can vote on the best location(s).

Teachers should print three copies of the rules for each student. Pupils sign one, indicating their commitment to an anti-bullying classroom. It can be tacked onto a

---

## Box 7.4: We Do NOT Do That Here

Eric Schaps described teacher Lincoln Olbrycht's reaction when his students laughed at a fellow classmate:

> Lincoln, who is quite laid back ordinarily, a flexible and accommodating person, stopped immediately. "Wait a minute," he said. "We don't do that here. We do NOT do that here." And he got as serious and stern as I ever saw him in eight years of observing his class. "Why don't we do that here?" he said a beat later, much more mildly, and right then and there, he facilitated a discussion around that question.
>
> Lincoln didn't lecture. What he did was to make clear that this was a critically vital issue for the life of their classroom. First, he signaled that there were real, serious ground rules and that they were morally based. Then, he gave the kids ownership of—and responsibility for—those ground rules by asking them "Why?"

(as cited in K. Smith, 2010, p. 1)

---

classroom bulletin board, taped to desks, or glued into notebooks. Send the two remaining copies home with a cover letter explaining the rules and their importance. Request assistance in upholding the guidelines. Parents and guardians sign one copy agreeing to periodically review the rules with their children. It is returned to school while the second copy remains in the household for discussion. In this way, parents are informed and involved.

Many times rule violators try to evade consequences by saying "I was only fooling around" or "I didn't mean to hurt anyone." Teachers should respond with "I'm glad that no harm was intended; however, that does not take away the pain you caused <the injured person> or the fact that a class rule was broken." The child should be held responsible. Accountability teaches youngsters that actions have consequences and it is wise to think before acting or speaking.

Children are works in progress and, as hard as they try, they might not reach the goal right away. Remain positive and praise efforts, attempts, and the process in addition to the final product. Youngsters will be inspired to work harder and will succeed sooner.

## Consequences

Historically, punishment has been the predominant form of discipline used in schools. That is interesting because punishment fails to teach prosocial behavior, appropriate ways to relate, or how to solve the underlying problem. It does not rebuild relationships that are harmed in spite of the fact that the parties have to live together in the close quarters of classrooms. Punishment does not examine the social context of bullying—what role others played that prompted or reinforced the actions of those who bullied—nor does it consider the needs of every group affected by antisocial acts. Misbehavior may temporarily stop, but it often returns with a vengeance because the punitive nature of punishment can incite anger, retaliation, and alienation. Who is on the receiving end of the wrath? Those who are bullied often find themselves hurt once for whatever reason and then a second time for retribution. Thus, a measure created to stop poor behavior can increase it. In fact, after reviewing 500 studies, Lipsey (1991) found that punishment was one of the "least effective responses to violence in schools" (as cited in Lewis, Sugai, & Colvin, 1998, para. 3).

School staff should always model anti-bullying behavior, yet punishment, in a way, is bullying:

- It is about a more powerful person who uses that power against a less powerful person.
- It tackles problems in a punitive fashion.
- It removes children from the activity, class, or school (e.g., time outs, detention, suspension, expulsion), which is exclusion, a behavior at the core of bullying.
- When separated, youngsters are deprived of positive role models and opportunities to develop appropriate social skills.

Examples of punishment include reprimands, writing sentences, removal of a favored activity (e.g., lunch, recess, sporting events, trips), extra duties (e.g., cleaning the classroom, lunchroom, or playground; working in the office or library), or standing next to the supervisor (e.g., during recess). These *punish*ments do not teach; rather, as the name states, they punish. Teaching sows change; punishment breeds bad feelings.

## Formative Consequences

Educators must tackle harmful behaviors with measures that keep members of the school community safe, help those who aggress, teach appropriate ways to get needs met, and rebuild relationships. Rule breaking and mistakes should be opportunities for learning, rather than antecedents to punishment.

Formative consequences fill these requirements. This method of discipline is not punitive, as with punishment, and does not provide natural consequences that come about as a result of an action. Instead, formative consequences are a carefully planned learning strategy that pairs discipline with misbehavior. Formative consequences provide awareness and insight, help youngsters think about their behavior and its impact on others, develop empathy, and teach prosocial ways to fill needs. For example, if a student bullies a peer because of ignorance about a disability, researching and writing a report about the disability educates and sensitizes the offender. There are many ways formative consequences can be applied:

- Write an account of the incident from the bullied person's point of view.
- Draw a picture of how a bullied student feels.
- Role play and reverse role play.
- Write a letter of apology, *only* if sincere.
- Write a letter to other students about why they should not bully.
- Read articles or books on bullying and write a composition about what was learned.
- Watch a movie about bullying. Identify the different types and how it affected the characters.
- Read a bullying book to younger children.
- Teach younger children about bullying.
- Lead a class discussion on the dangers of bullying, how to prevent it, and how to help those who are bullied.
- Research altruistic people (e.g., Dr. Martin Luther King Jr., Mother Teresa, Nelson Mandela, Mahatma Gandhi). Did their behavior differ from these role models? How can they act in similar ways?
- Interview adults or older students about their bullying experiences. How were they affected?
- Take an anti-bullying course.
- Enroll in a class that teaches prosocial behavior.
- Replace or repair damaged items.
- Become a buddy and/or teach younger children a skill (with adult supervision).
- Volunteer for community service or help others in some way.
- Take a course on empathy.
- Complete the Understanding My Behavior form (Figure 7.1).

Many of these strategies can be implemented by the classroom teacher. However, some might require a colleague with more expertise. In those cases, intervention should be carried out by the appropriate staff member.

Teachers have to tailor consequences, selecting the best approach for a particular child and offense. Formative consequences also require supervision during the process, but the minutes spent are an investment in terms of time and a child's future. This is illustrated in a story told by author and speaker Jodee Blanco when her teacher, Ms. Swenson, gave formative consequences to a duo who made cruel comments about Blanco. The educator:

> demanded each girl perform an unexpected act of kindness for a different person every day for two weeks. Each night before they went to bed, they had to record in their journals the kind act, the recipient's response, and how the response made them feel. Ms. Swenson required them to obtain signatures and phone numbers from the recipient so she could verify compliance.
>
> (Blanco, 2008, pp. 321–322)

Understanding My Behavior

Name _____   Date _____

What did I do?

_____

_____

How did my behavior hurt everyone involved?

The Person Bullied   _____

Bystanders   _____

Myself   _____

Would I want someone to treat me that way?

_____

Why was my behavior wrong?

_____

What goal was I trying to achieve or problem was I trying to solve?

_____

How can I more wisely reach my goal or solve my problem the next time?  (List two ways.)

1._____

2._____

How can I apologize and improve my relationship with the person I bullied?  (List two ways.)

1._____

_____

2._____

_____

*Figure 7.1* Understanding My Behavior form

It was not only Ms. Swenson's consequences that brought success but her approach. Instead of intervening immediately, she waited until school ended. Ms. Swenson and another teacher approached the girls, told the pair they cared about them, and noticed they were being unkind to classmates.

Compare Ms. Swenson's strategy and formative consequences to a punitive and demeaning approach. Several girls in another of Blanco's classes called her an "ugly bitch." Her teacher "overheard what they were saying and chastised them in front of the entire class, then sent them to the principal who doled out detentions" (Blanco, 2008, p. 319). The following day, the students threw stones at Blanco in an act of revenge.

## Restorative Justice

Restorative justice is another form of discipline. It compassionately and collaboratively obtains accountability from those who bully, helps those who are bullied heal, rebuilds damaged relationships, decreases the likelihood of repeated incidents, reintegrates those who aggress back into the classroom, and keeps schools safe. It is a method of problem solving that disapproves of misbehavior while affirming the worthiness of the person who bullied.

Relationships are at the core of restorative justice. It is based on the premise that relationships (a) are an integral part of life, (b) connect people, and (c) lead to a sense of belonging.

Restorative justice advocates argue that bullying is an indicator, signaling the breakdown of social relationships, not rules. Fix the broken relationships and bullying will disappear. Instead of asking "What happened?," restorative justice asks *"Who has been affected?"* Instead of asking "Who is to blame?," restorative justice asks *"What are his or her needs?"* Instead of asking "What is a just punishment?," restorative justice asks *"Who is responsible for repairing the relationship?"* It also asks *"What is everyone's side of the story?"* and *"How can we prevent this from happening again?"*

- *"Who has been affected?"*—Restorative justice recognizes that those who bully and those who are bullied are not the only people affected by abuse. Relationships with those in the school community and beyond (e.g., bystanders, fellow students, teachers, school personnel, parents) are also compromised.
- *"What are his or her needs?"*—The needs of those who were hurt and those who caused the pain are examined. In this way, healing begins and relationships are rebuilt.
- *"Who is responsible for repairing the relationship?"*—The person who bullied is held accountable. Fixing relationships begins when people who bully (a) acknowledge they made poor choices when they mistreated another person, (b) realize they affected someone who did not deserve to suffer, (c) repair the harm done to the person who was bullied, and (d) change the behavior that caused this violation of human rights.

● *"What is everyone's side of the story?"*—Restorative justice is concerned with the social, psychological, and relational injuries, as well as the physical and material losses. It gives voice to and respects everyone touched by the abuse:

– *The person who was bullied*—People who are bullied have the opportunity to say how they felt, describe the harm that was done, and ask the person who bullied questions. This forum helps return some of the control that was taken away by bullying.

Hearing the effects of bullying helps those who bully realize the damage they caused, increases empathy, and aids reconciliation.

– *The person who bullied*—People who aggress also have a chance to tell their story. Motives are explored because we cannot expect behavior to change without learning and addressing the underlying causes of misconduct.

– *Communities*—Affected members of the school and greater community are allowed to air their feelings.

● *"How can we prevent this from happening again?"*—Mediation and conferencing are two strategies used in restorative justice:

– *Mediation*—In many schools mediation has been unsuccessful because of the power imbalance and because it erroneously blames both sides for the problem. Mediation with restorative justice differs because those who bully must *first admit wrongdoing* and *accept responsibility* for their antisocial behavior.

After both parties speak, they work toward a mutually agreeable resolution. Participation is voluntary, with precautions taken to insure safety.

– *Conferencing*—Conferences open the meeting up to wounded members of the school and greater community. All in attendance have a chance to speak and tell how the bullying jeopardized their health and safety. Everyone is asked their thoughts for a just resolution, with amends jointly decided. Like mediation, conferencing increases awareness of the damage caused. Conferences give the person who bullied and the bullied person's support system front row seats, embedding them in the process.

People who are harmed are empowered by their roles, which includes deciding the guest list, the location of the conference, and who will talk first.

During "disposition circles" ways to mend the harm caused by bullying are discussed:

1. *Apology*—Apologies can be written or verbal. The person who bullied confesses wrongdoing, acknowledges the damage done, and may express regret. An important element is the shift in power. Control is given to the person who was bullied because this individual decides whether the apology will be accepted or not.

2. *Restitution*—The person who bullied can return or replace stolen or damaged items or provide monetary compensation. The person who was bullied helps calculate the value of the loss.

3. *Changes in behavior*—Negotiated agreements can outline steps that facilitate behavioral change. Examples include changing friends or environments, learning new skills, or enrolling in treatment programs.
4. *Community service*—An offender may go above and beyond and show sincere regret by performing community service.

(Centre for Justice & Reconciliation, 2008; National Center for Mental Health Promotion and Youth Violence Prevention, 2009; National Centre for Restorative Justice in Youth Settings, n.d.; Pranis, n.d.; Zehr, 2002.)

## Documentation

Teachers should keep records of all bullying episodes. Reports leave nothing to memory, serve as documentation, inform pertinent parties, and provide clues about the abuse.

### Bullying Incident Report

Teachers should complete a "Bullying Incident Report" for each bullying episode. It shows students that adults take their rules and bullying very seriously. Include information that explains what happened, shows patterns, prevents future abuse, and improves student–student relationships. The report is a first step and *not necessarily proof* of bullying because some student reports may not meet the criteria for bullying or are fabrications. An investigation can ascertain accuracy and veracity.

- *Name of student who was bullied*—Does this person have a history of being bullied by the person who aggressed during this incident? By other students? Would social skill training help the youngster?
- *Date*—Is there a pattern of dates? Does the bullying appear to happen randomly or at certain days during the week or month? What happens in the life of the child who bullied during those periods? Could he or she be watched more closely at those times?
- *Time of incident*—When did the episode occur? What happened around that time? Was it toward the end of the day when children might be tired? During a particular class? During unstructured periods?
- *Location*—Did the abuse occur at known bullying hot spots? Was it during an unsupervised activity or in a secluded area of the school building? Could school personnel be stationed in those areas?
- *Name of student who bullied*—Has this child been involved in bullying before? If so, is the youngster targeting the same child or randomly attacking different students? What is the reason? Can training improve deficient skills or would counseling help? Can certain children be separated?

# Bullying Incident Report

Student Who Was Bullied _____Date_____

Time of Incident _____ Location _____

Name of Student Who Bullied

_____

Description of Episode

_____

_____

_____

Event(s) Preceding or Provoking the Incident

_____

_____

_____

Bystander Name(s) and Roles

_____

_____

_____

_____

Consequences or Resolution

_____

_____

_____

Referral to_____

Teacher Filing this Report_____

*Figure 7.2* Bullying Incident Report

- *Description of episode*—What type(s) of bullying were seen? Did one person bully or was it a group?
- *Event(s) preceding or provoking the incident*—What preceded the bullying incident? Did anything motivate the episode? If yes, how can it be avoided in the future?
- *Bystander name(s) and roles*—Who were the bystanders? Were they in attendance during previous bullying episodes? What role(s) did they play? Should certain children be separated or paired with more prosocial students? Is bystander education needed?
- *Consequences or resolution*—What worked in the past? Repeat it. What failed? Discard it.

## Notice of Bullying Form

The Notice of Bullying form is a way to let parents know their child participated in bullying. It should be completed after an investigation confirms that bullying occurred. It is signed by three parties. The student's signature shows that those who bully will be held accountable. Parents sign to verify that they are aware of their child's involvement in bullying. It is a subtle way to encourage parents to promote prosocial behavior. The teacher's inclusion shows a commitment to provide a safe and positive learning environment.

It would be prudent to have the principal review all forms to insure that they are appropriate for the specific school and its personnel.

# Supervision

Olweus (1993a) discovered an inverse relationship between supervision and bullying. Increase surveillance and abuse decreases. When adult presence diminishes, bullying rises.

The logical solution of adding more supervision sounds deceptively simple; however, it is not easy because budgets are shrinking while class sizes are ballooning. The majority of bullying is missed by teachers because one set of eyes can only watch so many students. As a result, educators intervene in one in five bullying incidents in the classroom and one in six on the playground (Craig, Pepler, & Atlas, 2000).

## Extra Help

Extra help can be found with a little creativity:

- *Recruit parents*—Larger classes mean greater pools of adults who might be willing to invest in their children's education by volunteering a few hours each week.
- *Supervise a student teacher*—Student teachers increase classroom monitoring and teaching.

---

**Notice of Bullying**

Student Who Bullied  or Was Bullied_____

Date of Incident_____

Description of Episode

_____

_____

_____

_____

Consequences or Resolution

_____

_____

_____

Administrator Student Was Referred To_____

Child's Signature_____ Date_____

Parent's Signature_____ Date_____

Teacher's Signature_____ Date_____

---

*Figure 7.3* Notice of Bullying form

- *Education majors*—Solicit education majors who are not ready for student teaching. They might want a head start in the classroom.
- *Service learning*—Older students might receive service learning credits for assisting in lower grade classes.

- *Senior citizens*—Capitalize on the experience and wisdom of the older generation.
- *Students*—Do not overlook *the most powerful group* you can enlist: children. They are the experts in knowing where bullying occurs. Ask them. Then, you can strategically position yourself at the scene of a potential crime. Youngsters *have the power* to affect their peers' behavior. Pupils should do the supervising and policing, *if they will not be at risk*. They can tell classmates that bullying is wrong, that it is against class rules, and they want it to stop. Objecting to bullying as a group works well. If the consensus frowns upon abuse, the minority will fall in line because most children conform to the status quo and do not want to jeopardize their social status.

## Other Ways to Increase Supervision

In well supervised classrooms teachers do not "sit on top on the kids"; rather, they are like flies on the wall observing and ready to fly in, if necessary. That is because they anticipate problems and use strategies that forestall trouble. These educators might give colleagues the following advice:

- Avoid standing in one place or sitting at a desk for long periods of time.
- Continuously look up and scan the room when working with individuals or groups.
- Eliminate unsupervised free time.
- Listen to children's public conversations.
- Separate those who bully from those who are bullied.
- Bar students from unsupervised areas.
- Instruct pupils to record their destination, departure, and return times in a log book whenever they leave and re-enter the classroom. This discourages bullying and lingering.
- Look for changes in behavior, for example a sedentary child who becomes fidgety, an energetic student who becomes subdued, a talkative youngster who becomes quiet, a shy boy or girl who acts out, a calm child who becomes angry, a social butterfly who withdraws, or a studious student whose schoolwork declines.
- Keep an eye on youngsters who have a history of intimidating or bullying.
- Pay extra attention to students who were in arguments or altercations, or are frustrated.
- Investigate crowds.
- Provide extra supervision at bullying zones identified by students.

## Beyond the Classroom

Supervision should extend beyond classroom doors because problems occurring outside the room travel into the class.

Precorrection and active supervision can reduce discipline problems when children move around the school building (entering, exiting, lunch, recess, gym, specials). Precorrection includes "verbal reminders, behavioral rehearsals, or demonstrations of rule-following or socially appropriate behaviors that are presented in or before settings where problem behavior is likely" (Colvin, Sugai, Good, & Lee, 1997, p. 346).

Four elements are important in active supervision—moving, scanning, escorting, and interacting.

1. *Moving*—Continuous movement around all parts of the supervised area, as opposed to remaining stationary.
2. *Scanning*—Visual observance of students at all times, whether the person is standing still, moving, or talking.
3. *Escorting*—Accompanying students from one area to another.
4. *Interacting*—Greeting students, short conversations, explaining rules, discussing violations, and praising good behavior. Interaction can be verbal (talking) or non verbal (smiling, gesturing).

"The activeness of supervisory behaviors is more important than the number of supervisors" (Colvin et al., 1997, pp. 348–349, 359).

## Play Fighting vs. Bullying

Play fighting can occur anywhere: in the classroom, hallway, lunch room, school bus, or playground. Adults often have difficulty distinguishing between play fighting and bullying because of the similarities between the two—hitting, kicking, wrestling, holding, escaping, and chasing. However, there are many differences.

Play fighting is an enjoyable activity in which two friends with equal power voluntarily participate and take turns dominating. Play can be stopped at any time. Smiling, laughter, and happy sounds are seen and heard. There is never any intent to hurt playmates and any blows that land are soft. Injuries are rare. Play fights do not usually have an audience and can be played out near adults (Boulton, 1993a, 1993b; Schafer & Smith, 1996).

In contrast, bullying involves a power imbalance, with one party wanting to dominate and hurt the other. The targeted child is an involuntary partner, who does not enjoy the activity. This can be seen by fearful and nervous body language and cries or sounds of pain. The action continues even if the youngster is upset or hurt. Physical blows connect and cause injury. Bullying is usually done in front of crowds of peers and away from adult vision. Opponents are usually not friends before or after the episode.

Careful monitoring is necessary because almost one third of play fights turn into real fights (Schafer & Smith, 1996).

## Instructional Style and Bullying

A teacher's instructional style can affect classroom bullying. In one study, 65% of bullying occurred while students were involved in solitary tasks, 23% while working in groups, and 12% during teacher led tasks (Atlas & Pepler, 1998). Followers of social architecture can use these findings to suppress classroom bullying by increasing teacher led instruction and by decreasing solitary tasks.

## Cooperative Learning

Students learn via one of three methods: individually, cooperatively, or competitively. Over 900 studies showed cooperative learning is more effective than individualistic and competitive methods (D.W. Johnson, Johnson, & Stanne, 2000).

Cooperative learning receives negative reviews by those who mistakenly think it involves giving assignments to groups of students, with orders to complete them. In many cases, a few youngsters do the work while the rest do nothing and undeservingly receive credit.

There are five elements necessary for a true cooperative learning experience: individual accountability, group goals, positive interdependence, face-to-face positive interaction, and social skills. Individual accountability and group goals lead to positive interdependence—when students have to learn the assignment *and* are also responsible for other members learning the material. When each person's success is dependent upon others everyone is motivated to work hard, cooperate, and share resources (R.T. Johnson & Johnson, 1994; Slavin, 1991).

### Cooperative Learning and Bullying

Cooperative group work is incompatible with and a deterrent to bullying:

- Students may be forced to work together when cooperative groups are first formed, but as students do they cannot help but get to know the person behind the different colored skin, "funny" accent, and "weird" clothes. They often realize their classmates are not as bad as they thought, and with time the ignorance of racism and stereotypes fade.
- Children have to listen and interact with others when they work, talk, brainstorm, plan, and solve problems together. In the process, they begin to see life from other people's perspectives and understand their thoughts, motivations, and behaviors. This leads to empathy.
- Cooperative learning is synonymous with inclusion, the goal of anti-bullying programs and social architecture.
- Participants develop positive feelings toward others through cooperative group work:

Whenever we *do* a favor for another person, we undergo a surge of liking for that person. The way we treat a person—helping him or harming him—leads us to justify our treatment of that person, which, in turn, intensifies our feelings about that person.

(Aronson, 2000, p. 155)

Those who bully do not target people they like.

- Friendships form when peers fraternize together, team up, teach, and help one another, as is seen in cooperative learning. Friends prevent, diffuse, and stop bullying.
- Prosocial behavior increases. A person cannot be prosocial and bully.
- Social skills that are sometimes deficient in youngsters involved in bullying are learned, developed, and reinforced with group learning. Students must communicate, listen, take turns, follow directions, stay on task, share, help one another, make decisions, manage themselves, and cooperate when they work in groups.
- Self-esteem rises. Bullied children gain confidence because they are the respected "experts," holding valuable information that is needed by classmates.
- Children's conflict resolution skills increase, which may prevent or defuse potential bullying situations.
- Many children who bully come from authoritarian homes. They are introduced to different social models with cooperative learning. All players equally collaborate, have the same say, and are esteemed parts of the team. Everyone has a key role—no one person can control or dominate the group because no one is privy to anyone else's research.
- Most children who bully refuse to be held accountable for their actions, but in group learning they must or they will be letting down members of their group. The warm feelings that develop through cooperative learning or peer pressure prompt children to take responsibility.
- Disrespect can have severe consequences. Someone who abuses may see that cooperatively working together has rewards far greater than aggression (Aronson, 2000; R.T. Johnson & Johnson, 1994; Sapon-Shevin, Ayres, & Duncan, 1994; Slavin, 1991).

## Different Cooperative Learning Methods

Academic Controversy, Cooperative Integrated Reading and Composition, Cooperative Learning Structures, Jigsaw, Learning Together, Student-Teams-Achievement-Divisions, Team Assisted Individualization, and Teams-Games-Tournaments are a few examples of cooperative learning methods (D.W. Johnson et al., 2000). Instructions for the Jigsaw method can be found online (www.jigsaw.org/steps.htm).

## Cooperative Learning Grouping

The ideal group is made up of a diverse mix of students but power differentials should be kept in mind because they can sway group dynamics. Youngsters who bully should not be placed with targeted peers, antisocial children, or followers. High status students are the most likely to intervene so they should be dispersed among all groups and encouraged to stop abuse. Bullied pupils should be placed with prosocial youngsters.

Running a successful cooperative learning program sounds deceptively simple but requires practice and experience. Cooperative learning literature found in books and on the internet can be helpful. The best resource may be a fellow teacher who can share his or her knowledge and experiences.

# Chapter 8

# Seating and Grouping Assignments

Students should *not* be allowed to choose their seats or groups. What is wrong with giving pupils free choice? It is simple, easy, and pleases students.

Look at seat and group assignments from a bullying perspective. If given a choice, youngsters will want to be near their best friends. That leaves out bullied and unpopular classmates who are on the edge of the social periphery. The very essence of bullying is exclusion. Social architecture promotes inclusion. The goal is to move marginalized children from the border of the classroom into the center to foster friendships. This is achieved by carefully planning seating and grouping placements and by breaking up cliques.

As a sidebar, dismantling cliques not only deters bullying but is a service to society. Exclusive structures lead to social stratification. Members of the top echelon consider themselves superior and privileged and anyone not part of their "in" group is considered below them. Prejudice, discrimination, and intolerance follow.

Seat and group students near peers they would not ordinarily associate with because physical proximity has an important influence on the development of relationships. Children have opportunities to talk, work, share, help, and get to know one another when they are next to each other. Friendships naturally form along the way. When seats and groups are changed, pupils build friendships with their new neighbors, after a period of transition (Rizzo, 1989). Bullied children should also be seated and grouped with students who will support and defend them (PREVNet, 2007b).

While it is advantageous to place certain youngsters together, it can be just as beneficial to keep others far apart. Those who aggress gravitate toward peers who have

---

## Box 8.1: Take a Bite Out of Bullying

Historically, pupils at Black River Falls Middle School (WI) were allowed to choose lunchroom tables. Cliques, exclusion ("You don't belong here"), and disruptive and disrespectful behavior were the main courses.

A quartet of eighth grade student council members approached Principal Dave Roou with a solution—random seating assignments. They believed the present system contributed to bullying and cliques, preventing the class from building unity. Initially, some protested the new computer generated table assignments, but the foresight of these youngsters proved that change can bring improvement. There was an increase in cross-cultural interactions and friendships; bullying was reduced; and a more pleasant and inclusive atmosphere developed (Roou, 2004).

---

antisocial behaviors. They respond positively to deviant talk, compare notes, teach each other the "tricks of the trade," compete with one another, get into power struggles, and are negative role models. If given a choice, educators will find them at the back of the room, as far away from the teacher's view as they can get. Place kids who support violence as close to the educator as possible. Divide these youngsters up and always group three or four prosocial students with each child who bullies (Dishion, McCord, & Poulin, 1999; Kamps & Kay, 2002).

Also separate those who bully (including "bully victims") from anyone they will bully (those who are bullied and "bully victims"). Bystanders can be interspersed between these children, serving as human barriers (Bisenius, 2005). This leads to lower levels of bullying because distance reduces bullying opportunities and provides cooling off periods (Kochenderfer-Ladd & Pelletier, 2008). Followers and children who are easily influenced should not be near those who can persuade them to participate in aggressive activities.

Teachers should constantly move around the classroom because their presence puts youngsters in a "We better not do anything wrong because the teacher is watching" frame of mind. It also keeps students on task and allows easy access to the educator. It is the nature of a teacher's job to talk as they have to disseminate information, but they should also take time to listen. If so, they will learn about their children, the social hierarchy, who has the power, and who is marginalized. This information can become the basis of seating and grouping arrangements.

## Survey Instruments

How do teachers know the wisest organization for seating and grouping students? It will be difficult during the beginning of the school year because educators do not know their children very well. As the days pass, teachers can learn about the social sides of pupils by carefully watching, talking to, and listening to their youngsters during structured and unstructured periods of the school day. Colleagues who teach your class and school aides can provide additional information. Surveys, maps, and sociograms also provide objective data. Put together, these sources will paint a picture of the social ecology of your class.

## Class Bullying Surveys

School wide surveys are often the first step in identifying the extent of bullying in a school. Class questionnaires can tell teachers the amount, type, and location of bullying in their classrooms. They also raise students' awareness about bullying and open up lines of communication between students and teachers.

How can teachers introduce a survey? First, discuss (or review) the definition, types, and dangers of bullying. Then, tell the children that you need their help to make the class safer. You will hand out a survey and want their honest responses. They do not have to write their names on it.

Children will be more cooperative if the instrument is kept as short as possible; anonymity is insured; understandable terminology is used; tick boxes are included; and the questionnaire is tailored to the age, ability, culture, and specific circumstances of the class.

Pupils can be queried four to six weeks into the term, with interventions based on the findings. The effectiveness of anti-bullying initiatives can be learned by repeating the poll at three to four month intervals.

Are surveys helpful? Bullying dropped almost 50% in one school by moving staff to high risk areas that were identified in its anti-bullying questionnaire (Roberts Jr., 2006).

## Maps

Teachers can also increase student safety by mapping out bullying hot spots. This strategy pinpoints frequent bullying locations in classrooms, school buildings, and grounds. The information can be obtained using several methods:

- Teachers walk around the classroom or school with the class. "Stop" should be said each time pupils arrive at an area where bullying occurs. A pre selected secretary records the information on a copy of a class or school map.
- Students draw a map of the class or school and mark off bullying zones.
- The children note bullying locations on a copy of a class or school map, in an age appropriate way:
    - Younger students color bullying areas red and safe zones green.
    - Red "Bullying area" and green "Safe zone" squares and circles are glued onto the corresponding spots.
    - Older students make an "X" or write remarks where bullying takes place.

Teachers make changes based on the findings.

**Class Bullying Questionnaire**

Have you ever been bullied in this classroom? ☐ Yes ☐ No

Where did the bullying occur? ☐ Desk ☐ Coat Closet ☐ At line up ☐ Other_____

What type of bullying occurred? ☐ Physical ☐ Verbal ☐ Relational ☐ Cyberbullying

When did the bullying occur? ☐ Morning arrival ☐ During teaching ☐ At recess ☐ At group work ☐ During line up ☐ Bathroom ☐ Dismissal ☐ Other_____

How long did the bullying last? ☐ Few minutes ☐ Few days ☐ Week ☐ Month ☐ Longer

Were bullying episodes repeated? ☐ Yes ☐ No

What did you do when bullied? ☐ Ignored it ☐ Walked away ☐ Told the person to stop ☐ Told the teacher ☐ Hit the person ☐ Yelled at the person ☐ Other_____

How did the bullying make you feel? ☐ Did not bother me ☐ It hurt a little ☐ It hurt a lot ☐ It was so painful I did not want to go to school ☐ Other_____

Were bystanders present? ☐ Yes ☐ No

If yes, what did the bystanders do? ☐ Watched ☐ Joined in ☐ Told the person to stop ☐ Walked away ☐ Ignored the bullying ☐ Got help ☐ Other_____

Did you tell anyone? ☐ Yes ☐ No If yes, who did you tell? _____

Who bullied you? _____

Is anyone in the class bullied? ☐ Yes ☐ No If yes, who _____

If yes, what type of bullying? ☐ Physical ☐ Verbal ☐ Relational ☐ Cyberbullying

What are the names of classmates who bully?

_____

What do you do when you see bullying in class? ☐ Watch ☐ Join in ☐ Walk away ☐ Ignore ☐ Tell the person who is bullying to stop ☐ Get help ☐ Other_____

Do you feel safe in class? ☐ Yes ☐ No If no, explain_____

What can the teacher do to make the class safer?

_____

What can you and other students do to make the class safer?

_____

Figure 8.1 Sample Class Bullying Questionnaire

5. Read one response. Find the writer's name on the horizontal axis.
6. Looking across vertically, find the name of the "chosen" peer.
7. Plot an "X" in the square connected to the two names.
8. Repeat for every student in the class.

The information can be graphed in numerous ways, with each disclosing different data. For example, a bull's-eye graph shows the most and least popular students:

1. Draw several circles, each larger than the last, organized so they look like a bull's-eye target (see Figure 8.3).
2. In Figure 8.3, five rings were drawn for a class of 20 students. Five was written on the bottom and inside of the inner ring. Four was printed on the bottom and inside of the second ring. The numbering was repeated with three, two, and one.
3. The names of the children were plotted by placing them in the ring that corresponded to the number of nominations received. For example, Brianna was

| SOCIOGRAM DATA | David | Micah | Brian | Joshua | Jose | Danny | Ethan | Sanjay | Anthony | Ayden | Jasmine | Sophia | Madison | Debra | Emily | Maria | Isabella | Olivia | Abigail | Brianna |
|---|---|---|---|---|---|---|---|---|---|---|---|---|---|---|---|---|---|---|---|---|
| David | | X | | | | | | | X | | | | | | | | | | | |
| Micah | X | | | | | | X | | | | | | | | | | | | | |
| Brian | | | | X | X | | | | | | | | | | | | | | | |
| Joshua | | | X | | | | X | | | | | | | | | | | | | |
| Jose | | | X | | | X | | | | | | | | | | | | | | |
| Danny | | X | | | | | X | | | | | | | | | | | | | |
| Ethan | | | | X | X | | | | | | | | | | | | | | | |
| Sanjay | | | | | | X | | | | X | | | | | | | | | | |
| Anthony | | X | | | | | | | | X | | | | | | | | | | |
| Ayden | X | | | | X | | | | | | | | | | | | | | | |
| Jasmine | | | | | | | | | | | | | | X | | | | | | X |
| Sophia | | | | | | | | | | | | | | | X | | | | | X |
| Madison | | | | | | | | | | | | | | X | | | X | | | |
| Debra | | | | | | | | | | | | | X | | | | X | | | |
| Emily | | | | | | | | | | | X | | | | | | | | | X |
| Maria | | | | | | | | | | | X | | | | | | | X | | |
| Isabella | | | | | | | | | | | | | X | | | X | | | | |
| Olivia | | | | | | | | | | | | | | X | | | | | X | |
| Abigail | | | | | | | | | | | | | | | | | X | | | X |
| Brianna | | | | | | | | | | | | | | | X | X | | | | |
| TOTALS | 2 | 3 | 2 | 2 | 3 | 2 | 3 | 0 | 1 | 2 | 2 | 0 | 2 | 3 | 2 | 2 | 3 | 1 | 1 | 4 |

*Students in Class*

Figure 8.2 Sociogram data

The School Crime Operations Package (School COP) is a software applicat. allows teachers to map, record, and analyse bullying incidents occurring in and schools. It is free (www.schoolcopsoftware.com/index.htm).

## Sociograms

Sociograms, also known as friendship charts, provide visual representations of the s relationships in a group. They provide up-to-date information about a group's s dynamics: how children view each other, the most popular and least pop youngsters, the isolates (students who do not get any nominations), and cliques.

Sociometric data is gathered by charting pupils' responses to questions such "Who would you like to sit next to?," "Who would you choose as a partner f project?," or "Who would you invite to your birthday party?"

Sociograms eliminate subjective trial and error and are most effective if used conjunction with observations, surveys, and talks with students and staff.

## How Sociograms Help with Bullying

Information about the social milieu puts children who are at the greatest risk for bullying on the radar screen. It also draws attention to popular students who can be tapped for their leadership abilities.

Teachers can use the findings to develop and improve social interactions, for example by buddying less popular youngsters with admired peers, forming groups based on relationship needs, or separating cliques.

Unpopular or sensitive youngsters may be upset if their names are not among the popular selections. This can be avoided by instructing students not to share their answers. Scheduling the assignment before busy times limits chances for chatting. Periods prior to lunch and free play should never be used for data collection as opportunities for discussion are greatest during unstructured activities.

Injured feelings can also be prevented by keeping the results confidential and developing the sociogram with positive phrases. For example, ask "Who would you invite . . .?" rather than "Who would not be invited to . . .?"

## How to Construct a Sociogram

1. Children write their names at the top of a sheet of paper.
2. Pupils privately choose two classmates they want to play with (or sit next to, study with, vacation with, invite to their birthday party). Emphasize there are no right or wrong answers. Students write their selections on the paper and are told to keep their responses confidential.
3. Collect the papers.
4. Using graph paper, write each student's name across the top (horizontal) and left (vertical) axis (see Figure 8.2).

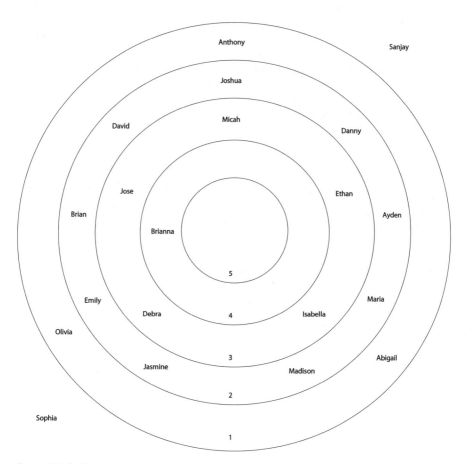

*Figure 8.3* Bull's-eye sociogram

selected four times so her name was placed inside ring number four. Jose, Micah, Ethan, Debra, and Isabella were named three times so their names were recorded inside ring number three. The procedure was repeated for all pupils.

Students closest to the center of the target are more popular. In this case, Brianna, Jose, Micah, Ethan, Debra, and Isabella are liked the most while Anthony, Olivia, Abigail, Sophia, and Sanjay are the least popular. Notice that Sophia and Sanjay are isolates because they received no nominations. In this case, it would be helpful to bring Sanjay and Sophia into the group, perhaps by seating them near admired students.

A group graph translates the data into student groupings:

1.   Write each student's name on a small rectangular piece of paper.
2.   Arrange the papers on top of a large sheet of paper, placing children who are named near classmates who were selected.
3.   When done, draw an arrow from the writer to each selected peer (→).
4.   Draw a line with an arrow at each end if two children mutually choose one another (↔).

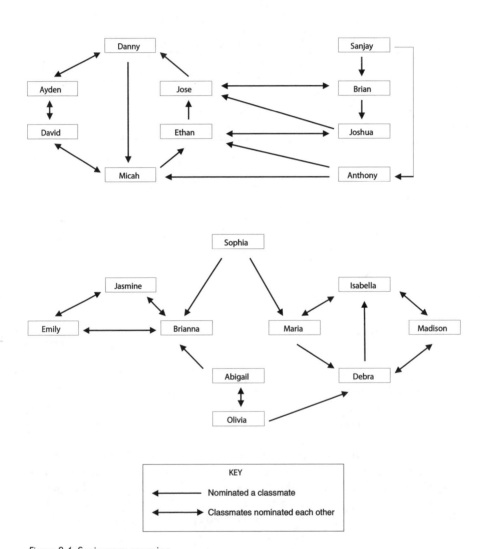

Figure 8.4 Sociogram grouping

In the example shown in Figure 8.4, the girls form several distinct groups. Jasmine, Emily, and Brianna comprise one; Isabella, Maria, Madison, and Debra make another. Teachers should break up these cliques. The boys form a larger group (Danny, Ayden, David, Micah, Ethan, and Jose) but some members play with Brian and Joshua. Anthony, Olivia, and Abigail (each receiving one nomination), and Sanjay and Sophia (no nominations) are on the edge of the social ecology. Teachers should pair, seat, or group these children with favored students.

---

### Box 8.2: Making the List

Principal Joe Bailey and the Graham Elementary School (Naperville, IL) took a proactive approach to helping students who did not have friends. They asked pupils to "name three kids they most like to do things with, three kids they don't like to do things with, and three kids they think most need a friend" (as cited in Dell'Angela, 2001, para. 8). Teachers are not often surprised by the youngsters identified as needing help but "Still on every class list, there was at least one eye-opener—a sweet, no-trouble kid who was inexplicably invisible to or unpopular with classmates" (para. 13). The teachers applied the findings by pairing friendless children with popular classmates for homework, strategically assigned seats, and established a club that would bring students with the same interests together, providing social connections (as cited in Dell'Angela, 2001).

# Chapter 9

# Bystanders/ Upstanders

A bystander is anyone other than the person bullying or the person being bullied who is present during a bullying episode. In school settings bystanders include students, teachers, administrators, librarians, coaches, hall monitors, lunch aides, cafeteria workers, custodians, secretaries, security guards, parents, bus drivers, and other support staff.

Students make up the majority of bystanders in schools; in fact, children are present during 85% of bullying incidents (Atlas & Pepler, 1998).

## Bystander Roles

Like actors on a stage, bystanders play different roles in bullying that begin, influence, reinforce, or end the violence. *Every* person present is a participant in the bullying:

- *The person who bullies*—The person who harms a targeted individual.
- *The person who is bullied*—The person who is the object of the aggression.
- *Assistant of the person who bullies*—This person does not initiate the bullying but will assist by hitting, holding, pushing, catching, or serving as a lookout. He or she may write graffiti, send hurtful emails, spread rumors, or refuse to give adults details about the bullying incident.
- *Reinforcer of the person who bullies*—This person provides positive feedback, inciting the individual or group by laughing, cheering, gesturing, smiling, commenting, or encouraging others to watch.
- *Defender of the person who is bullied*—This person helps those who are bullied by trying to stop the bullying, get help, or comfort the injured afterward.

- *Outsider*—This person quietly stands by and watches the bullying (Salmivalli, 1999; Salmivalli, Lagerspetz, Bjorkqvist, Osterman, & Kaukianen, 1996).

The roles are not fixed and can vary. For example, on Monday a child can be an outsider, but on Tuesday he or she could become the target. The same youngster might be a reinforcer on Friday.

Bystanders stand by. Upstanders stand up, speak out, and help those who are bullied. Defenders are upstanders. Bystander education helps transform bystanders into upstanders.

## The Power of Bystanders and Upstanders

It is imperative that educators understand the role bystanders play because they can be the solution to the problem. Why?

- Peers are almost always present during abusive incidents. Adults do not witness the bulk of bullying episodes.
- Children outnumber adults. Classrooms average about 15–30 students whose eyes and ears can pick up bullying vs. one teacher.
- Students know their peers better than adults.
- Students have "insider" information to which adults are not privy.
- Bullying is motivated by the attainment of power and status in the peer group so it makes sense to target the group that assigns the power and status.
- Youngsters have more influence over their peers than adults.
- Children determine the norms of social behavior.
- Most students do not support bullying.
- It is easier to influence the behavior of bystanders than to change those who aggress.

Youngsters possess a lot of power.

- Bullying stops in 10 seconds or less 57% of the time when upstanders intervene.
- The longer bystanders remain, the longer the abuse continues. When audiences walk away bullying ends.
- When bystanders join in, they reinforce those who bully (O'Connell, Pepler, & Craig, 1999).

One would think that children would use their power to stop bullying but that is not what happens most of the time. For example, an investigation found that peers spent three-quarters of the time watching or supporting those who bullied and helped targeted children only 25% of the time. Thus, more time is spent reinforcing aggression than stopping it (O'Connell et al., 1999).

Most people think they are not guilty of any wrongdoing if they do not throw a punch, yell an insult, exclude, or hurt someone. It is a misleading and harmful myth. Bystanders are *not* neutral. They reinforce those who bully and ignore the plight of the bullied. Those who aggress interpret the presence of onlookers as a sign of support, while those who are attacked view attendance as abandonment. Witnesses also add to the humiliation of the bullied and make it hard for anyone to save face. Neither side wants to back down when peers are watching.

Those who stand by and watch are "card carrying" members of a social system that gives consent to bullying. *There are no innocent bystanders.* This includes teachers. If they do not intervene they become part of the problem.

Adults often overlook the role of onlookers because their attention is focused on those who bully and those who are bullied. Doing so gives those who abuse an upper hand.

Teachers can use social architecture to (a) educate students about the roles they play so children can learn how they contribute to bullying, (b) teach safe upstander intervention skills, (c) alter social milieus that reinforce and reward bystanders and isolate bullied youngsters, and (d) create classroom climates that value inclusion, tolerance, diversity, acceptance, and peer intervention.

## Why Bystanders Do Not Intervene

Children do not like bullying, feel uneasy when they watch, and want to stop the abuse. Why, then, do they intervene a minority of the time (O'Connell et al., 1999)? Why is there a huge difference between a bystander's thoughts and actions?

- *Fear of retaliation*—Bystanders are afraid of becoming the "newest kid on the butcher block." Their fears are valid because those who bully viciously seek retribution. The irony is that helping an individual who bullies does not guarantee safety. If someone attacks one person without conscience, he or she will think nothing of assaulting another, including a bystander or "friend."
  *Social architecture*: Bystander education can be the catalyst that transfers power from those who aggress to onlookers. Learning ways to safely and effectively intervene can shift the power imbalance (see "Thirty Ways Bystanders Can Become Upstanders," page 130).
  Fears of retaliation will also lessen if teachers insure informers' anonymity, provide protection, and apply effective consequences.
- *Telling is tattling*—Society and those who bully have successfully brainwashed the public into thinking that telling is tattling. How many times have children been told by well meaning adults "Don't tattle"?
  *Social architecture*: Teachers need to do what they do best: teach. Educators must explain the differences between telling and tattling. Telling helps a person get *out* of trouble and keeps people safe. Tattling gets people *into* trouble and can be harmful (see "Telling vs. Tattling," page 122).

- *Experiences social pressure not to intervene*—Many youngsters allow abuse to continue because intervening can cost them status and friendships. Children will conform even if it means hurting someone because they want to be "in" and belong to a peer group.

  *Social architecture*: Social pressure *not to* intervene occurs when bullying is a norm. Teachers need to shift their classes' norms from "It is cool to bully" to "It is cruel to bully." If educators succeed, there will be pressure *to* intervene. Change begins with education.

- *Does not know how to respond*—Students have to be taught how to effectively handle bullying situations. It does not always come naturally. Knowledge provides children with the confidence to act.

  *Social architecture*: Strategies to prevent, diffuse, and stop abuse have not been part of school agendas. Just as students need to learn how to read and write, they also need to learn how to competently combat bullying. These lessons can be blended into academics, or learned during circle time, in assemblies, or during anti-bullying events.

- *Does not want to lose his or her position in the social hierarchy*—Children work hard to rise in the social hierarchy. Defending and intervening during bullying episodes can be interpreted as taking sides with the disliked bullied child over the more "popular" peer who aggresses. Action is often seen as an act of treason. Intervening can be social suicide.

  *Social architecture*: Teachers need to recognize "the social hierarchy and the strategies that students use to preserve the boundaries of their peer groups" and "create a climate that downplays social status by promoting activities that positively reinforce students' acceptance and tolerance of each other" (Farmer et al., 2006, p. 42).

  Inclusive, anti-bullying climates develop when everyone is accepted and included whether they excel in academics or have difficulty learning, whether they are athletically inclined or physically challenged, whether they are easy to get along with or irritating, whether they follow the rules or break them, whether they are in the "cool" group or considered an "outsider." One way to accomplish this goal is to organize activities where everyone is an equal and valued partner. For example, all students can participate in a class play whether it be acting, building props, sewing costumes, playing music, or controlling lights. Everyone works toward the common goal of an outstanding performance.

  Dismantle cliques by seating or grouping students with those they do not normally associate with. Select teams and groups so youngsters will not stack activities with members of their cliques. Bystander intervention would increase if thinking changed from "me" and "them" to "we" and "us" because perceptions would be altered from an attack on an outsider to an assault on one of our own.

  Helpful ideas for teaching tolerance can be found in "101 Tools for Tolerance," which was developed by tolerance.org (www.dec17.org/101_tools.pdf).

● *Does not want to lose "protection"*—Some children align themselves with those who abuse because they are afraid of becoming a target. Thus, they seek protection from being bullied by those who bully.

*Social architecture*: Once again, teachers need to educate students. "Protection" is an illusion because there are no assurances that those who aggress will not turn on their assistants. Supporters are pawns in a self-serving game of power, control, and domination. One day, they can be jumped. This is because there never was a true friendship. There is only one foolproof way of being "protected": end bullying.

● *Thinks he or she does not have the power to stop bullying*—Some students wonder how one person can have an impact, especially if bullying exists despite all the expertly designed anti-bullying intervention programs found in schools today. The thinking that nothing can stop abusive behavior can lead to an unhealthy future. If children accept bullying in school, they are on the road to accepting sexual, dating, domestic, and other forms of abuse as they travel through life.

We know that upstander intervention is successful in more than half the instances (Hawkins, Pepler, & Craig, 2001). Why? When peers challenge the wrongdoings of those who bully, there is potential for the power and reputations of those who abuse to decline. They back down rather than chance a loss.

Similarly, those who hurt others select rejected, unpopular children because bullying this population minimizes any loss of status or affection among peers (Veenstra, Lindenberg, Munniksma, & Dijkstra, 2010). This shows that youngsters have the power to control the behavior of those who bully.

At the very least, children can change how they respond to bullying. When they relinquish support, bullying diminishes. Bystanders can use their weight to shift the power imbalance.

*Social architecture*: In one of research psychologist Dr. Ervin Staub's experiments, subjects who volunteered for what they thought was a study on personalities were paired with one of Staub's associates ("confederates"). During the experiment a loud crash was heard from the next room, followed by crying and groans. When the confederates said "That probably has nothing to do with us" (Goleman, 1993, para. 12) about 25% of the volunteers investigated the commotion, but when "That sounds pretty bad—I'll go get the experimenter and maybe you should go check what's happening next door" (Goleman, 1993, para. 12) was suggested every single person investigated. "It showed me the power of bystanders to define the meaning of events in a way that leads people to take responsibility" Staub said (Goleman, 1993, para. 13).

What type of student has the courage to openly oppose bullying? Those with high social standing can defend targeted classmates with little social risk. It could be that defenders are admired because they help others or because their popularity precludes them from negative consequences (Salmivalli et al., 1996).

Sharing more research, creating similar experiments, and increasing bystander skills can help students realize they possess the muscle to put a choke hold on bullying. Children could band together with peers if lone activism is too daunting a thought. Greater numbers increase leverage and confidence.

●  *Does not think it is bullying*—Children and adults do not always realize that certain actions are bullying. Most agree that physical attacks are abusive; however, behaviors such as name calling, gossiping, or exclusion are often thought of as normal "kid's play."

   *Social architecture*: The definition and different types of bullying should be described, demonstrated, and discussed with specific examples. Circle time is a natural setting for this exercise. For example:

   –  *Physical bullying*—Slow, gentle and *non injurious* re-enactments.
      o  Poking, playing salugi, restraining
      o  Pushing down books, putting signs on someone's back
      o  Blocking paths
      o  Stealing someone's property

   –  *Verbal bullying*—Comments.
      o  Culture, ethnicity—"Go back to where you came from."
      o  Sexual orientation—"Faggot!" "You're gay."
      o  Threatening—"If you tell anyone, you won't live another day."
      o  Hurtful jokes—"She can beat an elephant in a food eating contest."

   –  *Relational bullying*—Words and actions.
      o  Exclusion—"Don't invite him to the party."
      o  Manipulation—"I won't play with you, if you play with her."
      o  Spreading rumors—"She is in love with <name>."
      o  Non verbal communication—Rolling eyes, nasty stares, gestures.

   –  *Cyberbullying*—Cite situations.
      o  Tricking others into sharing their password—"Friends share passwords. If you don't tell me yours, then you are not a true friend."
      o  Excluding—"Don't give her the link to the site."
      o  Sharing personal information—"Ricky's password is . . ."
      o  Forwarding photographs—"I'm sending a picture of Marcy getting undressed in the locker room."

●  *Does not think he or she is hurting anyone*—Children often think bullying is fun and games. They do not realize the harmful consequences of their actions. In reality, they are being entertained at the expense of others.

   *Social architecture*:

   –  Review Figure 4.1: Bullying web of harm (page 38).
   –  Explain that injuries are not always seen by the naked eye. Hurt feelings are hidden inside the body. (See Box 2.1: Chip Away Bullying, page 7.)
   –  Tell students that people have different perceptions and sensitivities. What may not hurt one person can deeply upset another. They should be sensitive to other people's feelings and err on the side of caution.

## Box 9.1: Differences

The following exercise is a bullying adaptation from an activity in Helen Carmichael Porter's book, *The Bully and Me* (2006). It lets students feel what it is like to be bullied and engages children in a thought provoking discussion on bullying.

1. Write instructions on slips of papers. For example:

   a. Roll your eyes—at anyone who is not wearing sneakers
   b. Ignore—anyone who is tall
   c. Say "I don't like you"—every time you walk past someone who is wearing blue
   d. Laugh—when you pass anyone who has brown hair
   e. Glare—at everyone wearing eyeglasses
   f. Point and sneer—at everyone wearing jewelry
   g. *Gently* tap—anyone wearing a belt

2. Students select one slip and follow the directions.
3. Afterwards, lead a class discussion:

   a. How did it feel to be the recipient of bullying behaviors?
   b. How did it feel to demean someone?
   c. Does this happen in our class? Does it happen to you?
   d. How does this exercise reflect bullying and intolerance?
   e. Brainstorm "different" qualities people are bullied for.
   f. Do we all have some kind of "difference"? What is yours?
   g. Would you want your "difference" to be attacked or celebrated?
   h. How can we stop bullying because of differences?

- *Does not realize that watching is supporting those who bully*—Many bystanders equate bullying with action. They think they are not contributing to the abuse if they quietly observe. "I didn't do anything," they say. That's the problem!

   *Social architecture*: Shatter the myth of innocence by explaining that bystander presence is interpreted as support. Explore the bystander roles and how each influences bullying.

- *Will not be believed*—There are children who act like sweet angels in front of teachers but do a "Jekyll and Hyde" when backs are turned. Reports of aggression dished out by charismatic and favored students are sometimes discounted. This can be a mistake because research shows that popular students can be aggressive (Faris & Felmlee, 2011b). When asked what they would want their principals to know about troublesome behavior, more than half the middle and high school respondents wrote "Please let our principal know that 'good kids' can be mean and can harass" (Wessler, 2003, p. 41).

*Social architecture*: Teachers have been shocked to learn that youngsters they least suspect torment classmates. Educators should not think that certain students are above bullying. It is these "model," "popular," and "nice" children who are often in the middle of abuse. Preconceived opinions of innocence can relax an instructor's guard and objectivity. Even the best students can be influenced, have a lapse in judgment, or experience a bad day. Teachers must keep their minds open, drawing conclusions after thorough and impartial investigations.

● *Parents and adults tell children to stay out of other people's business*—There are many well intentioned adults who advise children not to get involved in bullying. They erroneously believe such action violates boundaries.

*Social architecture*: These adults speak out of ignorance. Research shows that the venomous arms of bullying poison those who bully, those who are bullied, bystanders, teachers, the community, and society. Explain how everyone is negatively impacted by bullying. We *all* pay the price.

● *There are no expectations to act on bullying*—Bullying flourishes with laissez-faire attitudes. Upstander behavior rises with expectations; more children intercede when they are expected to do so.

*Social architecture*: Just as educators insist that children line up quickly and quietly for fire drills, not call out or run in class, teachers have to *insist on respect, tolerance, kindness, and inclusion* and stop the class for a teachable moment *every* time there is a lapse. For the most part, students will comply if these are *not negotiable expectations*. When teachers insist on upstander behavior, give continuous feedback, challenge inappropriate activity, and effectively respond to bullying, anti-bullying values become class norms.

● *Moral disengagement*—Bandura's social cognitive theory of moral agency explains why good people commit cruel acts. According to this theory, sociocognitive processes justify and rationalize antisocial behavior. They may include "the cognitive restructuring of harmful behavior, obscuring or minimizing one's role in causing harm, disregarding or distorting the impact of harmful behavior, and blaming and dehumanizing the victim" (Hymel, Rocke-Henderson, & Bonanno, 2005, p. 2).

When Hymel et al. (2005) performed research examining Bandura's theory and bullying, the subjects said bullying was acceptable (cognitive restructuring) and claimed bullied students were deserving of the maltreatment (blaming). Those who admitted to bullying others had the highest levels of moral disengagement; however, the majority of subjects showed varying degrees of this behavior. Disengagement can follow a progression that parallels the diminishment of self-censure; the severity of the acts increases as disapproval declines.

*Social architecture*: Hymel et al. wrote "Efforts to counter moral disengagement with strategies that inhibit such negative behavior need to be established, perhaps through efforts to enhance empathy for victimized students and/or raise bystanders' sense of moral *agency*, thereby increasing the likelihood that they will intervene on behalf of victims" (2005, p. 8).

- *Desensitization*—Repeated exposure to violence anesthetizes people. Desensitization can also lead to the imitation of bullying behaviors.

   *Social architecture*: Classroom discussions about the harmful effects of bullying can show its dangers, sensitize children to the feelings of others, and complement empathy training. Implementation of effective anti-bullying measures decreases the number of bullying incidents, which in turn lessens desensitization.
- *Deindividualization theory*—According to the deindividualization theory, people in large groups or crowds can lose their individuality, inhibitions, and self-restraint, which can cause them to act in ways they normally never would. As assemblies increase in size, more people are swept into the crowd's acts of aggression and take little or no responsibility for their hostile actions (Festinger, Pepitone, & Newcomb, 1952). This may explain, however not justify, why children who would never hurt anyone become aggressive in crowds. Group bullying can be more dangerous than one-on-one abuse because normal moral constraints disappear.

   *Social architecture*: Lack of self-awareness, lack of accountability, and anonymity play roles in deindividualization. If group members are aware of deindividualization, there is less chance of becoming part of the tide that carries them along with the crowd. The knowledge gives them control over their choices: whether to congregate with a potentially hostile group or pass, whether they can exert enough self-control to overcome the phenomenon or stay home, or whether they should warn an adult or not.

   Anonymity increases the likelihood of deindividualization because there is less risk of being identified and held responsible. "Telling" classes strip off the veil of secrecy, making participation public knowledge.

   Those who have higher levels of arousal are more susceptible to deindividualization, so it is advisable to keep a closer eye on these students.
- *Diffusion of responsibility*—As the number of bystanders increases, the chances of someone intervening decrease because (a) people feel less personal responsibility to help if others who are present are capable of assisting, (b) bystanders may believe that other onlookers have alerted or will call for help, and (c) the responsibility to intervene and any guilt for not doing so are diffused among all observers.

   *Social architecture*: Psychologist John Darley's research found that diffusion of responsibility can be negated if the person who is hurt selects "a specific person for help—'You there, can you help me'" (Keltner & Marsh, 2006–2007, Why People Help section, para. 7).

   People are also more likely to help those who are similar to them (Bystanders: Passive or active, 2009). Activities can accentuate commonalities.
- *Pluralistic ignorance*—Pluralistic ignorance occurs when most of a group privately disagrees with a norm but falsely assumes that others accept it. As a result, a norm the majority would ordinarily reject is publicly supported. In bullying situations, we see children go along with abuse, thinking they are the only ones who disapprove. In reality, the majority of youngsters think bullying is wrong, yet the (mis)interpretation of the silent majority is that bullying is endorsed.

## Box 9.2: Simon Says "Who Are You?"

Linda Starr (2004) developed a fun way to help students learn about each other (www.educationworld.com/a_lesson/00-2/lp2061.shtml):

- Explain to students that they will play a version of Simon Says in which only some students will respond to each command.
- Tell students that they must watch carefully as they play the game because, at the end, each student must tell one new thing they learned about a classmate.
- Lead a game of Simon Says. Provide such directions as:

    - Simon says "Everyone with brown eyes, stand up,"
    - Simon says "Everyone who has a dog as a pet, put your right hand on your head,"
    - Simon says "Everyone whose favorite sport is soccer, stand on one foot,"
    - Simon says "Everyone who speaks more than one language, jump up and down,"
    - and so on. Choose categories appropriate for your students.

- At the end of the game, have students sit in a circle. Ask each student to name one way in which he or she and another student are alike. The trait they share must be something they didn't know before playing the game. Students might say, for example, "I didn't know that Katie spoke Spanish" or "I didn't know that Jose was left-handed" (Starr, 2004).

*Social architecture*: A teacher can share the results of a class Bystander Survey (Figure 9.1), which explores the feelings of spectators. If the results are in line with research, students will learn that their peers are not supportive of bullying and wish others would speak out against it. This information can give children the confidence to act.

Circle time also provides an opportunity to discuss feelings associated with being a bystander. Reading a bullying book or relating a bullying incident can be a perfect segue into an exploration of feelings:

- "What do you think the bystander was thinking?" / "What were you thinking?"
- "How did the bystander feel?" / "How did you feel?"
- "What actions did the bystander consider?" / "What options did you consider?"
- "Why do you think the bystander acted that way (or did not act)?" / "Would you act that way (or not act)? Why or why not?"
- "What are some strategies that could turn bystanders into upstanders?"

---

### Bystander Survey

1. Is bullying a good or bad activity?                    ☐ Good      ☐ Bad

2. Do you like to watch bullying?                          ☐ Yes       ☐ No

3. How do you feel when you see bullying?                  ☐ Happy     ☐ Sad

                                    ☐ I do not care        ☐ Angry     ☐ Helpless

4. Do you wish you could end bullying?                     ☐ Yes       ☐ No

5. Do you like it when peers speak against bullying?       ☐ Yes       ☐ No

---

*Figure 9.1* Bystander Survey

Reading (e.g., newspaper, magazine, internet articles) or watching (e.g., documentaries, DVDs, news reports) firsthand stories of bystanders in action show children that others share their anti-bullying views.

We also see pluralistic ignorance in situations where the calmness of witnesses is interpreted as meaning there is no emergency. When others do not act, onlookers think they are misinterpreting events or overreacting (Keltner & Marsh, 2006–2007). In these instances, Darley recommends making needs clear. "I've twisted my ankle and I can't walk; I need help" (Why People Help section, para. 7). Now, there can be no pluralistic ignorance because the injured person is clearly telling bystanders that he or she is in distress and requires assistance.

## What Conditions Motivate Bystanders to Act?

While it is helpful to learn why bystanders remain in the bleachers, it is equally important to unearth factors that bring upstanders onto the court:

- *Loyalty to friends*—Children say they will help if a friend is in trouble but probably will not get involved if they do not know the person.
- *Expectations of friends and parents*—Students are more likely to intervene if friends and parents expect them to act.

  *Social architecture*: Relationships must be built first. They can be developed by teaching friendship skills, cooperative learning, pairing with buddies, frequently changing work partners, circle time, peer support programs, embracing differences and diversity, highlighting the talents of all students, and encouraging extra-curricular participation. Discussions about friendships should emphasize that friends stand up, support, and help one another. Children should be sensitized to the fact that we have a moral obligation to help people in need.

When parents learn about the devastating consequences of bullying they are more likely to support anti-bullying initiatives. Educate parents. Tell them to share information with their children and endorse bystander intervention.

- *Success in past interventions*—The more successful past efforts are, the greater the likelihood of future assistance.
- *Self-efficacy*—Poyhonen and Salmivalli (2007) tell us that "self-efficacy for defending has a unique *positive* association with supporting the victim. In the same time, it is *negatively* related to staying outside bullying incidents and not taking sides with anyone" (as cited in Salmivalli, Karna, & Poskiparta, 2010, p. 443).

  *Social architecture*: Arming students with non aggressive and effective bystander skills increases self-efficacy, intervention, and success.
- *Empathy*—Chances of giving aid are greater if spectators put themselves into the bullied person's position.
- *Feelings for the child who is bullied*—The odds of acting on behalf of someone are increased if the person being abused is liked.

  *Social architecture*: Training in empathy, friendship, and social skills will increase bystander intervention. The decision to intervene or abstain should not be based on relationships but on the safety of those who are bullied.
- *Bullying is wrong*—Some students intervene because bullying is wrong and unfair.
- *Positive view of self*—Others defend peers because they view themselves as good people.
- *Future benefit*—The thought of future gain, for example making a new friend, motivates some youngsters to act.

  *Social architecture*: Character education can facilitate support.
- *Being in a group*—Youngsters are more likely to intervene when they are in a group and less likely to speak out if they are alone.

  *Social architecture*: Develop anti-bullying norms and demonstrate the power of bystanders. Create anti-bullying clubs, patrols, and projects.
- *Thinking the person may be seriously hurt*—Chances of aid increase if onlookers think there is a serious injury.

  *Social architecture*: Discuss the harmful consequences of bullying, pointing out that the harm is not always seen (see Box 2.1: Chip Away Bullying, pages 7–8).
- *Social norms*—Children are more likely to intervene if anti-bullying and bystander intervention is the norm.

  *Social architecture*—Awareness, education, modeling by adults, expectations, and a strong anti-bullying program can change norms (Haffner, McDougall, & Vaillancourt, 2007; McLaughlin, Arnold, & Boyd, 2005; Rigby & Johnson, 2005, 2006).

## Box 9.3: Bystander Commercials and Videos

These short videos can be springboards for discussions on bystander intervention:

"Anti-Bullying PSA: The Price of Silence"
By Shake State Productions in association with The Museum of Tolerance
**www.youtube.com/watch?v=wY7Gvq0P4hc**
*This ad illustrates the powerful effect of upstanders.*

"The Cool Table"
By Family Channel and Bullying.org
**www.bullying.org** (Click on "I Want to Share," then "Your Voices," then "Multimedia," then "The Cool Table.")
*This video promotes upstander behavior and shows children how they can make a difference. An accompanying lesson plan can be found at*
**www.bullyingawarenessweek.org/pdf/teachers_guide_family_ channel_bullying.org.pdf**

"Tell Someone," "Words Hurt," and "Walk Away"
By Concerned Children's Advertisers (CCA)
**www.cca-kids.ca/psas/bullying_prevention.html**
*These anti-bullying commercials encourage children to tell adults about bullying and urge them to take action. Teachers can download related lesson plans.*

## Telling vs. Tattling

Telling (about bullying episodes) can be the difference between a class overrun by bullying and a bully free room. Yet, anti–bullying efforts are stonewalled because most children will not report bullying. It is not surprising because in our culture telling on another person is taboo and peppered with negative connotations. It is "tattling," "snitching," "ratting," "squealing," "being a narc," "turning in," "being a fink," and seen as betrayal. There is an ironclad code of silence among school children. No one wants to break it, lest they become labeled or the new "punching bag."

There *is* a difference between telling and tattling. The distinction needs to be explained, stressed, and reinforced. Coloroso (2003) wrote the simplest, yet clearest, definition in *The bully, the bullied, and the bystander.*

Tattling gets someone INto trouble

Telling gets someone OUT of trouble

---

### Box 9.4: Differences Between Tattling and Telling

| Tattling | Telling |
|---|---|
| Gets someone INto trouble | Gets someone OUT of trouble |
| Tries to hurt someone | Tries to keep someone safe |
| Does not involve a dangerous situation | Can stop/prevent a dangerous situation |
| Can be used to get attention | Is used to help another person |
| May be used to threaten or manipulate | Helps and protects |
| The person can handle the situation by themselves | Adult assistance is required |
| Not important | Important |

---

It is *tattling* if one student notices a classmate texting on a cell phone and tells the teacher because the informer is getting someone INto trouble. However, it is *telling* if a pupil sees a child hitting a youngster who is unable to defend him- or herself, because the reporter is getting someone OUT of a troublesome and dangerous situation. Davis takes telling one step further: "It's not tattling, it's being a witness to a crime" (as cited in Wilde, n.d., What It Means section, para. 5).

Give students examples of times adults tell. If their parents saw a pedestrian injured in a hit-and-run accident, would they ignore the person in need or call 911 and *tell* what happened? If an uncle worked in a store and saw a customer steal merchandise, would their relative turn his head? Some might but many would *tell* the owner. If teachers saw a colleague break a student's arm, would they make believe it did not happen or *tell* the principal? Telling is the *right* thing to do. It is not cowardly to tell; in fact, it is an act of courage and bravery.

If children mistakenly believe they are helping those who mistreat others by keeping quiet, they should think twice. Their misguided allegiance hurts those who abuse because unchecked childhood bullying continues into adulthood and can lead to a life of relationship and criminal problems. Telling school authorities is a way to help troubled students.

Teachers should strive to make their class a "telling class." Convey and get students to internalize that it is *their responsibility* to tell.

## Nineteen Ways to Encourage Telling

In classrooms governed by social architecture teachers set up and nurture environments that encourage the sharing of information.

1. *Keep confidences*—Retribution is the top reason students withhold information. Children are eager to help but will be tight lipped if there is a chance their identities will become public knowledge. They are understandably afraid of being beaten, ridiculed, excluded, or labeled. Youngsters feel safer and are more apt to report when confidences are kept.
2. *Offer protection*—Educators must assure the safety of reporters. Protection increases the number of students who tell and decreases bullying because those who aggress do not want to be held accountable for their harmful behaviors.
3. *Take bullying reports seriously*—Teachers should not act bothered or minimize any report and should follow up on each account, no matter how trivial or minor it may appear. Saying "Let them handle it themselves," "Ignore it," "They're just playing," "Mind your own business," or "It's nothing" discourages disclosures. These statements discount pupils' feelings and make them regret speaking up. Dismissive attitudes tell youngsters they cannot count on educators for support.

   Teachers can encourage reporting by thanking children for making their class safer, investigating, and issuing fair and effective consequences.
4. *Take action when bullying is seen*—If teachers act when they witness abuse or are told about it youngsters will be more inclined to report. Quick responders show children that bullying is unacceptable and will not be allowed in their class. Educators who turn their heads are intimidated or controlled by children who bully.
5. *Hold those who aggress accountable*—Students will not see the point of reporting if teachers do not hold children who hurt others accountable for their actions.

   Without consequences, those who bully have nothing to lose so they continue their established patterns of delinquent behavior. Even worse, when other students see that bullying is allowed they surmise that bullying is okay. Instead of one child, there can potentially be a class full of children who bully.

   Teachers have a responsibility to act once an incident is reported or seen. It is their moral, professional, and legal obligation.
6. *Apply effective interventions*—"Effective" is the operative word because many students think teacher interventions make situations worse. Under these circumstances, children conclude that telling does not help; instead, it hurts. Formative consequences and restorative practices are successful because they are related to the offense, create awareness, teach, and change behavior.
7. *Employ fair consequences*—Students want teachers to stop abuse. They also want fairness and justice to guide discipline. Reporting will be minimal if consequences are punitive or harsh. For example, youngsters shy away from reporting in schools with zero tolerance policies.
8. *Be alert to bullying*—The best anti-bullying teachers move around, keep their eyes and ears open, and are constantly on the lookout for misbehavior. This gives them a visible presence and makes it easier to report bullying.
9. *Keep a closer eye on those involved in bullying*—Altercations can be prevented or short circuited if teachers are present. If students repeatedly see a teacher, they will think he or she cares and will be more likely to talk about bullying episodes.

10. *Be in the right place at the right time*—Teachers can use an informant's information to advantageously position themselves in potential bullying areas. For example, they can stand by a lunch table that someone who bullies hounds or keep a close eye on a recess ballgame. In this way, those who bully cannot blame tipsters; it was the teacher who spotted the abuse.

11. *Praise*—Praise youngsters for being brave enough to tell adults about bullying. It gives reporters a well deserved pat on the back and motivates them to continue helping. Recognition and commendations also encourage other bystanders.

12. *Teach responsibility*—Unfortunately, safety in classrooms is not guaranteed. All students must pitch in to keep their class free from danger. It is important to let children know that they have a responsibility to others in their classroom community. Part of that responsibility is a duty to report when someone is being hurt. If youngsters tell peers to report abuse because "Bullying is wrong" maltreatment will decrease and bystander assistance will increase because of conformity. It also says that students will not allow their classrooms to become theaters of terror.

13. *Explain the plight of bullied children*—Children might be more likely to report bullying if they realize that those who are bullied need their help because they cannot defend themselves, which is the very reason they are targeted.

    Teachers can also explain how it feels to be bullied. This lesson becomes more powerful if the bullied child does the talking.

14. *Provide a way to tell*—Teachers need to show students ways they can safely report:

    – *Bully boxes*—Some schools use "bully boxes" where notes about bullying-related concerns, incidents, and suggestions are placed. However, anonymity is compromised when classmates see their peers putting messages into the box. Requiring students to write something about any topic on a weekly

---

## Box 9.5: A Newsworthy Lesson

Find a thick newspaper. Remove two sheets and draw a face on each. Tell the class to think of the faces as two children in their class. Put one aside.

Give a student the remaining "face" with directions to bully it (rip it in half). It should be an easy task. It is easy to rip someone to shreds if he or she is alone. Now, pick up the second "face" and place it in the middle of the newspaper. Tell the class that the newspaper represents a group of children surrounding a target (the face). Ask the student to rip the entire paper. It will be very difficult, if not impossible, because there are many layers that strengthen and protect it. It is the same with bullying. Targeted youth will be protected if surrounded by upstanders. Upstanders will be safe, too, because groups have more power than individuals.

basis circumvents this drawback. It could be about how they feel, things they like or dislike, ideas, or about bullying. No one will know who reports abuse if each pupil is required to place some kind of comment into the box. Teachers will also learn more about their students. The box can be named "The Thoughts Box."

Another problem some schools encounter with bully boxes is that some reports are not legitimate cases of bullying. This can be prevented by teaching students the definition, types of bullying, and the differences between bullying and non aggressive behavior.

- *Private meetings*—Students can privately meet with their teacher.
- *School mailbox*—Notes about bullying can be put in the teacher's school mailbox.
- *Email*—If youngsters want to remain anonymous, they can email information about bullying using a generic email address that conceals their identity.
- *Snail mail*—Pupils can snail mail letters to teachers at the school's address.
- *Text messages*—If cell phones are allowed, students can text when danger is imminent or occurring.
- *Help from friends*—Children can ask a friend to tell the teacher about a bullying episode or accompany them.
- *Parents*—Parents can inform the school about abusive incidents.
- *Anonymous questionnaires*—White Pines Middle School (Ely, NV) principal Aaron Hanson created an anonymous questionnaire asking students for the names of children who bullied in school. He met with everyone who was listed and helped them solve their problems. They no longer take their issues out on others (Bully Police USA, n.d.).
- *Professional anonymous reporting systems*—Some schools hire companies that specialize in anonymous reporting systems. Depending upon the service, children and parents anonymously call a phone number, text, or make online reports. They can tell about bullying, gangs, threats of violence, suicide, cheating, substance abuse, depression, self-mutilation, sexual harassment, date rape, illegal activities (e.g., drugs, guns, theft), and any other problems students may not feel comfortable talking about face-to-face.
- *Group discussions*—Circle time can provide a safe forum for reporting, depending on the group and how it is set up.
- *Journal writing*—Assignments that relate to bullying can be reservoirs of information. Journaling provides an open line of communication that helps teachers stay in touch with their students and solve problems during early stages.

15. *Create trusting relationships*—Youngsters are more likely to share information with adults they trust. Begin developing relationships on the first day of school because it takes time to build rapport and earn respect. The bonds must be in place *before* problems arise.

16. *Educate and raise awareness*—Explain that silence gives those who bully permission to hurt others and has been equated to bullying itself. It is an acceptance of bullying. On the other hand, telling says that bullying is wrong and the person does not want anyone to be hurt. Children need to understand how telling stops bullying, what happens when bullying is not reported, safe ways to tell, and about the power they possess. When fear handcuffs children, they should realize they are giving their power to, and being controlled by, those who bully. Is that what they want?

17. *Focus on the group*—One child can make a difference but there is power in numbers. Encourage youngsters to object to bullying together. Telling becomes a class norm when the majority of students follow this practice. If so, classroom bullying will have a natural death.

18. *Explain that telling can be done safely*—Most adults who witness crimes will not confront the criminals; rather, they contact the police department. Why? They fear getting hurt. In the same way, children can remain safe by privately telling school personnel and asking them to keep confidences.

19. *Spend time with students*—School staff participating in the NEA survey (see Chapter 1) found a positive correlation between spending time with students and being told of bullying incidents: the more time they interacted with students, the more likely they would receive bullying reports (Bradshaw et al., 2011).

## Ten Ways to Create Upstanders—Suggestions from Experts and More

Why do we expect children to intuitively know upstander strategies? Few youngsters will spontaneously help without bystander education, which may bridge the gap between what students want to do and what they actually do.

Different techniques have been proposed to promote upstander behavior. The best educational program for a particular class is dependent on its population, problems, needs, and resources. Experts in the field of bullying have made the following suggestions:

1. Salmivalli (1999) recommends several ways to increase upstander intervention:

   – *Awareness-raising*—Salmivalli stresses the importance of explaining:
      o the different roles students play and how their behavior contributes to bullying;
      o group mechanisms (e.g., conformity, group norms) and why people sometimes act in ways that are out of character for them;
      o the difference between their beliefs and behavior;
      o the responsibility of everyone to deter bullying.

- *Self-reflection*—Bystanders can review the roles they played during bullying episodes.
- *Role playing*—Awareness, recognition, and information are vital building blocks in bystander education. However, there is a difference between cognition and action. Role playing provides safe opportunities to learn, practice, rehearse, and fine tune responses that can carry over into real life situations. It also allows participants to explore feelings associated with the different roles.
- *Assertiveness training*—Bystanders should learn how to withstand peer pressure and share their beliefs, even when they differ from the majority.

2. Hazler and Carney (2002) argue that building awareness by providing information is not enough. "It is emotional awareness more than thorough knowledge that motivates people to give close attention and take personal responsibility for their actions" (2002, p. 135). This requires the use of "created experiences" that can be achieved through videotapes, books, readings, or speakers who personalize the abuse. That is why presenters such as John Halligan are so powerful. Halligan tells the story of his son, Ryan, who bullycided after years of bullying. He gives mistreated children a face and shows the reality of bullying. There is resistance to stirring youngsters' emotions because they can be hard to control, but thoughtful discussions before and after presentations help audiences safely digest the painful facts of life.

3. Twemlow, Fonagy, and Sacco (2001) describe a plan that helps students become aware of the roles each person in the class plays during bullying episodes. For example, a student (the person who aggresses) throws a spitball at a teacher (the person being bullied), and the class laughs (bystanders). The educator shows how every member of the class contributed—they may have caused, perpetuated, reinforced, or stopped the aggression. This approach increases insight while downplaying blame. Discussion and reflection periods reinforce the message.

4. Rigby (as interviewed in Wilde, n.d.) provides some important recommendations:

   - Help youngsters see that they are not the only ones who disagree with bullying. Knowing peers feel the same way gives children the courage to act.
   - Show pupils that intervention will make a difference.
   - Encourage a dialogue in which students tell what they would do if a bullying incident happened in their presence.

5. Macklem (2003) suggests creating a list of behaviors that are supportive of bullying. It clarifies the actions, eliminates confusion, and provides clear expectations.

6. Cowie and Sharp (1994, p. 64) use the following exercise:

   "Have you ever known that someone is being bullied but not done anything about it?

   - In groups of 4 or 5, share your stories. How did you feel? Were you comfortable or uncomfortable?

- In pairs, one person take on the role of the bullied pupil; the other take on the role of the bystander who did not help. Bystanders try to explain why you did not help; what dilemmas did you face?
- Re-enact the bullying scene, but this time intervene. How did you feel? How effective were you?

Discussion points:

- How does it feel to be a bystander?
- Are inactive bystanders as bad as the bully?
- How do bystanders make the bullying worse?
- What can bystanders do to help the bullied pupil?"

7. Alberti (2008) suggests that teachers help children see that bullying is "uncool." If successful, students will confront those who aggress, defend peers who are bullied, and report bullying. Alberti also says that bullying should be reframed as child abuse and informants should be rewarded for telling. The idea is similar to police tip lines that provide rewards for information.

8. Hirschstein, Van Schoiack Edstrom, Frey, Snell, and MacKenzie found that destructive bystander behavior and bullying can be reduced by coaching. "Coaching entails prompting, reinforcing positive social behaviors over time, and dispensing consequences in the context of real events and personalities" (2007, p. 16).

9. Bullying discussions can eliminate ignorance and motivate bystanders. Some topics include:

- How to recognize the different types of bullying.
- Bullying myths.
- How bullying hurts the person who bullies, the person who is bullied, bystanders, the school, community, and society.
- The power of bystanders and upstanders.
- How to form an alliance of upstanders.
- How to distinguish between dangerous and non dangerous situations.
- When to intervene.
- Safe and effective ways to intercede.
- How to talk to those who bully.
- Removing someone who is bullied.
- Telling vs. tattling.
- Encouraging peers to help.
- Supporting bullied students.
- Ways to lessen or eliminate bullying in the classroom and school.

10. Children emulate celebrities and athletes. Many of these "stars" have been bullied themselves and preach anti-bullying messages. For example, singer Justin Bieber's public service announcement tells bystanders to help (http://ellen.warnerbros.com/resources/united_against_bullying/?adid=ellen_hp_fav).

## Thirty Ways Bystanders Can Become Upstanders

Intervention can be increased by teaching children *specific* strategies and the language needed to prevent or stop bullying. The knowledge raises self-efficacy, which leads to upstander behavior.

Teachers must stress that good intentions will not prevent harm. *It is actions that count.*

The comprehensive list that follows has interventions tailored to every child. Some youngsters will be comfortable with a few of the strategies, and many can easily carry out more, but there are ways *every* child can lend a hand. Helping protects targeted peers, bystanders, upstanders, and the entire school community. It also shows pupils they are not helpless and have the power to prevent or stop aggression. *Remind students that their safety always takes precedence.*

1. *Develop an array of helpful upstander skills*—Students need to be equipped with a variety of strategies because (a) a youngster may be at ease using one technique but be nervous with another, (b) those who aggress might respond to one method while another fails, or (c) an idea can work well in one situation but be unsuccessful in another.
2. *Empathize*—Empathy can be the catalyst for advocacy. Bystanders should ask "How would I feel if I were bullied?" and "Would I want someone to help me?"
3. *Tell the person who is bullying to stop*—The following statements may prematurely end bullying episodes:

   "Stop!"
   "We don't bully in this classroom."
   "Leave my friend alone."
   "Why are you saying mean things?"
   "Bullying is wrong."
   "Bullying makes you look bad."

   It is important to be assertive, not aggressive.
4. *Tell an adult about the bullying*—Pupils should seek adult assistance when (a) someone is being hurt and nobody present can handle the situation, (b) danger develops, or (c) there are illegal activities (e.g., weapons, abuse, drugs).
5. *State the consequences for bullying*—Telling those who bully that they will get into trouble may make them think twice. For example:

   "You'll get detention."
   "Your parents will be called."
   "You'll miss the school trip."
   "You'll be dropped from the baseball team."
   "You'll be suspended from school."

6. *Reason*—People can have difficulty thinking straight when they are angry. When someone tries to reason it helps those whose emotional states block clear thinking to see "options or consider the consequences of their actions" (Phillips et al., 2008, p. 196). For example, "He is really annoying but if you hit him he'll get hurt and want revenge, plus you'll be expelled. Telling a teacher will take care of the problem."

7. *Distract the person who is bullying*—Distraction may take the minds of those who aggress off bullying, lessen the tension, or provide time for the targeted person to escape. Children can make a joke ("Listen to this riddle . . ."), start a new conversation ("Did you watch the Yankee game last night?"), shift attention ("Can you show me how to do this math problem?"), or suggest an alternative activity ("Let's play basketball.").

8. *Warn that help is on the way*—"I think someone went to get a teacher" can put the brakes on bullying. Those who are abusing will appreciate the heads up and those who are being bullied will be relieved if the confrontation ends early.

9. *Refuse to go along*—There are many ways to avoid participating in bullying. Say "I think it's wrong to bully anyone," walk away, change seats, log off the internet, and do not pass gossip.

10. *Practice balancing*—This technique "involves countering a negative comment with a positive comment in order to balance . . . a put-down" (Phillips et al., 2008, p. 192). It is not an attack on the person aggressing. It simply states an opinion. For example, in response to "Carol is a nerd," an upstander could say "Carol was in my math class and taught me how to do the problems I didn't understand. I passed math because of her. I think she's kind, helpful and cool."

11. *Walk away*—Students should leave if they do not feel comfortable speaking up. Departing means they will no longer contribute to the bullying. If it is impossible to make an exit youngsters can turn away and occupy themselves with another activity. Poker faces should be used. Any emotion, laughing, or gestures can be (mis)interpreted as support.

12. *Walk away with a friend*—The quicker a crowd disperses, the faster abuse will end.

13. *Do not lend support to anyone who aggresses*—Ignoring, excluding, spreading rumors, writing graffiti, smiling, and watching bullying are endorsements of abuse. Cheering, restraining, assisting, being a lookout, and lying about the actions of the people who bully are also forms of involvement. If it is too difficult to abstain, bystanders should cut ties or distance themselves from anyone who bullies.

14. *Remove the person who is bullied*—People cannot be bullied if they are not present. Children should take the targeted person's hand and say, for example:

> "Mrs. Jones wants to see you."
> "There's a call for you in the main office."
> "I need help with my homework."
> "We need one more player for our game."

Walk away arm in arm.

---

## Box 9.6: Removal

McGruff, the National Crime Prevention Council's crime dog, shows viewers how to remove a peer from a bullying situation in the "Watch Bully Hotline" video (www.youtube.com/watch?v=NfzbnGQFx_8). Similar directions are provided on the ASKACOP.org site (www.askacop.org/school/schoolbullies.html).

In both, bystanders approach the bullying scene, put their arms around the bullied child, and walk away together.

---

15. *Ask classmates to help*—The chances of stopping abuse increase as the numbers of people who disapprove rise.

16. *Compliment those who stand up to aggression*—Commending peers who help others is a sign of recognition, appreciation, and support. It also encourages future assistance.

17. *Record bullying locations*—Youngsters can jot down areas where bullying is most prevalent and give the list to the principal. It is hoped that additional supervision will be assigned to spots where surveillance is deficient.

18. *Stop rumors*—Rumors continue because one person tells another who tells another who tells another. The chain can be broken by refusing to repeat false and hurtful statements. Say "This is wrong. I am not going to pass along lies." Do not add to harmful stories. Refrain from laughing, smiling, or commenting, and encourage others to follow your lead.

19. *Do not engage in cyberbullying*—It is a person's presence and contributions that encourage cyberbullying, just as in offline bullying. Youngsters should not visit any internet sites where people are abused. They should not participate in conversations or polls that are hurtful; or pass along nasty emails, photographs, instant or text messages.

20. *Comfort the person who was bullied*—When targeted youngsters are repeatedly bullied they begin to believe that no one likes them, the insults are true, bullying is their fault, and they deserve the abuse. Support offsets these thoughts and lets bullied children know they are valued.

    Ask compassionate questions and make caring comments, for example:

    "Are you okay?"
    "Is there anything I can do to help you?"
    "I'm sorry he did that to you."
    "You didn't deserve it."
    "I don't know what he was thinking. I really like your shirt."
    "You can sit with me."

Pick up books and other items that were knocked down, brush off dirt, and escort the child to the school nurse if medical attention is needed.

21. *Participate in a peer support program*—A peer support program provides education, skill building, friendship, and support. It lets children who are abused know that they are not alone, that others care, and that others disapprove of bullying. (See Chapter 11, "Peer Support Programs.")

22. *Brainstorm ways to end bullying*—Upstanders can invite friends to brainstorming sessions that are dedicated to finding solutions.

23. *Help bullied classmates develop skills*—Students can teach skills to prevent, deal with, or end bullying.

24. *Sit or stand next to the person who is bullied*—Sit or stand next to those who are bullied in class, at lunch, in the schoolyard, in the hallways, and on the school bus. If you are sitting or standing next to a target, the person who bullies cannot. It is a sign of support and lets others know you want bullying to stop.

25. *Begin a friendship with a bullied child*—Children who do not have friends are like bull's-eyes on dartboards. Friendships decrease the odds of being pierced. Even better, invite the bullied person into your group of friends.

26. *Escort vulnerable children through bullying zones*—Youngsters *who feel safe* can accompany those who are susceptible to bullying through known bullying hot spots. The presence of another person or group of people decreases the risk of an attack.

27. *Include targeted peers in activities*—Chances of being picked on are decreased when children are included in activities. Students do not have to like everyone but they should not purposely exclude anyone.

28. *Talk to the person who bullies, in private*—If peers privately ask those who aggress to stop bullying they may be receptive to the request. Explaining why bullying is harmful, that hurting others is not "cool," and that bullying negatively affects those who bully may change behavior.

29. *Clean graffiti*—Graffiti that smears others is ongoing bullying because it remains and continually hurts the targeted individual(s). Erasing graffiti can limit pain.

30. *Save evidence*—Nasty notes, bullying emails, humiliating photographs, damaged property, and other pieces of evidence should be saved and given to teachers.

Students must *always consider safety first*. They should not do anything that will jeopardize the health of those bullied, those who bully, bystanders, teachers, or themselves. Seeking adult assistance is the prudent course of action if bullying gets out of control.

Reviewing the list of ways students can help should be a first step, not a lesson with an endpoint. After the methods of intervention are introduced, they should be taught, demonstrated, role played, and practiced. Feedback should be given. Children can rehearse in school with their classmates, at home in front of a mirror, or with family members. Youngsters will become more proficient and more likely to intervene if time is spent learning these strategies.

The most common goals of bystander intervention are to stop bullying, prevent abuse from reoccurring, and change antisocial behavior; however, those are not the only objectives. Upstander action also supports bullied children by minimizing some of the harmful effects of bullying and buffers against future attacks. Help from peers also decreases feelings of exclusion, negates thoughts that everyone supports bullying, lets those who are bullied see that others care, and shows those who are targeted that they belong (Salmivalli et al., 2010).

In addition, upstander behavior motivates targeted children. "When you feel helpless and alone, you are less likely to resist," Staub said. "Actions by bystanders—even simply protesting what's being done—empower the victims, while passivity adds to their suffering" (as cited in Goleman, 1993, paras 27–28).

## What Can Bystanders/Upstanders Say?

The Training Active Bystanders (TAB) program for youth and adults was developed by Quabbin Mediation (n.d.), a non profit mediation and training organization, Staub, and hundreds of members in the community, including youth (www. trainingactivebystanders.org). In TAB, the trainers (many of whom are youths themselves) lead discussions in which participants plan for what they could do or say when they find themselves in various bystander situations, for example:

| | |
|---|---|
| Call attention to a situation | *Hey! What's going on?* |
| Offer help | *Is there something I/we can do?* |
| Express disapproval | *Stop that!* |
| Recruit allies. Make suggestions for what other bystanders might do | *You go get help and I will stay here.* |
| Stop negative bystanders | *When you laugh you encourage them.* |
| Support the target | *Do you want them to stop that?* |
| Raise the target's spirits | *I am sorry this happened/that they did that.* |
| Support the harm doer in non harmful action | *Can I help you figure this out?* |

## What if Someone Wants Their Friend to Bully?

Youngsters are placed in awkward positions if friends pressure them to participate in bullying. Children often succumb to peer pressure because they do not want to lose friends. Students could be afraid to say no because they don't want to be rejected, left behind, laughed at, or targeted. Others might be curious or do not know how to say no. Advance planning averts sticky situations.

- *Think before you act*—Is the action wrong, hurtful, or dangerous? Will it compromise your principles? What are the consequences? Are they worth it? How will you feel afterward?
- *Be assertive*—State your feelings: "I don't want to do that." "It's wrong." If the person insists, repeat your statement.
- *Recommend another activity*—If the suggestion is appealing, the person might abandon bullying.
- *Walk away*—You cannot participate if you are not present.
- *Ask yourself*—"Do I really want to be friends with someone who is pressuring me to do something I don't want to do?"
- *Choose friends who have similar values*—They will not put you in difficult positions.
- *Hang around peers who share your views*—It is easier to say no when you are with someone who is in agreement.
- *Stay with a large group*—The more people with you, the less chance of being pressured.
- *Become friends with people from several different social networks*—The loss of friends from one group will not hurt as much if you have friends in other groups.
- *Know your position on issues*—It is easier to bow to pressure when you are not sure how you feel.
- *Plan responses beforehand*—It increases confidence and decreases anxiety.

## Effective Responses

The Friendly Schools and Families program is an evidence based bullying reduction program. Its website provides examples of effective responses that show that the speaker does not want to participate in bullying (www.friendlyschools.com.au/about. php; How Do I Say "No" section, para. 3), such as:

- "I still want to be friends; I just don't want to do that."
- "Let's go and play basketball instead."
- "I don't want to be involved."
- "I don't believe in bullying."
- "I don't see the point in hurting other people."
- "The more friends we have the better."
- "I am not going to help you bully someone."
- "How would you feel if someone did that to you?"
- "Why not just let her join in?"
- "I can't help you take someone else's belongings."
- "I don't think it is fair to tease someone about that."
- "I don't see the need to make her feel bad."

## Bystander/Upstander Pledge

There are many bystanders who will not instigate bullying but will jump into the ring once the bell sounds. Even more support abuse by watching. If students sign a "Bystander/Upstander Pledge" they might think twice. Figure 9.2 provides an example of such a pledge. Students can cut out the pledge and paste it into their planner for daily reflection. Children do not have to check a box if the statement makes them feel uncomfortable.

# Additional Thoughts for Teachers

Upstander education should begin as early as possible. Generally speaking, the earlier a problem behavior receives intervention, the greater the odds that it will be changed. Kindergarten is an opportune time to shape views and norms because young children believe teachers can stop bullying and have not yet surrendered to peer pressure. They are more receptive to anti-bullying messages and enjoy helping. This is not to say that upstander work cannot be done with older children. It can and should. The job may be more challenging because some behaviors and beliefs have been set. However, human beings are flexible and changing, not made of concrete that becomes a permanent slab once poured. Success can prevail if teachers tap into their students' empathy, humanity, and sense of justice.

## Differences

Children pick on peers who are "different." Interestingly, it is the person who bullies who decides what is "different" and defines the norms, thus establishing relationships of dominance and subordination. Everyone does not think there is anything wrong with Overweight Oliver, Smart Sarah, Awkward Alvin, Foreigner Farrah, or Wheelchair Willy. Yet, youngsters accept the cruel behavior dished out by those who abuse and jump onto the bullying bandwagon. It is crazy in the sense that children are going along with . . . who??? They are blindly following those who viciously hurt others. These are the people parents want their offspring to stay away from, not follow!

The excuse "Everyone is doing it" is just that, an excuse, and a poor one. Everyone does not bully; nor do they think it is okay. Hurting people is wrong.

Bystanders are deluding themselves if they think they are safe because all people are "different" in some way. When a whim strikes, a judgmental person will easily find a new person to bully. Everyone is fair game. Those who bully turn on friends, acquaintances, strangers, and enemies.

Today, children may be anchored in a safe harbor; tomorrow they may be in the midst of a raging storm. Students are all in the same boat. One hole in the boat can cost the lives of every passenger. It is in bystanders' best interests to plug the leak. If onlookers do not challenge those who aggress today, they may become tomorrow's bully bait. Anti-bullying efforts are investments in everyone's future.

## Bystander/Upstander Pledge

### If I Witness Bullying

I will:

☐ Put myself in the bullied person's shoes

☐ Assertively ask the person who is bullying to stop

☐ Walk away

☐ Remove the targeted person

☐ Get adult help

I will not:

☐ Hit, push, hold, or stand lookout

☐ Laugh, cheer, smile, or encourage bullying

☐ Spread rumors

☐ Write graffiti

☐ Stand quietly

I will always:

☐ Try to help anyone who is bullied

☐ Include everyone in all activities

☐ Treat others as I want to be treated

Signature _____Date_____

*Figure 9.2* Bystander/Upstander Pledge

Protestant Pastor Martin Niemoller learned this lesson too late:

> In Germany they first came for the Communists, and I didn't speak up because I wasn't a Communist. Then they came for the Jews, and I didn't speak up because I wasn't a Jew. Then they came for the trade unionists, and I didn't speak up because I wasn't a trade unionist. Then they came for the Catholics, and I didn't speak up because I was a Protestant. Then they came for me—and by that time no one was left to speak up.
>
> (Martin Niemoller Quotes, n.d.)

*Social architecture*: Teachers have to challenge and correct inaccurate perceptions of the norm. The norm should not be the opinion of one or a few children, but the beliefs of the majority. Assign an essay asking students how they feel about bullying. Read some of the papers, without naming the authors, so pupils can see there are classmates who think bullying is wrong. Discussing the results of the Bystander Survey (Figure 9.1, page 120) and pluralistic ignorance (pages 118–119) will also help. Tell youngsters to speak to peers privately to find out who shares their viewpoints. Conversations can encourage children to join ranks and form an alliance against bullying. The assignment also increases the awareness of those who bully because they falsely assume that everyone supports bullying. It shows them that the opposite is true.

## Social Status

It is disturbing to learn that some who bully have elevated social status and are considered "cool," while targeted children find their names at the bottom of popularity polls and are pushed to the perimeter (Juvonen et al., 2003; Salmivalli et al., 1996).

All humanity is not lost because research also shows that those who aggress are not always liked. This apparent contradiction can be explained by analyzing the different methods of assessment. Perceived popularity is found by asking children to name the most popular and least popular students. It indicates social reputation. Sociometric popularity is found by asking youngsters to name peers they like and dislike. It indicates likeability among those surveyed. Thus, athletes can be considered "cool" for their athletic ability but may be disliked if they are aggressive (Cillessen & Mayeux, 2004). Bystanders may be supporting people they do not like!

*Social architecture*: Bullying continues when peers do not issue social consequences. Teachers need to show students that there is nothing wonderful about hostile behavior. Who wants to be bullied? Who wants to watch friends being hurt? What is good about causing a classmate pain? Those who bully are not the "hip" and tough people they portray themselves as because they will not pick on equals. There is nothing powerful about destroying a helpless opponent. In truth, bullying is a cowardly act. Point this out to students. Giving social prestige to those who abuse feeds their frenzy.

No one wants to be labeled a follower but that is exactly what many bystanders unknowingly are. When students protest, ask "Would you bully on your own?" "Why do you participate in bullying when you don't feel comfortable doing so?" "Why don't you voice your opposition?"

Leviticus 7:19 says ". . . flesh that touches any contaminated thing may not be eaten, it shall be burned in fire. . . ." One interpretation of this statement is that people should distance themselves from behavior they wouldn't want to participate in because humans are influenced by their environment. If not, they will find themselves taking on that behavior (Lieberman, 2006). If we apply this lesson to bullying, children should stay away from abusive behavior because, whether they intend to or not, sooner or later they will engage in the same hurtful activity. If all students followed this advice those who bully would lose any social status they have and youngsters would be true to themselves.

## Heroes

Heroes display kindness, try to right wrongs, and support others. Heroes are courageous people who perform brave deeds and are role models. Heroes stand up for those who are not able to help themselves.

Upstanders are heroes because they speak out against bullying and assist disadvantaged peers.

*Social architecture*: Upstander behavior should be framed as "heroism." Replace "ratting" and other negative connotations with the inspiring "hero" term and activism will become more appealing.

What type of child is brave enough to campaign on behalf of others and be successful? Pellegrini et al. argue that some interventions "are unlikely to be effective if not led (and perhaps initiated) by high-power prosocial children" (2010, p. 209). Educators should solicit help from popular and well liked students in their classrooms. These influential pupils are in advantageous positions to stand up, protect, and condemn bullying because they are central in their social networks and admired. Peers listen to them. If they model anti-bullying behavior or intervene, others will follow (Salmivalli et al., 2010).

Children are always vying for the highest spots in the social hierarchy. Point out that supporting rather than stabbing is a far better way to earn respect and popularity. The good feelings derived from helping are an added bonus.

It takes only *one* child to galvanize the troops. One person who heroically takes a stand can inspire others to follow. However, individuals are not the only heroes; groups can also perform heroic acts. When outnumbered, those who bully quickly back down and will not retaliate because there are too many peers to challenge and the social consequences are high.

Heroism can be integrated into the curriculum and held up as a quality to strive toward. For example, in history, teaching about the Holocaust usually focuses on Nazi Germany. The inclusion of those who hid Jewish people, helped them escape, and gave assistance shows heroes in action. Explore the reasons these heroes risked their lives for others. What motivated such courageous acts? These are role models children should emulate.

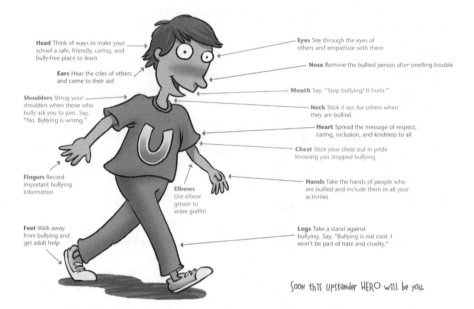

*Figure 9.3* The Upstander Hero (Goldstein & Verdick, 2012)

Courage should be discussed, with examples of the different types explained. For example, "It takes courage not to follow the crowd . . . to go against the social norm . . . to stand up for someone who is a target . . . to control our own emotions and not . . . bully someone else" (Froschl & Gropper, 1999, p. 74). Courage is the opposite of conformity.

Children can create their own "Upstanders Hero" diagrams (Figure 9.3). Educators can create a "Wall of Heroes" listing the names of students who help others. These activities help build altruistic classroom cultures.

## Demonstrate the Consequences of Inaction

Curtis Taylor was tripped, ganged up on, and had chocolate milk poured over him. The eighth grader's possessions were knocked out of his hands, vandalized, and stolen. Students kicked the cast on his broken foot. The bullying continued even though Curtis's father spoke to school officials. After three years, the youngster could no longer take the abuse. Curtis shot himself.

The school held a memorial service and taped a large sheet of paper onto Curtis's locker for student comments. Many wrote that Curtis was nice. When Curtis's dad, Bill Taylor, read the statements he thought "Where were you kids? Why weren't you his friends?" (Greene, 2001, para. 21).

*Social architecture*: A tragedy could have been averted if students had befriended Curtis and pulled the plug on bullying. If they had, Curtis would not have spent the last three years of his life tormented, in fear, and filled with pain. Curtis would be alive today.

Some children think bullying is "fun and games." Teachers can read news reports that illustrate the dangers of abuse. Documentaries depicting bullying can be shown. Guest speakers who share the damaging consequences can make a powerful impact. It is not being dramatic. It is telling the truth.

It is true that a minority of bullied children end their lives but isn't one death one too many, especially in light of the fact that it can be prevented? We cannot always control cancer or accidents but teachers *can* control bullying. How would you feel if it were your son or daughter, niece or nephew, or a student in your class who committed suicide? It will not happen, you say. There is not one parent or teacher who expected their child to bullycide. They found out too late.

## The Power Imbalance

Teachers also need to be sensitive to the fact that the power imbalance that exists between those who bully and those who are bullied may also exist between those who bully and bystanders. Expecting bystanders or upstanders who are overmatched to stand down more powerful students could jeopardize their health and social status. The power gap can be bridged by:

- Arming students with effective and safe intervention strategies.
- Encouraging children to join together—it only takes a few united youngsters to switch the power advantage.
- Helping students realize that they create the power imbalance. The power of those who bully is gained from their accomplices. The more followers they have, the greater their power. If students withdraw their support, the power of those who aggress will disappear.
- Changing the cultural norms in the classroom from acceptance of bullying ("Bullying is fun") to rejection of bullying ("We don't bully here").

# Chapter 10

# Friendship

## Importance of Friendship

Friendships are essential to children's healthy growth and development. They provide companionship, nurturance, intimacy, recreation, and support. Friends encourage, advise, help, share, and build self-esteem. In the process, social skills and competencies are developed. "Best friends contribute more to a child's acquisition of social skills than parents, teachers, or even organized groups like Scouts" (Freedman, 2002, p. 194).

In terms of bullying, friendship provides a very important function: protection (Bollmer, Milich, Harris, & Maras, 2005). Friends help prevent abuse, shorten its duration, defend against bullying, retaliation or ostracism, and teach skills needed for avoiding and countering attacks. Friends also serve as eyewitnesses, and provide comfort and support to bullied children:

- In one study, half of the students without membership in a peer group were bullied (Salmivalli, Huttunen, & Lagerspetz, 1997).
- The odds of being bullied lessen as the number of friends increases (Hodges, Malone, & Perry, 1997).
- Even one friend can reduce the possibility of being attacked (Bollmer et al., 2005).
- Bullied youngsters who have at least one good friend develop fewer emotional, behavioral, and psychological problems (Hodges et al., 1997).

The quality of a friend has to be taken into consideration. A friend who stands up for and defends a pal offers more protection than someone who hides in the corner (Goldbaum, Craig, Pepler, & Connolly, 2003; Hodges et al., 1997). A friendship with someone who has internalizing problems, is weak, or is bullied can increase the probability of being abused. If targeted children have a friend it is often someone who is also the recipient of maltreatment, and thus unable to deflect abuse.

Higher quality friendships also have an effect on those who bully. Children with externalizing behaviors who had a higher quality best friend were less likely to hurt others. Close friendships may serve as a model for healthy peer relationships, encourage prosocial behaviors, help develop empathy, or provide opportunities for learning and practicing appropriate social skills (Bollmer et al., 2005).

Social isolation is one of the most painful parts of bullying. It tells youngsters they are unwanted. No one wants to sit next to them, or eat lunch or play with them. No one wants them in their group, on their team, or at their party. If teachers learn the basics of friendship they can restructure the social architecture in their classes by skillfully applying their knowledge. Striving for the goal "Each child in my classroom will have at least one friend" goes a long way toward decreasing bullying and increasing academic performance.

## Building Blocks of Friendship

Children are attracted to people who have qualities they admire. While personal differences vary from individual to individual, there are some characteristics that most humans value:

- *Being complimentary*—Compliments make people feel good. Praising someone's ability, personality, clothes, or efforts; or saying "Good game," "Great job," or "Thank you, I appreciate you" are positive remarks appreciated by all.
- *Helpfulness*—Help can be given in many ways. For example, it can include listening, teaching an activity, explaining a difficult assignment, standing up for a bullied peer, offering advice, or helping a buddy feel better when he or she is upset.
- *Fairness*—Fairness involves taking turns, cooperating, compromising, or seeing a disagreement from the other person's perspective.
- *Having similar interests*—People like to participate in activities they enjoy. The fun increases when others share their interests.
- *Honesty*—True friendships are based on honesty where each party is truthful when things are going well but will also tactfully provide constructive criticism during difficult times. Lying destroys trust.
- *Reliability*—Friends should be dependable, available, and people whom they can rely on, in good and bad times.
- *Kindness*—Kindness is a selfless act that lets others know that someone cares. It can be achieved with words or actions and leaves the recipient with good feelings.
- *Empathy*—Everyone wants to be around empathetic people. They put themselves in their pals' shoes, are understanding and supportive, and follow the Golden Rule—"Treat others as you want to be treated." They also validate feelings.

- *Being a good listener*—Good friends let their buddies talk. They listen carefully.
- *Acting as confidant*—Close friends share secrets and keep each other's confidences.
- *Being welcoming*—Friends happily greet each other. It can be done with a smile or a "high five," or by verbally saying "It's good to see you." Warm receptions make people feel cared for and wanted.
- *Loyalty*—Friends stick up for one other. They also remain friends during stormy times.
- *Acceptance*—True friends accept one another as each is; they do not try to change the person. Differences are respected.
- *Encouragement*—Friends provide encouragement and are cheerleaders when their buddies are faced with challenges.
- *Ability to apologize*—No relationship is ever 100% perfect. There will be disagreements and conflicts. True friends try to understand their companion's point of view, apologize, and compromise. They also accept apologies and forgive those who hurt them.
- *Positivity*—People want to spend time with those who are optimistic and cheerful, see the best in others, and are positive.
- *Sharing*—Close friends share possessions, time, thoughts, and dreams.
- *Sense of humor*—Sense of humor involves the ability to make others laugh, laugh at another person's jokes, or laugh at oneself.

Oden and Asher (1977) coached socially isolated children in several social skills during five sessions over a four week period. The skills they covered were:

1. Participating in a game or activity.
2. Cooperating (e.g., taking turns and sharing materials).
3. Communicating (e.g., talking and listening).
4. Validating or supporting (e.g., giving attention or help).

These particular areas were selected because they are related to peers' acceptance and the establishment of friendships. The participants' acceptances among contemporaries rose after the sessions and were higher one year later. Focusing on these areas may be a way teachers can open the doors to friendship.

## Friendship Busters

There are qualities that are obstacles to friendship building:

- *Putting people down*—Constantly criticizing and hurting feelings.
- *Fighting*—Physically or verbally attacking others, constantly arguing, or disagreeing.
- *Bossing others around*—Telling people what to do and thinking he or she is always right.

- *Bragging*—Constantly boasting and showing off. Thinking he or she is better than everyone else.
- *Excluding*—Purposely preventing others from joining.
- *Cheating*—Disregarding rules, or being dishonest or deceptive.
- *Being a sore loser*—Not being able to accept defeat graciously, or blaming others or circumstances for losses.
- *Lying*—Not telling the truth, being misleading, or being two- aced.
- *Dominating conversations*—Not letting others get a word in. Having to be the center of attention.
- *Ignoring others*—Not paying attention to anyone's thoughts, feelings, interests, wants, or wishes. Being insensitive to their needs.
- *Not considering friends' interests*—Only wanting to talk about and participate in activities he or she enjoys. Relationships are one way.
- *Complaining or being negative*—Constantly finding fault with, or being pessimistic about, themselves, others, activities, or life.
- *Being possessive*—Not letting their friend have other friends.
- *Being a rumormonger*—Maliciously spreading rumors or gossiping about others.
- *Bullying*—No one likes being hurt or excluded.
- *Isolating*—Children cannot make friends if they are not around other children.

## How to Make Friends

Some children intuitively know how to make friends while others need a few pointers. The good news is that there is a pool of potential friends available. It is a matter of knowing what to say and do and putting oneself in the right place at the right time. Friendless students who are bullied can benefit from the following guidelines:

*Beforehand*:

- *Develop the "building blocks of friendship"* (see pages 143–144)—The more characteristics possessed, the greater the chance of making friends.
- *Increase interests*—The more interests you have, the more attractive you will be to a greater variety of people. Observe the activities of others. Try them. If they are not enjoyable, find something that is more fun.
- *Practice good hygiene*—Nothing turns a person off quicker than bad hygiene. Bathe daily; wash and brush hair, teeth, and nails; and use mouthwash, if needed. Dress in clean and neat attire.
- *Look around for those in a similar position*—Are there students who are shy, sitting alone, or friendless? They are more likely to welcome friendships. "Popular" peers already have a lot of friends, so the odds of them looking for new friendships are reduced.
- *Observe others*—Look at pupils who have lots of friends. What do they do? How do they treat others? Imitate positive qualities.

- *Give yourself a pep talk*—Tell yourself that you are a good person, worthy of anyone's friendship. There are wonderful people out there who also want to make new friends. It is a matter of finding them. Be determined and persistent.
- *Look for friendships based on who you are, not on which group people are in*—Most people want to be part of the "popular" group but that group is not always the best or right fit for everybody. Popular means one thing to one person and has another, totally different, meaning to someone else. Find friends based on your personality.

*Approaching others*:

- *Check your body language*—be aware of non verbal communication:
  - Stand tall. Do not slouch.
  - Stand about an arm's length away—not too far and not too close.
  - Smile.
  - Make and maintain eye contact but do not stare.
  - Keep your hands at your sides and your body still.
  - Speak in a volume that can be heard. Do not yell or whisper.

  Teachers should keep in mind that children from other cultures may have different mores. They should be respected.
- *Congregate with children*—You cannot make friends if you are not around peers. Sit and stand near people so they can see and talk to you. Volunteer. Join clubs, teams, and extracurricular, community, and recreational activities. Participation will help you find others with similar interests.
- *Smile*—Smiling lets others know you are friendly and interested. Humans gravitate toward happy people.
- *Start a conversation*—There are many ways to begin a conversation:
  - Say hello.
  - Introduce yourself.
  - Compliment the person.
  - Ask if you can help.
  - Ask what they are doing.
  - Ask their opinion.

  Open ended questions encourage conversation. Close ended questions bring one or two word responses. How would people respond to the following questions?

| Close ended questions | Open ended questions |
| --- | --- |
| Did you have a good weekend? | What did you do this weekend? |
| Was there a fight on the school bus? | Why do you think fights occur on the school bus? |
| Was anyone hurt? | What happened? |
| Do you know how to do the math problem? | What steps did you take to solve the problem? |

As you can see, close ended questions bring "yes," "no," or short replies while open ended questions require longer answers. Words such as what, why, how, and describe are used with open ended questions.

● *Continue the conversation*:

  – Ask questions—it shows people you are interested.
  – Listen to what people say and validate their feelings.
  – Rephrase what the person said.
  – Take equal turns speaking.
  – Talk about interests you both share.
  – Point out commonalities.
  – Share something about yourself. It encourages others to tell about themselves.

● *Extend invitations*—If the conversation is going well and you think the person is interested, ask if he or she wants to play with you, do homework together, or come to your house after school.

*Key points*:

● *Keep track of names and interests*—People feel good when others remember details about them.
● *Be yourself*—If you try to act like someone you think people will like, you will not be genuine. You might be able to disguise your true self for a while but the real you will be discovered in time. Friends will be disappointed because you were dishonest. You are no better or worse than anyone else. Believe in the person you are.
● *Be patient*—It takes time to find good friends but they are worth the wait. Choose peers who will be true friends.
● *You are a good person*—Friendlessness does not mean there is anything wrong with you. It means you have not found the right people, yet.
● *Do not settle*—Real friends are always kind and caring to one another. *Do not enter or stay in a relationship where the "friend" is cruel, mean, or abusive.*
● *Help is available, if needed*—Ask for help, if you have followed the guidelines and still have difficulty developing friendships. Teachers, guidance counselors, social workers, psychologists, parents, siblings, and relatives can offer additional suggestions.

## Joining a Group

Group entry is a difficult task for onlookers, even for children with high status. In one study, popular youngsters were more successful entering groups than their unpopular peers, but were still ignored or rejected 26% of the time (Putallaz & Gottman, 1981). Entering groups is an important skill to learn, especially for those who are bullied. Research shows that frame of reference, group size, and group status impact acceptance or rejection:

- *Frame of reference*—Popular children who shared the same frame of reference as group members, that is the informal rules and norms of the group, had more success breaking into groups. They first quietly observed and then went along with the status quo by mimicking the words and actions of the participants. In contrast, unpopular children who tried to redirect the group's attention to themselves had less luck breaking into groups. They were disagreeable, tried to control the group by changing the conversation, asked irrelevant questions, and made self-statements (Putallaz & Gottman, 1981). Teachers can help students infiltrate groups by teaching them the "rules of the game."
- *Group size*—Groups of two and three were hardest to enter, with trios being the most difficult. Acceptance was higher when entering groups of four or more. Approaching a single child yielded the best results (Putallaz & Wasserman, 1989). Educators can organize groups of four or more to make entrance easier and suggest initiating activities with children who are alone.
- *Group status*—The status of a group also has an effect on admission. Unpopular children had more favorable outcomes when entering unpopular groups and experienced more difficulty becoming part of popular groups (Putallaz & Gottman, 1981).

## Additional Tips for Joining Groups

- *Watch different groups*:
    - Look for groups that seem friendly and inviting.
    - Look for groups whose members have interests and skills that are similar to yours.

- *Time your comments and entry*:
    - Do not interrupt.
    - Wait for a lull in the conversation or action.

- *Let your interest become known*:
    - Smile, stand tall, and make eye contact.
    - Say "This looks like fun."
    - Ask "Can I join?"
    - Ask relevant questions about the activity or conversation.

- *Read the verbal and non verbal communication of the person(s) responding*:
    - What do their faces say? Are there annoyed looks? Friendly looks?
    - Wait to be invited into the group. Do not run in.

● *If accepted into the group . . .:*

    – Go along with the rules or conversation. Do not try to change things right away. Give the group time to get to know you.

    – Do not try to control or take charge of the group. Go with the flow.

● *If you are ignored or rejected . . .:*

    – Do not argue, yell, call names, beg, cry, stomp your feet, throw yourself on the floor, or insult group members.

    – Realize that "no" might mean "The time is not right, now. Maybe another time."

    – Look for a more welcoming group or person.

    – Remind yourself that rejection is not a reflection of the person you are; rather, it is about individuals who have not yet learned about inclusion, diversity, and respect. It can also be poor timing.

    – In private, let teachers know that students are excluding others.

## Where to Find Friends

Children's friendship networks are made up of classmates, other peers in the school and neighborhood, siblings, relatives, members of extracurricular and out of school clubs, teams, and organizations.

Youngsters who have a hard time making friends in their classes may fare better with pupils from other classes. Students who participate in extracurricular activities can find peers with similar interests. For example, the art club would appeal to those interested in art. Likewise, those who enjoy playing ball will find others who like sports on athletic teams. It is easier to befriend someone with similar interests.

Children who cannot make friends in school can decrease their chances of suffering from depression, anxiety, low self-esteem, and other negative consequences of friendlessness and bullying by developing friendships outside of school. Sometimes joining an activity where the child is not known is a better plan as it gives the youngster a fresh start. There are no reputations to dispel and it can give the child a place to try out new strategies. Check the Boy or Girl Scouts of America, Campfire Boys and Girls, 4-H, Police Athletic Leagues, YMCAs, colleges and universities, museums, libraries, community centers, parks and recreational programs, places of worship, drama, dance, art, gymnastics, karate, music, sports teams and clubs, and volunteer opportunities. These pastimes connect children.

Youngsters who have abusive "friends" should be encouraged to end those relationships. Many children stay and accept maltreatment, believing that having any "friend" is better than having no "friends." It is faulty thinking because friends do not hurt each other. Remaining reinforces thoughts that they do not deserve better. Staying is an acceptance of mistreatment, which can set up an unhealthy pattern of abuse that continues throughout their lives.

## How Teachers Can Alter the Social Ecology to Help Develop Friendships

There are many ways teachers can develop classroom relationships:

- *Show students that you like, accept, and enjoy unpopular children*—When educators show distaste for a particular child, the class interprets the action as permission to reject their classmate. When teachers display a fondness and interest in the youngster, his or her "social stock" rises and peers rethink their negative views (Chang, 2003; Lavoie, 2007).

- *Put the disliked child's skills and special talents on center stage and praise their abilities*—Everyone has special talents or knowledge in one area or another. Isolated children have little opportunity to share theirs with classmates. Peers can learn about someone they may never have approached when teachers provide time for pupils to display their skills. Youngsters may identify or admire the ability, want to learn more, or want to get to know the child better (Lavoie, 2007; PREVNet, 2007b).

- *Assign competence*—When low status children do well on an academic task, the teacher can publicly praise the student, making sure high status peers hear the compliment. If the praise is specific and accurate and the relevance is explained, then high status classmates and the child will expect competency in this and other abilities. The result is an increase in participation and influence of the low status child. Research also shows that expectations for competence are transferred to other situations (Cohen & Lotan, 1995).

- *Give collective rewards*—The opposite of collective rewards is the more familiar collective punishments, where privileges for the entire class are withdrawn because of the misconduct of one or a few pupils. According to Takekawa (as cited in Yoneyama & Naito, 2003) collective punishment can cause bullying.

  The reverse happens with collective rewards. All students are rewarded when a classmate performs well (Lavoie, 2007): "Class, I can see how hard Freddy worked today. He did an exceptional job on the project. I am so pleased that I will let the class have five extra minutes of recess." Freddy now becomes a hero.

- *Give socially isolated children positions of importance*—Give low status students coveted positions that provide recognition and increase status, for example the "foreman," who is in charge of assigning prized jobs to classmates. Children will be nice to their peer in attempts to secure highly regarded assignments. The kind treatment may be temporary or can forge a path to friendship. At the very least, rejected students feel special and have elevated status during the time they are in the prestigious role. Points to keep in mind are (a) give children jobs they are capable of doing, and (b) make it social in nature so the youngster can interact with other students (Gronlund, 1959; Lavoie, 2007).

- *Integrate friendship building activities into the curriculum*—A school that was testing activities for a new curriculum had students build "a block wall, with each block representing a barrier to friendship. They problem solve about what they can do to take away each block" (Froschl & Gropper, 1999, p. 72). They also role played students being bullied because they wanted to be friends and drew and told stories describing a time they were courageous enough to defend a friend (Froschl & Gropper, 1999).

- *Group children according to interests*—Children are often grouped according to academic abilities. Teaming children with similar interests provides opportunities to share commonalities which can lead to friendships (as cited in Dewar, 2009; Lavoie, 2007).
- *Organize children into small groups*—Breaking large classes into smaller groups positively affects student interactions.
- *Pair potentially compatible students*—Likes attract, but they have to find one another first. Teachers can be matchmakers by bringing pupils with similar personalities or interests together. Suggest afterschool play dates to parents whose children are compatible.
- *Pair popular children with those who are less popular*—When high and low status students are seated next to each other or placed together in groups they talk, work, share, and help one another. In the process, they get to know each other (Rizzo, 1989).
- *Point out strengths*—Children may not realize the talents and abilities they possess. Help students discover their assets, particularly ones that are beneficial to friendship making.
- *Increase children's self-esteem*—Everyone can use a self-esteem boost. It is especially important for bullied youngsters because self-esteem plunges with repeated rejection. High self-esteem protects against bullying. How can teachers build self-esteem?

  - Encourage children to pursue interests—Their skills will naturally develop.
  - Allow youngsters to make mistakes—Mistakes are learning experiences.
  - Ask students to help—Ask as often as possible. It makes them feel valued and respected.
  - Give children responsibilities—It shows confidence and breeds feelings of importance. Pride is also taken in jobs that are well done.
  - Have high expectations—Youngsters rise up to the expectations of teachers and parents.
  - Promote independence—People learn and grow by engaging in new, different, and challenging experiences.
  - Set up situations where students can succeed—Success builds self-esteem.
  - Break large projects into small steps. Children will enjoy a string of successes.
  - Compare youngsters' accomplishments to their past. They will see progress and growth.
  - Build upon students' small and large efforts, failures, and successes—Each attempt is a stepping stone of growth that should be applauded.
  - Respond to children's behavior, not to their personalities—It is inappropriate actions that need to change, not the child.

- Ask youngsters what they like about themselves—Make a list of 10 qualities.
- Focus on positives—Replace negative thinking and false thoughts with uplifting affirmations and truthful facts.
- Listen to students—It shows you value and respect them.
- Accept children—Do not judge.
- Spend time with youngsters—Talk and play with them.
- Be your students' biggest cheerleader.

● *Encourage friendless children to take risks*—It can be scary to walk up to another student, especially if one lacks social skills and has been rejected. However, children will not find playmates if they isolate themselves. Advances have a very big upside: A friendship might develop. If it does not work out, children are in the same position they were before the attempt. Risks can be lessened if friendship and social skills are learned beforehand.

● *Help children get to know one another*—There are many different ways to help children learn about each other. Pairing students, seating or grouping pupils near one another, circle time, and cooperative learning were previously mentioned. Projects such as a collage, book, or essay about a child can be shared with classmates. Show and tell can introduce children's interests. Play games such as "Moving Toward Friendship" (Box 10.1).

"Play and Friendship" (Cooper, Cappasola, Green, Baskette, Bhoothalingom, & Randall, 2003) describes over 60 friendship building activities. It can be found online (http://faculty.unlv.edu/jgelfer/esp728/Play&Friendship.rtf).

---

## Box 10.1: Moving Toward Friendship

The following activity will help children find commonalities, share interests, increase self-awareness and self-esteem, and interact with others in a group.

1. *Preparation*:
   a. Create a list of interests or favorite activities that are appropriate for your class, for example:
      i. Sports—e.g., baseball, basketball, football, soccer, lacrosse, bowling, tennis, golf, roller blading, swimming, horseback riding, fishing, paint balling, dancing, karate.
      ii. Hobbies—e.g., computer or internet, video games, talking on the phone, texting, instant messaging, shopping, arts and crafts, cooking, gardening, photography, drama, magic, writing, remote control cars, trains.
      iii. Collections—e.g., dolls, cards, coins, rocks, stamps, model cars, CDs, action figures.

      iv.  Games—e.g., Wii, Xbox, Playstation, checkers, chess, cards, Candyland, Chutes and Ladders, Connect Four, Twister, Clue, Battleship, Yahtzee, Trouble, Life, Monopoly, Sorry, Guess Who, Uno, Concentration.

      v.  Favorites:

- Food—e.g., pizza, hamburgers, hot dogs, tacos, french fries, pasta.
- Color—e.g., red, pink, blue, green, purple, black.
- Season—e.g., fall, winter, spring, summer.
- Fast food restaurant—e.g., McDonalds, Burger King, Taco Bell, Wendy's, Kentucky Fried Chicken, Arbys, Boston Market, Subway, Blimpie, Dominos, Panera Bread, Nathans, Sonic.
- Subject—e.g., English, math, social studies, foreign language, physical education.
- Other topics may include internet sites, television shows, stores, books, songs, or musical groups.

  b.  Post colored squares along the perimeter of the room, evenly spacing them apart. For example, tape a red square in one corner, a blue in another, white in the third, and green in the fourth corner. Tape different colored squares on the walls, midway between the corners.

2. *Activity*:

  a.  Assemble students in the center of the room. Ask them to bring a pencil and paper.

  b.  If pupils have the same interest or favorite as the one the teacher mentions, they proceed to the stated area—e.g., "If you like baseball go to the red square," "If you like collecting coins go to the white square," "If your favorite food is pizza go to the blue square."

  c.  After the children move to an area, tell them to look at the other students who occupy the same space and record their names and the interest or favorite.

  d.  Students remain in the spot they are in, if the next named interest or activity is not applicable to them.

  e.  Repeat for about 10–15 minutes. By that time, youngsters will have accumulated a list of classmates who share commonalities with them.

3. *Discussion*:

  a.  How did you feel moving from area to area?

  b.  Are there some classmates on your lists who frequently occupied the same area as you? What does that tell you?

  c.  Some names on your lists are friends. Are there others who you do not normally hang out with? Did that surprise you? Why or why not?

  d.  Are similarities important in friendships?

4.  Assignment:

    a.  Pick two students you share a common interest or activity with, who are not in your friendship circle. During the next week, start a conversation, or eat with, play with, or telephone the person.
    b.  Write about the encounters. Did they lead to friendship? Why or why not?

- *Organize group work*—Diversify groups, being careful not to place a child who bullies near one who is targeted. Periodically change members so pupils can work with a variety of students.
- *Give two children the same monitor job*—Youngsters will work, cooperate, and spend time together while executing the job responsibilities. A friendship could develop.
- *Set up situations where children help one another*—Research shows that people like those who help them (Aronson, 2000).
- *Encourage participation in after school activities*—If children want to develop friendships they have to be where the action is. Recommend extracurricular activities and community offerings.
- *Form a club that brings friendless children together*—The club can introduce marginalized students to one another and provide opportunities to talk, play, build self-esteem, and learn social skills.
- *Teach anti-bullying skills*:

    - *Social skills*—Listening, conversation skills, entering groups, body language, sharing, taking turns, complimenting, or reading social cues.
    - *Friendship skills*—Qualities that help build friendships, qualities that block friendships, how to make friends, or where to find friends.
    - *Assertiveness skills*—How to be assertive, not aggressive.

- *Point out appropriate and inappropriate behavior and consequences*—Point out actions that prevent children from making friends: "Latisha, I noticed that you took all the building blocks and did not let anyone use them. If you share the blocks with others they might want to play with you."

    Help the child see the benefit of a particular behavior. "How do you think Marc felt when you shared the blocks with him? Do you think he will play with you again?"
- *Do not allow children to sit out*—Many times, shy children or those with poor social skills want to be part of a group. They remain on the periphery because they do not know how to join in or fear rejection. Teachers can help these youngsters by (a) teaching the necessary skills, (b) bringing them into conversations, or (c) inserting them into activities.

    Educators can involve youngsters in valuable roles, regardless of abilities. If they cannot jump rope, they can turn the rope. If they cannot throw a ball, they can be the scorekeeper. If they cannot play an instrument, they can be an equipment manager.

- *Set up the activity*—Adults have told students who have difficulty socializing to "join in." They have ordered peers to "let him play with you." Reverse that thinking; instead, ask what the low status youngster likes and set up an activity that facilitates that interest. Then, round up classmates who also enjoy the pastime.
- *Let students tutor or teach skills*—The time spent tutoring or teaching others can help build relationships and increase the "teacher's" self-esteem. Children can be identified as "experts," with the "Who Is Good in What in Our Class" described in Box 7.3 (page 80). For example, if Jessica needs help with math, she would refer to such a resource and see that Robin is listed as being proficient in that subject. Jessica would then ask Robin for assistance.

  It is commonsense to ask someone who is skilled to teach. However, educators might consider other possibilities. What about a child who is deficient in a skill? For example, a fifth grader who is not up to par with peers in a sport will most likely have greater proficiency than a first grader to whom he or she can teach some skills. In the process, the "coach" may work harder to improve his or her weak area. This can be done with any academic subject, sport, or activity.

- *Encourage responsibilities for other children*—Stress the expectation that children should include, stand up for, and take care of one another. Give students specific examples such as asking a shy child to take the field, inviting an unpopular classmate to their lunch table, walking to class with a lonely peer, stopping someone who bullies from hurting a student, or comforting someone who was bullied.
- *Select appropriate games*—Organize games that require many children, are more fun with a lot of players, are easy to learn, can be joined midway, and promote social interaction. In this way, no one will be left out; in fact, everyone will be wanted. Games that have no winners or losers prevent cutthroat competition, exclusion, and increase enjoyment.

  One example suggested by Brown, Ragland, and Bishop (1989) is a variation of an old-time favorite game, musical chairs. Children compliment or make friendly statements when the music stops, instead of rushing to find a seat. Those who are "out" sit in a circle of chairs and interact with one another. Thus, everyone continues to have positive social experiences and opportunities to build friendships (as cited in W.H. Brown, Odom, & Conroy, 2001).

- *Organize pull out times*—Time pull out services (e.g., extra help, speech, and other types of therapy) so they will not conflict with free play or recess. Children without friends cannot afford to miss opportunities for socialization. Pull out times are determined by the overall schedule of a school but perhaps the need for socialization can be discussed with the individual in charge of scheduling.

# Chapter 11

# Peer Support Programs

Youngsters who have trouble developing relationships are marginalized. Their position on the edge of the class prevents them from establishing friendships and social skills, which pushes them further away from peers.

Children can escape this cycle by enrolling in peer support projects. Peer programs where students help other students provide support, education, skill building, problem solving, and friendship, and decrease bullying. Peer support helps those who bully too.

This approach certainly makes sense because (a) children are a natural resource in schools, (b) childhood rejection is a relationship problem between youth, (c) students turn to peers when they need support, (d) youngsters may create solutions that adults would not consider, (e) contemporaries are readily available, (f) pupils have similar experiences, (g) children belong to the same culture, (h) students may be aware of problems sooner than adults, and (i) peers may be more understanding than the older generation.

Peer support is not a replacement for the professional services schools offer. Rather, peer helpers give children an additional source of support.

## Peer Support Programs and Bullying

Empirical evidence shows that student-on-student support programs are valuable additions to anti-bullying initiatives. Peer support:

- prevents and reduces bullying (Menesini, Codecasa, Benelli, & Cowie, 2003);
- reduces the damaging consequences of bullying (Naylor & Cowie, 1999);

- helps targeted children cope with bullying (Cowie & Hutson, 2005);
- increases inclusion (National Children's Bureau, 2004; Whitaker, Barratt, Joy, Potter, & Thomas, 1998);
- raises empathy (Menesini et al., 2003; Whitaker et al., 1998);
- improves problem solving, decision making, and stress management skills (Peer Support Australia, n.d.);
- elevates self-confidence (Peer Support Australia, n.d.);
- discourages peer helpers from bullying (Peer Support Australia, n.d.);
- gives bystanders a way to assist (Sharp & Cowie, 1998);
- decreases pro bullying attitudes (Ellis, Marsh, Craven, & Richards, 2003);
- creates climates of caring (Naylor & Cowie, 1999).

Peer support tells the student body that bullying is not an acceptable norm.

## Befriending

Befriending is the most common form of peer support. It occurs when a peer or older pupil voluntarily agrees to "be friends" with a particular student. This one-on-one relationship provides friendship and support to vulnerable and usually isolated children. It can be an informal program where the participants spend time together doing whatever they wish or a formal set up such as playground buddies.

### Befriending and Bullying

Befriending lessens the stress associated with abuse and provides a friend who can help deter future bullying. It also increases friendship, interpersonal and social skills, which may prevent, diffuse, or end bullying. Feelings of belonging, self-esteem, and confidence increase while isolation and loneliness decline.

Befriending also stunts the growth of bullying behaviors and attitudes. In one study, sixth grade students increased their defender roles and anti-bullying attitudes. The "short-term intervention was able to break the conspiracy of silence and to enhance responsibility and empathetic feelings among pupils" (Menesini et al., 2003, p. 11). Unfortunately, the benefits were not duplicated with older students, which highlights the importance of beginning anti-bullying work during the younger grades.

## Circle Time/Class Meetings

Circle time/class meetings are community building activities where students explore, think, and reflect during discussions, exercises, or games. Pupils assemble in circular formation because circular patterns have no beginning or end, with no point having greater importance than another. Sitting around a circle shows participants that each is an equal and valuable part of the group where no one is any better or worse than the next. All are included and can be seen. The teacher's place in the circle signals that he or she is not teaching but facilitating the process. A "talking stick" or another object can be passed to the speaker; it signals that the holder has the floor. It can give quiet students a feeling of power, making it easier to talk.

Areas that have been covered during circle time/class meetings include anger management, assertiveness, bullying issues, communication skills, conflict resolution, feelings, self-esteem, and events or problems that occurred in the class, school, or world.

Teachers may lead circle time/class meetings in the beginning but as time goes on students gradually take the reins. Fifteen to 30 minutes is recommended in the lower elementary grades and can be lengthened to 30–40 minutes for upper elementary and middle school students.

## Circle Time/Class Meetings and Bullying

The thought of squeezing one more anti-bullying activity into an already bulging school day makes the addition of circle time/class meetings as appealing to teachers as speaking to a parent who denies his or her child's involvement in bullying. However, discussing bullying topics pays huge dividends because declines in bullying mean more time for academic work.

Circle time/class meetings provide opportunities to share information on bullying, develop anti-bullying rules, brainstorm strategies for peaceful resolutions, and role play. It also lets those who bully see that classmates do not approve of hurtful behaviors. Children can increase awareness and understanding of their feelings, reactions, and concerns during circle time. As a result of the process, youngsters become more accepting of differences, develop friendships, and build empathy.

Are class meetings effective?

- Olweus and Alasker (1991) found that teachers who regularly used class meetings in their anti-bullying work had greater reductions in class abuse compared to colleagues who used meetings to a lesser extent or not at all (as cited in Bisignano, Lockard, & Randel, 2009).
- Physical and verbal bullying decreased while positive problem solving strategies rose in a study of first graders who participated in class meetings (Browning, Davis, & Resta, 2000).
- A fourth grader who had been called names recalled one particular class meeting. "In that meeting (on name-calling), people started to listen to how I feel about being called names. Since then, . . . haven't had much name-calling" (Emmett & Monsour, 1996, Results and Conclusions section, para. 6).
- Roxann Kriete, executive director of Northeast Foundation for Children (Greenfield, MA), told about a child who bullied who hated the morning class meeting. "He was getting to know his classmates, and to like them, which made picking fights with them less satisfying" (as cited in Langland, 2003, para 12).

## Bullying Discussion Topics

- What is bullying? What are the different ways people bully?
- Does bullying hurt? How?
- Have you ever been bullied? What happened? What did you do? How did you feel?
- Did you ever bully anyone? Why? How did it feel? Was there a better way to accomplish your goal(s)?
- Why do some children hurt others? Are there better ways to get needs met?
- How can we help someone who bullies change his or her behavior?
- Did you ever see anyone bullied? What happened? How did you feel?
- What did you do? Would you do the same thing or something different now?
- Is it wrong to silently watch a bullying incident? Why or why not?
- What could you say or do to stop bullying?
- How could you help someone who is being bullied?
- How could you help someone who was bullied?
- What is the difference between telling and tattling?
- Would it be better to have a bully free class and school? Why or why not?
- What can be done to make this an anti-bullying classroom and school?
- How can you protect yourself from cyberbullying?
- When should you ask for help? How?
- How can you make new friends?
- What are some helpful communication skills?
- How do you handle disagreements? What are the outcomes? Are there other ways to solve problems?
- What are problem solving skills? How can they prevent or stop bullying?
- What is the difference between assertiveness, aggressiveness, and passivity? How does each play a role in bullying?
- How can you handle anger? Does anger contribute to bullying? How?
- How can you protect yourself from peer pressure?
- How can you effectively deal with anxiety?
- How can you increase your self-esteem?
- What are some successful anti-bullying strategies?

Meetings should not be limited to a discussion format. The use of bullying-related literature, group work, games, media, and speakers keeps interest high.

Be forewarned that successfully running circles is a learned art that is honed with experience. Reading about circles, practicing with colleagues, and finding a mentor could lead to favorable outcomes.

---

## Box 11.1: Sharing

Children often think they are the only ones who are bullied. As such, they may hesitate to talk about the abuse because they are ashamed or scared, or think others will not understand. Teachers may be able to help these youngsters express their feelings by sharing a time when they themselves were bullied. Student volunteers can also dialogue about memories of being targeted. Hearing a teacher's or classmate's account of mistreatment may make speaking about a difficult topic easier. If personal accounts are not possible, a book, internet, media, or DVD on bullying can be used.

These stories can be followed up with several discussions—the different types of bullying, harmful consequences, how bullying felt, suggestions on ways to prevent abuse, bystander intervention strategies, and ways to support students who are harmed.

Teachers can explain that the class is like a family and each member is responsible for their classmates' welfare. Educators should emphasize that bullying is wrong, should never happen, and will not be allowed in their classroom.

This activity lets students know they are not the only ones who are bullied, peers share similar experiences, and everyone does not endorse bullying. It also tells those who bully that classmates do not support abuse. It can turn bystanders into upstanders.

---

## Circle of Friends/Circle of Support

Circle of Friends/Circle of Support originated in Canada as a way to integrate students with disabilities into mainstream classrooms. A group of five to eight children provide emotional support, mentoring, friendship, and encouragement to a peer who is having difficulties, "the focus child." The circle and child in question brainstorm ways to decrease isolation, develop relationships (within and beyond the group), and improve social skills and behavior. They help the focus child learn about feelings, control anger, read body language, and defuse potentially explosive situations. Circles meet regularly for six weeks, a half term or semester, and also surround those who bully (Barratt, Joy, Potter, Thomas, & Whitaker, n.d.; Sharp, 2001; Whitaker et al., 1998).

### How Circle of Friends/Circle of Support Works

1. The teacher meets privately with the parents and the potential focus child.

   ● Circle of Friends/Circle of Support is introduced and told how it can help.

2. The parents must consent to starting a circle.
3. The focus child must also agree.

4.  The focus child gives the teacher permission to speak with the class.
5.  The class talk about forming a circle is held without the focus child.

- Students are told that, although it is unusual to be talking about someone who is not present, permission was received from the child to do so.
- The teacher attempts to gain empathy by:
  - asking students how it would feel to be lonely and without friends;
  - exploring the role of the class's behavior.
- Pupils are asked to describe what they find difficult about the child.
- Positive characteristics are discussed.
- Suggestions on how to help their classmate are solicited.
- The Circle of Friends/Circle of Support is explained.
- Volunteers are recruited.

6.  During the first meeting of the Circle of Friends/Circle of Support:

- introductions are made;
- group members share the reasons they volunteered to be part of the circle, emphasizing the positive;
- positive characteristics of the focus child are voiced;
- areas that need work are discussed;
- strategies are brainstormed, with the entire group agreeing on which idea(s) to try.

7.  Future meetings involve exploration and problem solving.

All meetings of the Circle of Friends/Circle of Support include the focus child. Initially, teachers must plan and organize the group. However, the goal is to have students run the circle with adults playing a facilitator role (Barratt et al., n.d.; Sharp, 2001; Whitaker et al., 1998).

# Quality Circles

Five to 12 children as young as age seven are teamed together into quality circles. Students meet regularly and cooperatively work toward developing solutions to issues that concern them (Cowie & Sharp, 1994). The backbone of this intervention is a five-step problem solving method.

## How Quality Circles Work

Behaviour4Learning's (2005) article on quality circles provides an excellent overview of the process. The Behaviour4Learning site was closed but this material is part of public sector information licensed under the U.K.'s Open Government Licence v.1.0 (www.nationalarchives.gov.uk/doc/open-government-licence/):

*Step 1    Identifying the problem*

The circle makes a list of all the problems the circle wants to tackle. They then decide on the most serious problem they want to tackle.

*Step 2    Analysis of the problem*

The circle members consider possible causes of the problem using the "why-why" technique. For example:

"Why do people bully?"
"They want to hurt people"
Why?
"Because they don't like them"
Why?
"Because nobody plays with them"
Why?
"Because they cheat"
Why?
"Because they want to win and be the best"

Once having identified the causes of the problem the group selects one cause and tries to establish the extent of the problem by collecting data, which may take the form of observations, surveys or interviews.

*Step 3    Developing a solution*

Once one of the causes has been identified and analysed the circle members begin to suggest solutions using the "how-how" approach. It begins with a solution statement followed by the question how? For example:
"Show them how to be nice"
How?
"Show them an example"
How?
"One of the older children could show them how to be nice"
How?
"They could have a show"
How?
"Two people can be bullying one person in the show"
How?
"The teachers could organise them"
How?
"The people who are being bullied could take part"

*Step 4    Management presentation*

The quality circle members present their solution to a 'management team' who facilitate the implementation of the solution if possible. Students need to be helped [to] develop presentation skills and they need to be prepared to answer questions from the management team.

*Step 5    Reviewing the solution*
If the proposed solution is implemented there must be a review of how effective the solution has been. If agreement has not been reached to implement the solution, the management must discuss its reasons with the quality circle, who will then review their solution.

(Behaviour4Learning, 2005)

## Quality Circles and Bullying

Quality circles have been successfully employed in schools as anti-bullying interventions. Smith and Sharp (1994) report that 95% of 57 primary school students surveyed spoke positively about their quality circle experiences. More than half gained a greater awareness of bullying and were more likely to stop the abuse. Sixty-nine percent became more sensitive to their words and actions (as cited in Anti-Bullying Alliance, 2008).

# Other Peer Support Programs

Peer mentoring is similar to befriending but focuses on solving problems, while peer education gives students opportunities to teach peers and children in younger grades. Peer advocacy connects a group of students with someone who has a disability. Four to six children speak out on behalf of the abused peer. The idea can be extended to anyone who is severely bullied. Mental health professionals train students in the basics of counseling in peer counseling programs. Students become playground pals/ playground buddies when they volunteer to help make recess a safe, orderly, and happy time. Friendship benches or playground stops are areas where students can find companions if they do not have anyone to play or talk with during recess.

# Peer Support in Action

## Cool to Be Kind

Bullying hurts. Students at San Clemente High School in California learned this lesson a little too late. It took the bullycide of 16-year-old student Daniel Mendez for pupils to realize the damaging effects of bullying.

Mendez's best friend, Brenden Kim, wanted something positive to come from his buddy's death. With the help of Lizzie Heinze and other sophomores, Kim formed "Cool to Be Kind" or "C2BK," a peer based reporting system where students can report bullying and be helped.

"This has entirely changed my perspective on bullying," Heinze said. "I used to look away because I thought it was a joke. But it's not" (Garrett, 2009, para. 25).

## Tickled Pink

Twelfth grade students David Shepherd and Travis Price took action when a ninth grader was called a homosexual and threatened with physical harm because he wore a pink shirt on the first day of school. The duo purchased and distributed 50 pink shirts and emailed classmates asking them to join their cause. The next day, hundreds of pupils attended school wearing pink. The bullying stopped.

"If you can get more people against them . . . to show that we're not going to put up with it and support each other, then they're not as big a group as they think they are," Shepherd said (CBC News Online, 2007, para. 13).

## A One Woman Anti-bullying Force

Jamie Isaacs was physically, verbally, relationally, and cyberbullied for over six years. Some students formed an "I hate Jamie club" and a teacher even joined the bullying. After years of abuse Jamie decided to take action. She helped create, write, and pass two anti-bullying laws and formed an anti-bullying task force. The 15-year-old makes bullying presentations, has co-authored a book, *In Jamie's Words*, and started the Jamie Isaacs Foundation for Anti-Bullying (Mian, 2011). Jamie's future includes a bullying song and video, a documentary on bullying, campaigning for more laws and, of course, sensitizing the public to bullying. Jamie "wants to be the voice for all victims of bullying who do not have a voice" (Jamie Isaacs Foundation for Anti-bullying, 2010, para. 1).

## Teenangels

Teenangels are 13- to 17-year-olds who teach students, educators, parents, and elected representatives about online safety, privacy, and security. After training, the volunteers become researchers and public speakers, and write columns for websites, sharing information about responsible and safe ways to surf the internet. Teenangels are a division of WiredSafety.org (2012).

## Flying High on the Ground

Hitting, pushing, shoving, and throwing objects occurred on two buses driving students to a Texan elementary school. The principal asked the school counselor for help when three bus drivers quit. She came up with the idea of "Flight Attendants."

In the real world, these airline workers greet passengers, assist with luggage, locate seats, ensure safety guidelines are observed, attend to problems, and oversee safe and orderly boardings and debarkings. In the Texan school, each trained "flight attendant" helped four or five children board the bus, assisted with "luggage" (backpacks and lunch boxes), and reminded riders to stay in their seats and to take turns getting on and off the bus.

The program was a resounding success. There were fewer fights, safer rides, happier faces, and elevated moods. The Flight Attendant idea can be applied to other situations: "Food Service Specialists" (in cafeterias), "Traffic Controllers" (in hallways), "Counselor Helpers" (in the guidance office), "Office Workers" (in the main office), and "Junior Patrols" (at crosswalks) (Carns, 1996).

# Chapter 12

# Empathy

Empathy is the ability to place oneself into another person's shoes and feel what he or she is feeling. Feshbach (1983) breaks empathy into three parts:

1. The ability to identify and describe the affective (e.g., emotions, feelings) state of another person.
2. The ability to view the world through another person's eyes, seeing things from that individual's perspective.
3. The ability to experience and feel the emotions of that person.

Empathy must include both cognitive (1 and 2) and affective (3) responses. Affective empathy is by far the more critical factor when it comes to bullying.

Children who are aggressive possess low levels of empathy while non aggressive youths have high levels. Those displaying empathy demonstrate more prosocial behavior, view bullying in a negative light, and are less inclined to take part in abusive activities (Feshbach, 1983; Findlay, Girardi, & Coplan, 2006; Gini, Albiero, Benelli, & Altoe, 2007).

Why does empathy reduce and mitigate aggression?

- Seeing another person's perspective helps in understanding motivations, opinions, and actions.
- Awareness increases tolerance, acceptance, and respect.
- Empathetic people experience discomfort because they can feel the pain of others.
- Behavior is moderated because empathetic people are aware of the harm they cause.

# How Do People Become Empathetic?

Empathy has an innate component and, while we cannot control the number or type of physical and mental characteristics we receive from parents, we may be able to alter the degree. Modeling, training, role playing, and other methods can increase empathy. It *can* be taught.

## Matching Activities to Feshbach's Definition

*(1) The ability to identify and describe the affective (e.g., emotions, feelings) of another person—*Children must first know what feelings are and be in touch with their own feelings before they can become aware of the feelings of others. This can be accomplished by discussing feelings—anger, excitement, fear, happiness, jealousy, loneliness, pride, sadness, surprise, or worry. Ask children what feelings they have had and how they felt. This exercise can be made into a game by writing the names of feelings on slips of paper that have paperclips attached. Make a fishing pole with a magnet at the end. Children "catch" a feeling and tell about a time they experienced that particular feeling. During the game children begin to realize that they are not the only ones who have had these feelings. Classmates and others also share them.

Teachers can show the class pictures of different facial expressions. They can be drawn, clipped from newspapers, magazines and books, or taken from the internet. Ask children to identify the pictured feelings. Television or DVDs can also be used. Momentarily pause the action and ask students to label the emotions portrayed by the actors and actresses. The class can be divided into teams that alternate pantomiming and guessing feelings.

*(2) The ability to view the world through another person's eyes, seeing things from that individual's perspective—*The next step is asking students how they respond when they experience emotions. As peers listen they learn that others handle feelings in different ways and that there are many positive responses.

In Feshbach's program, children were asked questions that helped them see different points of view: "What would the world look like to you if you were as tall as Wilt Chamberlain—or as small as a cat?" "What birthday present would make each member of your family happiest?" (1983, p. 268).

Literature is another medium that helps children see through the eyes of others and provides a safe platform for discussing any aspect of bullying. Those who are reluctant to talk about their own bullying experiences sometimes open up when the conversation turns to abused characters in books. Counselor, author, and bullying speaker Stan Davis (Davis & Davis, 2007) recommends stopping at appropriate points during a story to ask how each character feels or acting out parts of the book. He suggests discussing decisions that confront the character(s) and brainstorming possible solutions and alternative endings. Davis also advocates comparing the book's cultural settings to the students' and asking questions that connect the story to their own lives such as "How does the story compare to bullying at our school?"

---

## Box 12.1: Learning with Literature

Literature can lock bullying out of the classroom. Below is a brief list of books and websites that suggest bullying books and lesson plans:

- C.J. Bott's *The bully in the book and in the classroom* (2004) and *More bullies in more books* (2009) offer a comprehensive list of K-12 bullying literature. They include summaries, activities/topics, and quotations for discussion.
- The elementary library teachers at Newton Public Schools (MA) compiled *Bullying K-5 recommended resources* (2006) (www.newton.k12.ma.us/libraries/documents/bullyingk_5.pdf). It includes summaries of anti-bullying books organized by subject area. Discussion questions are included.
- Free Spirit Publishing's *Safe & caring schools* series by Katia Petersen provides lesson plans and activity sheets that are used with bullying books. The lessons are based on the following books: *Enemy pie* by Derek Munson, *My secret bully* by Trudy Ludwig, *But names will never hurt me* by Bernard Waber, *Stop picking on me* by Pat Thomas, *Nobody knew what to do: A story about bullying* by Becky Ray McCain, *Say something* by Peggy Moss, *Just kidding* by Trudy Ludwig, *The meanest thing to say* by Bill Cosby, *Telling isn't tattling* by Kathryn M. Hammerseng, and *The ant bully* by John Nickle. The material can be downloaded for free (www.freespirit.com/files/other/SafeCaring_Gr3-5_bully.pdf).
  Other bullying downloads for educators complement Free Spirit Publishing's books (*Bully free classroom* by Allan L. Beane, *Good-bye bully machine* by Debbie Fox and Allan L. Beane, *Teen cyberbullying investigated* by Thomas A. Jacobs, *Bullies are a pain in the brain* by Trevor Romain, and *What's up with my family?* by Annie Fox). They are also free (www.freespirit.com/educators/downloads.cfm?subj_id=20).
- Stan Davis skillfully integrates literature with anti-bullying education by reading and discussing *The hundred dresses* by Eleanor Estes. He created a series of lessons that focus on bystander action. It can be found in his book, *Empowering bystanders in bullying prevention"* (Davis & Davis, 2007).

---

*(3) The ability to experience and feel the emotions of that person*—Role playing provides opportunities to see another person's perspective and feel what he or she is feeling. As the name implies, children put themselves into different roles. During the process, the role player must think about how the individual feels and how those feelings prompt them to act. Role play goes beyond the teaching of skills and empathy building. It also provides opportunities for practice, allows testing of different approaches, gives immediate feedback, helps children anticipate actions, and provides a safe place to express feelings.

Role playing can be performed one-on-one or with more students. Every role in bullying can be included. For example, students can simultaneously act out the part of the person who bullies, the child who is bullied, bystanders, and upstanders. The players speak as they would in an actual bullying episode, receive replies, and respond accordingly. Teachers can provide input if additional help is required. Actions, such as leaving the scene, are also practiced.

Reverse role play is a powerful way to increase empathy, especially with those who aggress. Those who bully and bystanders play the role of targets during the exercise. The goal is to help participants realize how their actions (or inactions) hurt others. This activity is more effective if the re-creation is as close to original events as possible.

Teachers should stop the exercise at strategic points to explore and clarify the actions. Educators should also have follow up discussions at the session's conclusion. For example, how did each of the players feel, what are some alternative behaviors (role play them), and what conclusions can be drawn? Continued practice helps responses become second nature, thereby increasing their effectiveness and use. Confidence rises with efficacy.

## Curriculum

Weave empathy lessons into the curriculum. Reading biographies, celebrating different holidays, speaking in other languages, and reading stories that depict different cultures help children appreciate diversity. The lessons can be brought closer to home when students make presentations about their ethnicities. Asking immigrant parents and grandparents to share their countries' histories, customs, lifestyles, music, clothes, recipes, and foods gives students a bird's eye view of other cultures. Projects that help needy, poor, and underdeveloped countries, such as fundraisers, food, and clothing drives help youngsters see that, while they are different, they are also similar in many ways. This is a helpful strategy because Zahn-Waxler, Hollenbeck, and Radke-Yarrow (1984) and Smith (1988) found that people have more empathy for those who are similar to them (as cited in Dewar, 2009).

---

### Box 12.2: Drama-tic Results

Teacher, journalist, and theater director Steven Haff asked a group of students to recreate bullying incidents they experienced or witnessed. The children discovered a common thread after acting out the scenes—there was always someone who was bullied, someone who did the bullying, a bystander, and sometimes an upstander. They used these roles to create a seven minute play that was performed twice for every class in their school during Bullying Awareness month. Viewers silently watched the first time. During the second performance, the audience was asked to stop the action if they had a suggestion or resolution to bullying situations portrayed during the show. The actors then improvised, acting out the spectator's idea. The project increased awareness, bullying knowledge, and self-esteem (Haff, 2009).

## Experiential Learning Using Simulation

Simulation comes as close as we can to the real life equivalent of walking in another person's shoes. The following activities help students understand the challenges facing children with disabilities:

- Youngsters string beads, pick up coins or buttons, tie shoelaces, or write their names and addresses while wearing stiff, bulky gloves. These actions simulate the difficulties encountered by children with fine motor activity deficits (Faherty, n.d.; Kelly, 2004).
- Placing petroleum jelly or wax paper over eyeglass or goggle lenses (or scraping the lenses) provides a look at what it is like to live with a visual impairment (Faherty, n.d.; Gundlach, 2009; Yenne, n.d.).
- Ask children to walk a taped line while looking through the wrong end of binoculars. Perception will be distorted (Faherty, n.d.).
- Earplugs simulate hearing loss (McVey, Davis, & Cohen, 1989).
- Walk blindfolded volunteers around the classroom or ask them to eat from a tray of food while their vision is blocked (Gundlach, 2009; Yenne, n.d.). They will learn the difficulties encountered by those who are blind.
- Show a taped segment of a movie or television show with the sound turned off, which is what television viewing is like for a hearing impaired child. Ask students what they think happened, and then replay the scene with sound (Bruce & Shade, 1996).
- Let students carry books, go in and out of doors and bathroom stalls, or bring a hot lunch to a table while sitting in a wheelchair, walking with crutches, or using a walker. The skill, strength, and challenges facing those with impaired mobility will be realized (Yenne, n.d.).
- The world of those afflicted with ADHD can be shown by asking the class to complete math problems or list every U.S. state with their non dominant hand while being distracted (e.g., strobe light blinking, radio, television, DVD playing). Children have to also keep their feet moving the entire time (Yenne, n.d.).
- Place one arm in a sleeve, tie the end, and ask the child to wrap a box. This exercise replicates the difficulty of everyday tasks when a person is physically disabled (Kelly, 2004).
- Ask pupils to look in a mirror while connecting dots or completing a maze. This activity simulates dyslexia (Kelly, 2004).
- Talking with a mouthful of marshmallows helps youngsters understand what it is like to speak with a speech impediment (Kelly, 2004).
- The frustration felt by a mentally retarded child can be shown by quickly giving a series of ten commands (e.g., stand up, turn around twice, clap your hands three times, count to ten, sing "Happy Birthday") (Bruce & Shade, 1996).

## Walking in Another Person's Moccasins

Krznaric (2010) tells how the Native American proverb "Walk a mile in another man's moccasins before you criticise him" can develop empathy. First, people must figure out the person or group who is the object of their strongest prejudice and then step into their moccasins. Simulation exercises are very effective if there is a disability. Other forms of prejudice take creative thought. For example, attending a support meeting for gay students would be beneficial if bullying is motivated by homophobia.

## Eliminating Competition in the Classroom

Players must concentrate on their needs, if they want to win the coveted award. If contestants focus on themselves, they cannot think of others. Thus, competition hinders empathy.

Bullying is a competitive activity because "the bully is competing for dominance over another person or for a position of high status in the peer group" (D.W. Johnson, Johnson, & Holubec, 2008, Bullying and Competition section, para. 1). Schools that value competitiveness may inadvertently promote bullying:

- Competition promotes a "winner/loser" mentality.
- Those who win or make the team see themselves as superior, which means others are inferior. It can lead to hierarchies with losers at the lower echelons. Losers become potential targets.
- Competition increases hostility and decreases empathy. How can warm feelings develop in an atmosphere of competition that pits student against student with each trying to outdo the other who is viewed as an obstacle to success?
- Competition makes success a higher priority than relationships.
- Cooperation is limited during competition. Opponents do not work together during competition; instead, they work against one another trying to outdo the other.
- Viewing the perspective of others, which increases empathy, occurs less in competitive individuals (Kohn, 1987).

Competition also sets up unfair and demeaning comparisons. It is ridiculous to think that everyone will be good at everything, yet competition constantly compares children to their peers. It judges and labels.

Some argue that competition is a motivator. The desire to work hard and excel should be intrinsic, not brought about because of external competition.

In reality, there is no need for competition because we are all equal. We can beat someone in one area but they can best us in another. Who is to judge that one skill is more valuable than another? Competition should be replaced with "efforts." Everyone who tries, everyone who participates, is deservingly a winner.

## Describing the Feelings of Others

Earlier, literature was recommended as an example of one way to explore the feelings of others. The lessons can be expanded by asking the class how they think individuals feel/felt when discussing current events, movies, historical figures, or real life happenings:

- "How do you think <the person who is/was bullied> feels/felt?"
- "Why do you think <the person who is/was bullied> feels/felt that way?"
- "How do/did <the bystander(s)> feel?"
- "How might <the bystander(s)> feel if he or she acted differently?"
- "How do you think <the person who bullies/bullied> feels/felt?"
- "Why do you think <the person who bullies/bullied> acts (acted) that way?"
- "What are some more appropriate ways to behave?"
- "What are some ways you might have helped the person who is/was bullied?"

## Educating Children About Differences

Children with disabilities, illnesses, and other differences receive a disproportionate amount of bullying. Many times, the mistreatment is due to a lack of knowledge. Education erases ignorance and increases empathy.

The story of Darla is one example of the success that a carefully planned educational program can bring. Darla was a fifth grade student who suffered from primordial dwarfism yet stood tall among her peers despite being less than three feet in height:

> Darla's mom prepared a slide presentation which she gave in every science class explaining what primordial dwarfism is and why some people are born with it. Then Darla answered all her classmates' questions about what her life was like, including some of the unexpected advantages of being tiny. The mom also wrote a letter to parents explaining the presentation, and asking them to reinforce the message of acceptance at home, which the principal printed on school letterhead and made sure was sent home with every student . . . When Darla and her mom took the mystery out of her dwarfism for her classmates, they also took away the fear.
>
> (Blanco, 2008, p. 371)

Darla became a popular, well liked student with many friends, thanks to the foresight of her mother and the cooperation of the school community (Blanco, 2008).

## Seizing Teachable Moments

Turn bullying incidents into empathy raising opportunities. Lickona's (2000) story illustrates this point:

When five-year-old Brian called a Jamaican classmate "tan man," the teacher took Brian aside and explained: "Brian, there are two kinds of hurts: outside hurts that you can see, like a cut or a bruise, and inside hurts that you can't see, like a hurt feeling. The inside hurts hurt more and last longer. When you call John 'tan man,' you are causing an inside hurt that makes him very sad. Do you wish to continue to cause this inside hurt?" Brian said that he didn't.

(Teach Empathy section, para. 1)

## Creating Teachable Moments

Bullying-related activities can increase empathy:

- *Art*—Create posters, drawings, or collages of what it feels like to be bullied. Discuss those feelings.
- *Bullying research*—Assignments can show the harmful consequences of bullying, how it impacts lives, and effective intervention strategies.
- *Interviews*—Interview an older student, sibling, or adult who experienced bullying and find out how it affected the person.
- *Movies*—Watch a movie on bullying and discuss the characters, consequences of their actions, and the feelings of the person who was bullied. What would you do if you were a bystander?
- *Books*—Read a book on bullying and write how the bullied character felt. Could you create a different ending that shows empathy?
- *Historical figures*—Report on famous people who were bullied and how it affected them.

## Reinforcing Empathetic Behavior

Teachers can point out and praise empathetic behavior. It is a well deserved thank you for the caring child. It also serves to motivate the entire class because youngsters love compliments and will work hard to earn them. The reinforcement also shows students that empathy is valued by their educator.

## Pointing Out Similarities

Teachers can help students learn about their similarities by asking them to list their likes, dislikes, interests, hobbies, and personality traits. Afterwards, the teacher can pair youngsters and ask them to use the information to complete a Venn diagram. The completed product will illustrate their similarities and differences. Activities such as those in Box 10.1: Moving Toward Friendship (pages 152–153) or Box 9.2: Simon Says "Who Are You?" (page 119) also help students find others with similar interests.

---

## Box 12.3: Mix It Up at Lunch Day

Millions of students at thousands of schools have participated in Mix It Up at Lunch Days. During the event, children switch seats at the noontime meal and eat with a new group of pupils. Schools can structure the event any way they want, from using ice breaker questions as introductions to having older students act as mentors.

Mix It Up at Lunch Days increase empathy, teach tolerance, decrease prejudice, break down barriers, and lessen misunderstandings that can lead to conflicts, bullying, and harassment. It helps children get to know one another and see they are more alike than different.

Teachers can download a K-6 or 6–12 organizers' guide, posters, fliers, and stickers from the Mix It Up at Lunch Day Foundation (www.tolerance.org/mix-it-up/downloads). All materials are free of charge.

---

### Using the Internet

There are many excellent anti-bullying websites that are a source of infinite information, advice, and support. A recent Yahoo search of "bullying" brought over 78 million hits. Table 4.2: Bullying sites on the internet (page 52) and Table 4.3: Internet safety and cyberbullying information from around the world (page 55) will provide readers with a sample of the unending material available.

### Music

Songs can be used to sensitize children to bullying. One particularly powerful piece of music is "Wanda's Song," written by Chris Reading, Eric Reading, and John Paul Laurence. It is sung on a YouTube video (www.youtube.com/watch?v=a5X2FJyjBxE) titled "The Readings—Wanda's Song." A class viewing of the video can be followed with a discussion on the impact of a person's actions, with particular emphasis on bullying. Ask students to put themselves in Wanda's place. How do they feel? Discuss the negative consequences of bullying. Have the children imagine they are one of the people who bullied Wanda. How do they feel? What would pupils do if a similar situation presented itself at their school? What are healthier ways to handle bullying?

Other songs that can be used in anti-bullying interventions include "Beautiful" by Christina Aguilera, "Caught in the Crowd" by Kate Miller-Heidke, "Don't Laugh at Me" by Peter Yarrow, "Hero" by Superchick, "Mean" by Taylor Swift, "Miss Invisible" by Marie Digby, "Perfect" by Pink, and "Who Says" by Selena Gomez.

## I Am Lovable and Capable

Sidney B. Simon's book, *I am loveable and capable: A modern allegory of the classical put-down*, presents a day in the life of 14-year-old Randy. In the morning Randy put on an invisible IALAC sign (abbreviation for: **I A**m **L**oveable **A**nd **C**apable) and wore it during the course of the day. Each time Randy received a "put down" a small piece of the sign was torn off. At the end of the day the sign was the size of a postage stamp. The story helps readers realize how words and actions can unintentionally hurt people (Simon, 1973).

The book appears to be out of print but copies can be obtained on the internet. Go to www.eric.ed.gov, find "Search Term(s)," type "IALAC", and click on "Search." The entry will appear. Scroll down and at the bottom left corner you will see "ERIC Full Text." Click on it.

Mendler, Curwin, and Mendler (2007) tell the story of a high school teacher, Mr. Aziz, who took on the role of Randy. He drew a picture of his body and pinned it onto his shirt. Aziz told his students that a person's actions can be supportive or disrespectful and he would rip off a part of his body (the paper figure) to show injury each time someone did anything he considered disrespectful. The exercise opened his pupils' eyes. There were many times they were unaware of being disrespectful. As a result, offensive behavior drastically dropped.

Entire classes can follow Aziz's example. They can make and wear a picture of themselves and rip off pieces of the figure anytime they are physically, verbally, relationally, or cyberbullied. Afterwards, teachers can ask "How did it feel to be bullied?" "Did your behavior change?" and "In the future, will you think 'How would I feel if someone said or did that to me?' before acting or speaking?"

The Gay, Lesbian and Straight Education Network and the National Association of Elementary School Principals created the *It's All in a Name* lesson plan, which discusses put ups and put downs (www.nonamecallingweek.org/binary-data/NoName Calling_ATTACHMENTS/file/86-1.pdf).

# Chapter 13

# Battling Bullying with Incompatibility

Bullying declines when teachers use incompatibility to alter their classes' social landscapes. Educators can review the following list and select activities that best fit with the teacher, students, particular bullying problems, time constraints, and budgets:

*Inclusion*—"Greater peer inclusion at the classroom level and positive teacher–student relationships were associated with fewer occurrences of peer aggression" (Doll, Song, & Siemers, 2004, p. 176).

Teachers should ask themselves the following questions:

- "Do all students participate or are those who are not up to par with classmates left out?"
- "Are marginalized youngsters actively moved away from the edges of the social ecology and guided toward the mainstream?"
- "Is exclusion forbidden and are instances used as teachable moments?"
- "Are seats, groups, and teams assigned by the teacher?"

In *You can't say you can't play*, kindergarten teacher Vivian Gussin Paley pointed out that educators attempt to stop hitting and name calling, yet statements such as "You can't play; don't sit by me; stop following us; I don't want you for a partner, go away" (1992, p. 14) are not always challenged. Thus, one child decides who is acceptable and who is not and determines the social fates of others.

The author conjectured reasons why one of her students played with certain classmates but not others. "They are outsiders, different in some way from the children she has known. No, this is not true. They are *not* different. What makes them outsiders is simply that they are treated as outsiders" (Paley, 1992, p. 68). Paley looked at a regularly used intervention and concluded:

> In general, the approach has been to help the outsiders develop the characteristics that will make them more acceptable to the insiders. I am suggesting something different: The *group* must change its attitudes and expectations toward those who, for whatever reason, are not yet part of the system.
>
> (p. 33)

Paley came up with a unique idea, the "You can't say you can't play" rule. Acceptance came slowly as hurt feelings declined and inclusion increased (Paley, 1992). "You can't say you can't play" should be a mainstay in every classroom.

Two other ways to increase inclusion are described by Sapon-Shevin (2005):

- The "family rule"—Students cannot ask their teacher a question unless they query all their cluster mates first. This encourages children to include, help, and support peers.
- Teachers can use recess to teach several pupils how to do difficult projects. This group then helps classmates complete the activity. Youngsters who are not "stars" are now seen differently and the educator has assistants who help instruct the class.

Schools understandably give precedence to bullying incidents. However, if personnel gave the same priority to complaints about being left out there would be a decrease in bullying.

*Kindness campaigns*—People display kindness when they say, do, or give of themselves to make another person feel good. A little creativity can motivate kind acts.

- Margaret Singleton (1997) instructed her students to perform a good deed everyday and write or draw their acts of kindness in a "caring journal."
- Sixth grade teacher Tania Walker's school made a "kindness chain." Students throughout the building wrote kind acts they performed or observed on strips of paper. They then taped the ends together creating links, and put them onto a "chain of kindness" that connected the classrooms (KindActs, 2000). This can be adapted to a classroom with the chain linking each student's desk.
- The Sloan Creek Middle School (Fairview, TX) created "87 Ways to Show Kindness." Students can brainstorm their own lists or add to Sloan Creek's (http://scms.lovejoyisd.net/Uploads/54/misc/K@CREEK87ways.pdf).
- Teachers can create a "Pay It Forward" project. As seen in the movie by that name, each person must be kind to three people. Each of those three do not pay

back the kindness to the giver but "pay it forward" by being nice to three other people, who in turn must "pay it forward" by being kind to three more people.

This assignment can be adapted to bullying. Students report on three acts of kindness that are related to bullying. For example, they can comfort a peer who is bullied, report a bullying incident, or ask a classmate to stop hurting someone. Children should try to track how far their acts of kindness travel. One person can create a chain reaction of kindness with the acts reaching billions of people (see Box 13.1: The Power of One).

● Although internal motivation is preferred, direct reinforcement may stimulate kindness. Rewards can include material items such as stickers, pencils, erasers, magnets, bookmarks, or inexpensive toys. Certificates (Figure 13.1) can be awarded during class presentations and award assemblies or viewed in newsletters and on websites. Privileges such as free time, line leader, special helper, no homework, and extra computer time can also reward kindness. Children enjoy popcorn, cookies, pretzels, and other edibles, as well as lunch with the teacher, phone calls, or letters home. Class parties or trips reward the class as a whole.

---

### Special Recognition Certificate

_____

made our class a safer, friendlier, more respectful, inclusive, and bully free place to learn

☐ Told someone to stop bullying            ☐ Walked away from bullying

☐ Removed someone from a bullying incident  ☐ Befriended someone who was bullied

☐ Asked an adult for help                   ☐ Told peers not to bully

☐ Distracted a person who was bullying      ☐ Stopped a rumor

☐ Reported bullying                         ☐ Cleaned hurtful graffiti

☐ Comforted someone who was bullied         ☐ Performed an act of kindness

☐ Refused to go along with bullying         ☐ _____


_____              _____
        Date                               Signature

---

Figure 13.1 Special Recognition Certificate

# Box 13.1: The Power of One

## The Power of One

If one person is kind to 3 people = 3 people will be touched by kindness

If each of the 3 people is kind to 3 people = 9 people will be touched by kindness

If each of the 9 people is kind to 3 people = 27 people will be touched by kindness

If each of the 27 people is kind to 3 people = 81 people will be touched by kindness

If each of the 81 people is kind to 3 people = 243 people will be touched by kindness

If each of the 243 people is kind to 3 people = 729 people will be touched by kindness

If each of the 729 people is kind to 3 people = 2,187 people will be touched by kindness

If each of the 2,187 people is kind to 3 people = 6,561 people will be touched by kindness

If each of the 6,561 people is kind to 3 people = 19,683 people will be touched by kindness

If each of the 19,683 people is kind to 3 people = 59,049 people will be touched by kindness

If each of the 59,049 people is kind to 3 people = 177,147 people will be touched by kindness

If each of the 177,147 people is kind to 3 people = 531,441 people will be touched by kindness

If each of the 531,441 people is kind to 3 people = 1,594,323 people will be touched by kindness

If each of the 1,594,323 people is kind to 3 people = 4,782,969 people will be touched by kindness

If each of the 4,782,969 people is kind to 3 people = 14,348,907 people will be touched by kindness

If each of the 14,348,907 people is kind to 3 people = 43,046,721 people will be touched by kindness

If each of the 43,046,721 people is kind to 3 people = 129,140,163 people will be touched by kindness

If each of the 129,140,163 people is kind to 3 people = 387,420,489 people will be touched by kindness

If each of the 387,420,489 people is kind to 3 people = over 1 billion people will be touched by kindness

and it keeps continuing!

*Acknowledge the positive*—Catch students being good and acknowledge prosocial behaviors. Compliment upstanders who help bullied peers, speak out against bullying, or get help. Praise those who bully when they peacefully walk away from potentially explosive situations or go one day without bullying. Honor a socially deficient youngster who learns a new strategy. Salute class members who join anti-bullying campaigns or contribute to bullying-related discussions. The attempts, the efforts, even the failures should also be complimented because it means the students are trying and that is the first step toward change.

The story of Ms. Jackson illustrates the power of positive thinking. Ms. Jackson taught in:

> a self-contained class of low achievers who had gained a negative reputation among teachers in the school . . . they didn't care about school. Yet they behaved differently with Ms. Jackson, their social studies teacher. She made each of her students actually feel good about making mistakes. As she returned an assignment to a student who received 60 percent, she said, "You did a great job on questions, 1, 6, 7, 8, 9, and 10. But I noticed that you didn't do the others. Those have to do with China and communism. I must not have done a very good job teaching that. I'll be reviewing that topic in the first few minutes of today's class. If you'd like to improve your grade, please redo those questions when I'm finished. Either way, congratulations on the answers you completed. They were done very well!"
>
> (Mendler et al., 2007, p. 86)

*Bullying-related art projects*—Cut leaves and ask students to write one way to help a bullied student on each leaf. Glue them to a paper tree. Or write anti-bullying messages on quilt squares and put them together (Anti-Bullying Alliance, 2006). The class can also write ways to prevent bullying on cardboard boxes. "Build a tower to show that, when we stand together against bullying, we're strong" (p. 3).

*High expectations*—Children will rise up, or down, to expectations of teachers. If educators tell children they can solve a math problem they will strive to accomplish the task. Efforts will cease if youngsters are told they are stupid or not capable of learning. Antisocial tendencies wane when teachers stress expectations of prosocial behavior.

*Test grading procedures*—Allowing students to grade each other's tests is a time saving idea. However, educators should reconsider the use of this practice. Children are bullied for being smart and children are bullied for not being smart. When pupils grade each other's tests they learn how well or poorly classmates perform. This can provide ammunition for bullying. Those who excel might "dumb down" because they do not want to find themselves on the chopping block. Academically challenged youths may withdraw.

*Volunteerism and charity*—Volunteerism and charity are the antithesis of bullying. There are countless volunteer opportunities open to children. Age appropriate activities should be selected:

- Bring cards, books, flowers, or toys to children at hospitals.
- Send books and care packages to servicemen stationed overseas.
- Collect food for local food banks.
- Help prepare and distribute meals at a soup kitchen.
- Befriend a child in a rehabilitation facility.
- Collect new and gently used clothes for the homeless or those who cannot afford them.
- Collect toiletries, clothes, blankets, books, or toys for survivors of earthquakes, floods, or hurricanes, or for people in shelters.
- Make holiday cards for, read or talk to, play games with, teach, or entertain residents in senior citizen centers, assisted living facilities, and nursing homes.
- Write letters for seniors who are unable to write. (Kids can transcribe the spoken words.)
- Recycle newspapers, pop tops, old eyeglasses, or hearing aids.
- Bring already read magazines to nursing homes and hospitals.
- Raise money for charities through bake sales, car washes, garage sales, and talent shows.
- Collect blankets, food, bowls, and toys for animals in shelters. Clean cages and help care for the animals.
- Donate new and used books to libraries.
- Sponsor a child.
- Use an allowance to purchase a holiday gift for a child in need.
- Clean local parks or community centers.
- Assist elderly neighbors with chores, spend time with them, or cook for them.
- Paint over graffiti or clean litter from streets.
- Read to or teach younger students.

*Service learning*—Service learning combines community service with education. Students volunteer and learn while they serve in community jobs that integrate and complement their academic curriculum. Many benefits are derived from participation in service learning. There are increases in social competency, responsibility, self-esteem, empathy, problem solving skills, respect between teachers and students, and acceptance of culturally diverse populations. There are decreases in lateness and behavioral problems, while attendance, grades, and school climates improve. These qualities are incompatible with bullying.

Service learning opportunities can be found in the community, by speaking to colleagues who are familiar with the program, or by visiting Learn and Serve America's National Service-Learning Clearinghouse (www.servicelearning.org/).

*Character education*—Traits that are taught, developed, and reinforced through character education are incompatible with bullying. Some include caring, citizenship, compassion, cooperation, courage, courtesy, equality, fairness, honor, integrity, kindness, knowledge, loyalty, respect for others, responsibility, self-discipline, self-respect, and tolerance.

---

## Box 13.2: Bullying is Stung by the BEE

One large public elementary school reduced self-reported aggression by 40% and self-reported victimization by 19% after implementing "The Five Bees" as part of their BEE Character Education Program: Be Respectful, Be Responsible, Be Honest, Be Ready to Learn, and Be Your Personal Best.

The elimination of name calling and teasing was one goal of the program. Signs were posted throughout the school and the "two put ups for each put down" rule was instituted. Each time children were observed putting down a peer, they were reminded of the school rule "Be Respectful" and asked to make two nice statements about the person who was disrespected.

Rewards were used to motivate students. For example, children who demonstrated prosocial behaviors were invited to lunch with their teachers or principal in the "Beehive Café," a decorated area in the corner of the lunchroom. Recognition was also publicized during morning announcements, in monthly newsletters, and by special awards (Orpinas, Horne, & Staniszewski, 2003).

# Chapter 14

# Stopping and Responding to Bullying Episodes

## Should Teachers Intervene if it *Appears* to be a Minor Incident of Bullying?

When teachers intercede they are saying "Bullying is not acceptable in this classroom (school) and we will not allow it to happen. Everyone deserves to feel safe." *Educators must stop* minor or major incidents of bullying, for a number of reasons:

- Bullying is not a conflict that students can work out together. It is an aggressive act by a person with greater power taking advantage of someone with less power who has difficulty defending him or herself.
- Teachers do not know the intent of the person who is aggressing. What may appear to be play fighting or fooling around can be bullying. Educators should not rely on their perception of intent because the reality is not known and human error can occur. Instead, look at the *behavior* because that is a known. If teachers have even one iota of thought that it might be bullying, they should go with their gut. In most cases, it will be bullying.
- Educators may think a bullying episode is trivial when in fact it can be a damaging act because actions that would not bother one person can be devastating to another.
- If students see school personnel ignoring abuse they will think teachers do not care, they cannot stop bullying, adults condone antisocial behavior, targeted

children deserve the abuse, power reigns over fairness, bullying is acceptable, violence is rewarded, there are no consequences for hurting others, or it is okay to join in.

- Students will lose faith in teachers' abilities to insure their safety.
- Children will lose respect for educators.
- If teachers do not intervene, students will not either.
- If unanswered, less serious forms of aggression (e.g., poking, pushing, hurtful remarks) may progress to more dangerous types of abuse. It is like a rolling snowball that gets larger and larger.
- If bullying is allowed to continue, mistreated youngsters may start believing that they deserve to be abused.
- Targeted children might think that nothing will change or the situation is hopeless.
- Teachers have a legal responsibility to protect students.

## How to Stop a Bullying Incident

Teachers are expected to handle bullying situations. It is not always easy to remain calm or make the right decisions when insults are sprayed, punches are slung, and emotions are flying. As challenging as it can be, and it can be quite challenging, educators need to maintain composure. Calmness helps de-escalate bullying episodes and adds to objectivity and professionalism. It is easier to remain level headed if a plan is in place.

A teacher's first response should stop the bullying. Investigations and consequences are secondary measures. Intervene *immediately*. It is easier to contain a small problem than one that has mushroomed out of control.

### First Response

1. Distract the participants. Loudly and firmly say "Stop," drop a heavy object (e.g., book or chair), clap, or blow a whistle. If distraction does not work, proceed to step 2.
2. Stand between the person being bullied and the person doing the bullying, *only* if it will *not* put you in danger.★ Block eye contact.
3. If numbers 1 and 2 do not stop the bullying, send a teacher or student for a security officer, dean, or the appropriate safety personnel in the school. Clear the area of all other students while you wait for assistance.
4. When the altercation has ended, name the behavior or state what you observed:

   - "*I heard you say. . .*"
   - "*I saw you hitting a student . . .*"
   - "I noticed you are not including everyone in . . ."

5.   Say why the behavior should end:

"<*Calling names, hitting, excluding*> *is against the class (school) rules. The rule states . . . The rules were made to respect and protect everyone in our class (school).*"

6.   Tell the student to stop, citing the behavior:

"*The* <*behavior—name calling, hitting, excluding*> *must stop now.*"

★ This controversial bit of advice is given by the U.S. Department of Health and Human Services (U.S. Department of Health and Human Services, Health Resources Services Administration, n.d.). The author thoughtfully considered the recommendation and included it as an option. Educators can choose to discard the suggestion or use it *if there is no risk of injury*. For example, stepping in between a pair of kindergarten children engaged in a verbal argument poses less danger than getting in the middle of two high school boys who are wrestling. Judgment should dictate responses.

## Rationale

| *Statement or action* | *Rationale* |
|---|---|
| Distract the participants. | Momentary distraction can break momentum, provide time to calm down, or allow the teacher to verbally steer children away from the aggression. It focuses attention on the educator and away from the battle. |
| Stand between the person being bullied and the person doing the bullying. | A human body placed between two people becomes a barrier, preventing contact. People are also less inclined to argue with someone they cannot see. As a point of emphasis, if there is *any* chance of injury, *do not put yourself into harm's way*. |
| Send a teacher or student for a security officer, dean, or the appropriate safety personnel. | Intervention may compromise the teacher's safety. Security officers, deans, or appropriate safety personnel are trained to handle confrontations. |
| Clear the area of all other students. | Removing spectators eliminates the audiences that those who bully want. It could shorten or end the bullying. It also keeps bystanders out of danger. |
| Name the behavior or state what you observed. | Most times, those who bully will deny any wrongdoing. The chances for denial diminish when educators say they witnessed the bullying. |

| | |
|---|---|
| Say why the behavior should end. | It is important to refer to the class or school rules ("The class rule states . . .") as opposed to saying "I" ("I want you to stop . . .") because it removes personalization. It is not the teacher saying the behavior is incorrect but a class or school rule. The statement is even more powerful if students created the rules. In most cases, phrasing words in this manner will prevent arguments, anger, or retaliation, because the teacher is not claiming ownership but merely enforcing a rule. |
| Tell the student(s) to stop, citing the behavior. | When teachers tell students to stop and name the action, they are succinctly and clearly letting children know the behavioral expectation. Misinterpretations and excuses (e.g., "I didn't know") are eliminated. |

Do not reprimand youngsters in front of peers:

- It is not wise to attribute fault because an investigation has not been performed.
- No one should be humiliated. It is the behavior that is inappropriate, not the person.
- Embarrassment can trigger angry responses.

Refrain from giving the child who appeared to be bullied too much public support. The peer group is watching and being labeled a "teacher's pet" can provide an excuse for future abuse.

## Second Response

Teachers should turn to the second response after all children are out of danger and the bullying episode ends. The names of everyone present should be recorded.

### The Person Who Was Bullied

- Send the child who was bullied to the school nurse if there are physical injuries. A school counselor should be considered if the student is very upset.
- If not, allow the pupil to go to the bathroom, an office, or another safe place to regroup. Ask the child's friend to act as an escort. If a friend is not available, assign a compassionate classmate.

- Do not ask for an account of the incident in front of everyone:

  - The student has been mentally or physically hurt. Give the youngster time to calm down, regain self-control, and feel safe.
  - Questioning children who are attacked in front of the people who abused them can cause revictimization. The children who bullied and their supporters will attack any explanation and spew blame.
  - The mistreated youngster might be accused of being a tattletale.
  - Fears of retribution will compromise honesty.

## The Person Who Bullied

- Do not ask for an apology immediately after a bullying incident. It will not be genuine. You also want the child to save face in front of peers.
- Tell the student you will meet together at a later point. You do not want to ask for the child's version of events in front of an audience because the request can feed into any needs for attention and power. It can also elevate social status.
- Keep the person who bullied with you until the abused child is safely away. Then, send the student back to his or her desk or class.
- Let the youngster know that you will be carefully monitoring future behavior.

## Bystanders

- If bystanders successfully intervened, compliment them.
- If bystanders tried to help but were not successful, commend their efforts, and review ways to effectively stop bullying.
- If bystanders did not intervene, say "Perhaps you didn't know how to stop bullying. The next time you might try <examples of successful ways to end an episode>."

## Third Response

An investigation is done during the third response. Teachers should interview the person who was bullied, the person who did the bullying, and bystanders privately. If possible, keep witnesses separated before questioning to prevent them from comparing notes, covering up, or fabricating events. Conduct interviews as soon as possible but not immediately after the incident. Allow time for emotions to calm down.

## The Person Who Was Bullied

- Praise bullied children. Thank them for having the courage to talk about the bullying incident. Assure youngsters by letting them know:

  - they have the right to be safe in school;
  - they are helping themselves and the entire school by talking;

- the problem will be solved together;
- you will do everything in your power to help.

● Do NOT ask bullied children "What did you do (to provoke the bullying incident)?" This is blaming them for the behavior of someone else. It wrongly reinforces the message of the bullying group—that bullying is the recipient's fault and he or she deserves to be abused.

● Tell bullied children that the bullying is not their fault and they do not deserve to be abused. Children who are repeatedly bullied often internalize perceived reasons for bullying, thinking they are worthless human beings who brought the maltreatment on themselves. It is understandable because the message bullying sends is "We don't like you, you aren't wanted, and bullying is your fault." Bystanders' silence and lack of adult intervention can, in a bullied child's mind, confirm those statements.

   Let these youngsters know "This is your school," "You have a right to attend," "You belong here," "You are a worthy person," "You are a valued member of the school community," "Everyone does not agree with bullying or what those who aggress say," and "You do not have the ability to control another person's actions but you *can control* your own reactions."

● Validate the children's feelings. Those who are bullied can experience fear, anger, anxiousness, abandonment, shame, helplessness, hopelessness, hurt, humiliation, isolation, powerlessness, rejection, or worthlessness. Encourage the sharing of these feelings.

   Regardless of whether a teacher agrees or disagrees, children have a right to their feelings. Try to empathize with the pain by stepping into the speaker's shoes and seeing life through his or her eyes. Be where the child is. Do not say "Things will improve" or "In twenty years those who bully will be in jail." It will not make the student feel better. The targeted are in pain *now* and must deal with *today's feelings*, not the future. Maintain objectivity and validate the youngster's feelings.

   The TeachSafeSchools.org website gives examples of questions and statements that validate and demonstrate empathy (Melissa Institute for Violence Prevention and Treatment, n.d., Demonstrating Empathy section):

- "I can see how upset you are. Why don't we talk about it and see if we can work it out?"
- "How tough was it?"
- "How did that make you feel?"
- "I understand why you would feel . . ."
- "What I see is someone who is really upset. If we talk about it, it will help you feel better."
- "This just hasn't been a good day, has it? But it doesn't have to keep on being that way."
- "It seems like . . . (you are frustrated, annoyed, angry)."

- "When friends (family members) do X, it is natural to want to get back at them (not back down, run away)."
- "Some problems seem so big that it seems as if no one can do anything about them."
- "Sometimes things seem terrible, but there are always ways to make them better."
- "Other students who have had this same thing happen to them have often had the same feelings."

- Assure children who are bullied that they will not have to meet with the person who aggressed, unless they want to. This will calm fears and avoid revictimization.
- Listen, take the narrative seriously, and record pertinent information. Assure children that conversations will be held in strict confidence. The only exception is if someone's safety is in danger. Allow youngsters to speak freely. Talking can increase self-esteem and help them "move out of a world of learned helplessness and toward one of empowerment and self-efficacy" (Roberts Jr. & Coursol, 1996, Listening Approaches section, para. 1).

  After students finish talking, ask questions to obtain additional information, clarify what was said, and/or double check your understanding. Teachers should find out who did the bullying, who was present, what happened, the time of the episode, where it took place, why the youngster thinks the abuse happened, what precipitated the bullying, any damage or injuries, and whether it was an isolated event or a repeated incident.

  Take all statements seriously, even if they do not appear to be legitimate. Something that initially does not make sense may become clearer after all pieces of the puzzle are put together.
- Give bullied children some sense of control. Bullying is an out of control situation for targeted children because they are at a disadvantage, they feel powerless, their objections are often ignored, they have to attend school, and many times they lack the support of the majority of peers and some teachers. Asking what will help or make the situation worse will give the child some sense of control.
- Create a plan that insures safety. Bullying, by definition, is a repeated activity. It will continue unless strategies that prevent future abuse are put into place. Let bullied students participate in the planning. It restores some control.

## The Person Who Bullied

Following up with those who bullied is of critical importance. Many students who aggress say teachers do not speak to them. They probably think they "got away with it," bullying is okay, or their actions are supported by adults.

- Know where the person who aggressed is coming from. Children who bully are not "bad kids." They are children in emotional pain. Most are bullied and have not learned how to appropriately express their feelings so they act out. These youngsters have no control over their abusive environments so, in a twisted way, bully to obtain some control and power.

The majority learn that violence is the correct way to handle feelings and solve problems. They are supported, reinforced, and rewarded for antisocial behavior and rarely face consequences. Many times, the only attention paid to them is when they act inappropriately. Negative attention is better than none at all.

- Do not judge but keep an open mind. Do not automatically assume any child is at fault. In many cases, those with bullying histories will be "guilty as charged," but not always.

The student could have been provoked, which does not mean it is okay to hurt another person but the information helps to understand motivation and points out areas needing improvement.

- Attentively listen to the child's version of events. Give the person who aggressed a free and uninterrupted opportunity to speak. Pay careful attention. As with the person who was bullied, the teacher should learn the specifics of the bullying incident—who, what, when, where, why, damage, and frequency. When the child finishes speaking, ask questions or make comments that fill in the blanks, clear up inconsistencies, aid in understanding, and confirm your interpretation of the report. Write down the details.
- Do not accuse the child of wrongdoing. Blaming will shut the student down. At this point, the primary goal is to establish a dialogue and obtain information. Treat the youngster with respect. Do not be critical or condescending, or show anger.

## Bystanders

- Tell bystanders that you need their help. You want to find out what happened so you can make the school a safe place for all students.
- Assure bystanders of anonymity. Assure children that their names will not be attached to any information provided.
- Interview bystanders. As with the bullied child and those who bully, find out the 5 Ws (who, what, when, where, why).

## Fourth Response

The fourth response explores ways to prevent future bullying and strengthen students.

## The Person Who Was Bullied

- Update bullied children. Let abused youngsters know the investigation is underway or completed, consequences were given according to the class and/or school's anti-bullying policy, and measures to insure future safety are in place.
- Consider the effects of bullying. Investigations are fact finding missions. However, the affective domain should not be overlooked. Find out if there was any

psychological harm done by the bullying and respond accordingly, which might include a referral to the school's mental health professional.

- Teach appropriate skills. Social scaffolding (teaching of skills) complements social architecture. Some areas to consider include anger or anxiety management; assertiveness training; communication, conflict resolution, friendship or social skills; how and when to ask for help; anti-bullying strategies; self-talk; and positive affirmations. Many of these topics will benefit all students and should be integrated into the curriculum.

   Discuss strategies that were used in the past. Were they successful? Stick with them. If not, discard them.

   Youngsters do not learn by osmosis. They need instructions, demonstrations, practice, feedback, more practice (in the classroom and then in actual settings and situations), additional feedback, and refinement. Practice increases proficiency and makes the application of skills habitual.

- Explore the child's strengths. Help youngsters identify abilities and talents they possess. Develop strategies around assets.

- Brainstorm anti-bullying strategies. It is empowering if children develop their own solutions. If they have difficulty, step in.

- Increase opportunities for socialization. Friendships are formed when students move off the sidelines and join groups, clubs, teams, and other social activities.

- Steer children into activities that increase self-esteem. Some ways to increase self-esteem include developing an existing skill, learning a new skill that is within capabilities, teaching peers or younger children, helping, or volunteering.

- Look at the big picture. Those who are bullied can brainstorm ways to change the bullying climate in their school. They can conduct school bullying surveys, ask teachers to create bullying-related projects, request anti-bullying clubs, or undertake similar initiatives. It is empowering because the successful completion of these ideas not only changes their current situation but that of every student.

- Keep a log of bullying episodes. Record keeping is a positive way of coping. It can empower the author and may prevent, lessen, or end bullying. Keeping logs is also a non aggressive way to deal with bullying, an assertive response that removes the need to fight, and eliminates problems with recall. These written records avoid negative attention children might get from telling and can serve as evidence (after an investigation corroborates the report). Logs may also help in seeing reality. Bullying may occur more or less frequently than thought.

   The following information should be included in the log: date, time, and location of the incident; what happened; who did the bullying; actions the bullied person took; injuries; other damages; and witnesses.

   Other ways to document bullying episodes include photographing injuries; keeping copies of correspondence, emails, letters, or notes; recording actions taken; saving medical records; and preserving damaged property (Goodstein, 2008).

- Ask permission to share information with school personnel. Explain that sharing gives adults in the school a heads up and increases vigilance. As a result, safety will improve. Honor children's wishes if they do not want you to talk to others, unless someone's safety is in jeopardy.

● Assign a safe adult. Help identify an adult in the school who the youngster can turn to in times of need. It can be a teacher, guidance counselor, aide, nurse, custodian, security guard, paraprofessional, secretary, cafeteria worker, coach, or any adult who can provide safety and advocate for the child. One caring adult can make a big difference.

● Follow up on bullying incidents. Targeted youngsters should be checked on at regular intervals to see how they are adjusting after the bullying episode and to find out if abuse is still occurring. If rapport is established they will have another person in their support system.

● Make referrals, if necessary. Targets might require additional support. Counseling may improve depression, anxiety, PTSD, and other psychological problems. Help with social skills, assertiveness training, making friends, or self-esteem may be beneficial, too.

● If bullying continues despite all efforts, it is better to change the class of the person who aggresses, *not the person who was targeted*. Research shows that abuse continues when bullied children are transferred into new classes but there is a decrease when those who aggress move to another class. The continuation of bullying might be because students who enter a class during the middle of the school year can feel fearful, insecure, and anxious. These feelings are compounded with those who are bullied because of their previous experiences. Fears are picked up by new classmates "testing" newcomers (Salmivalli, Lappalainen, & Lagerspetz, 1998).

● When you are with children *listen* with "not only open eyes and ears, but open hearts and minds" (Delpit, 1995, p. 46).

● Let abused children know that bullying is a temporary although extremely painful problem that will not last forever. Actions such as those outlined have to back up the words, especially with the bullied population because the frontal lobes of the brain do not fully mature until one's twenties. That means youngsters do not have fully developed higher level thinking, including the ability to foresee consequences caused by their actions, control emotions, make judgments, and solve problems. We see the unfortunate results with bullycides, school shootings, and other harmful acts.

## The Person Who Bullied

The message teachers should convey to those who hurt others is "adults aren't going to let you engage in this behavior because we care and because you are worth the time that it takes to teach you how to do it right" (Farmer et al., 2006, p. 40). Educators should not think of time spent with youths who aggress as an unwanted time consuming job but as an opportunity to help a child learn and grow.

- Describe the behavior. Assuming bullying did occur (a) clearly state the actions that constituted bullying, (b) review the rules of the classroom and school, (c) explain how the child violated those guidelines, and (d) describe how the offense affected the targeted person, bystanders, and the person who aggressed.
- Do not accept excuses or blaming. Those who bully rarely take responsibility for their actions and often blame others. "I was just kidding around," "It was her fault," "I didn't mean to hurt Katlin," "Big Steve pushed Sam into me," "Everyone was doing it," "She is so annoying," and similar lines are often heard.

  These are poor defenses for horrendous behavior. Erroneous beliefs will be reinforced if teachers entertain these false statements. Immediately respond with "There is no excuse for bullying or hurting another person" and "We do not allow bullying in our school." Repeat the phrases as often as is necessary.

  What if a child admits misconduct and tries to justify it? Validate any expressed feelings and explain that the behavior was inappropriate. For example, "I understand why you were angry. You had a good reason to be upset, but hitting someone is the wrong way to handle anger."
- The person who aggressed needs to realize that bullying has consequences, that it is unacceptable, and that frustration (or whatever the reason for bullying) can be dealt with in healthier ways. Formative consequences and restorative practices hold the youngster accountable, increase awareness, provide insight, help change behavior, and are connected to the crime.
- Getting someone who bullies to accept responsibility is a major goal of successful interventions. It may be accomplished by having the student complete the Understanding My Behavior form (Figure 7.1, page 89) or by verbally answering the questions. A discussion should follow.

  The Attorney General of Delaware developed a 16 page "Bully Workbook" that is completed by those who bully (attorneygeneral.delaware.gov/schools/bullypack.pdf). The objectives are to (a) help offenders think about their actions and its effect on others, (b) correct faulty thinking, and (c) change harmful behaviors.
- Ask if something is bothering the youngster or if he or she is being bullied. Let the child know you want to help. This shows you care.
- Explain prosocial options. It is easier to extinguish an inappropriate behavior if it is replaced by an incompatible behavior. In the case of bullying, antisocial behavior cannot be performed simultaneously with prosocial alternatives.
- Brainstorm amends with the pupil.
- Stand by as the youngster telephones parents to explain how he or she bullied a fellow student and the consequences for the transgression.
- Shift to an attitude of concern. Explain the negative consequences of bullying such as reprimands, detention, loss of privileges, rejection, and decreased popularity.
- Commend popularity and strengths. Point out that the person already has popularity and leadership abilities so it is not necessary to bully. It would be in everyone's best interests to use the power in positive ways.

● Find the function of the bullying. Barbetta, Norona, and Bicard (2005) warn teachers against defining behavior solely by its appearance (e.g., stealing from someone). Those who do will miss the total picture. Observations do not reveal the reasoning behind acts, which is vital information if behavioral change is the goal. According to Barbetta et al., misbehavior occurs either to get something or to avoid something. Discover the purpose of the bullying and remove the payoff or make it too costly to continue. Find prosocial ways to fill needs:

  – Are those who bully rewarded with material possessions? Create rules that prevent theft: (a) Expensive possessions should be left at home, (b) money should not be brought to school, (c) write names on all property using permanent markers, and (d) there should be a "No borrowing rule"—students can no longer say "I was only borrowing it."

  – Do those who aggress seek power and dominance? Channel needs in positive directions. Let those who bully use their leadership abilities to teach skills, lead a class project, help the less fortunate, share anti-bullying information with those in lower grades, or captain a team. Adults should supervise all activities.

  – Is the person who bullies ignorant of social, cultural, physical, or psychological differences? The child and/or class can do a research report or attend a presentation on the topic. Students can be put into the bullied child's shoes with a role playing or simulation exercise.

  – Is bullying seen as fun and entertainment? Empathy training, role playing, and simulation exercises can show that being bullied is not amusing.

  – Is bullying used to alleviate boredom? Boredom can be overcome with quick transitions between activities and classes, assignments for those who finish early, equipment for each child, making learning participatory and interesting, and holding students up to high academic standards.

  – Does bullying fill a need for praise or acceptance? Create a culture that does not reward bullying. Teach students to speak out against abuse, refuse to participate, leave the scene, or get help. Bullying would be passe if popularity, accolades, and approval were not given to those who abuse.

● Build a relationship with the child. Research shows that those with difficult and frustrating behaviors receive less support from educators (Berkowitz & Benbenishty, 2012; Demaray & Malecki, 2003) so teachers need to be especially sensitive to and aware of how they treat students who bully. This is the population that needs the most help from teachers.

  Teacher–student relationships can be the difference between a child going nowhere or one who succeeds in life. Teacher, administrator, and staff development specialist Dennis Loftus uses the "2 by 10" strategy from a program called "Discipline With Dignity." The teacher spends two minutes a day talking to a child for 10 straight days. The educator might ask "How are things going?" "How is your family?" "What did you do last night?" or "Do you have any concerns?" In the beginning, students may be leery and reluctant to respond but they become more receptive as time passes. Short answers become longer when pupils realize the questioner cares. Connections build:

> "If you get a kid who is not carrying out what he said he'd do, instead of chastising the kid, you want to keep a relationship," Loftus says. "'Did you do what you said you'd do? If not, what do you think caused you not to do it? Are you happy with that choice? Did it help you get where you want to go?' You want to be able to teach the kids that life is a series of choices—some are successful, some are unsuccessful."
>
> (Curtis, 2003, 2 by 10 section, para. 1)

Youngsters who aggress will be more willing to listen, cooperate, and change if they share warm relationships with those giving guidance and suggestions. There is a greater chance of influencing troubled children if adults establish rapport *before* they misbehave.

- Give empathy training. Many times those who mistreat others do not realize the consequences of their actions. In the case of ringleaders, it is probably because they lack empathy. In the case of followers, it may be because they never spent a few minutes thinking about the ramifications of their behavior. Ask them how they would feel if they were bullied? How would they feel if their younger or older brother, sister, or cousin were bullied? Interject empathy training and role playing when working with individuals who bully.

- Teach appropriate skills. Those who bully may need work with aggression, expressing feelings, communication, conflict resolution, empathy, social skills, misreading actions, or finding more appropriate ways to get their needs met.

- Involve those who bully in role play. Reverse role play can demonstrate what it is like to be on the receiving end of abuse. Those who aggress can also practice more appropriate ways to respond to frustration, getting needs met, and other causes of bullying. For example, situations can be set up in which a student is annoying or peers pressure the person to bully.

- Thinking errors can contribute to bullying. For instance, a clumsy classmate may accidently knock into a peer. The peer could misinterpret the body contact as an aggressive act and want to "right the wrong." Teaching children to think about the circumstances and intentions before they respond can defuse aggression.

- Teach acceptance of differences. Differences, proclaimed by those who ruthlessly seize power, are used as excuses for bullying. Those who aggress should be challenged in a non confrontational manner.

  Teaching about other cultures and diversity normalizes foreign looks, customs, clothing, interests, languages, and other differences. It is these variations that color our world. Differences should be respected, not attacked.

- Draw up behavior contracts. Behavior contracts are written agreements jointly negotiated and signed by a child and teacher (parent, mentor, coach). They are a form of behavior modification designed to eliminate inappropriate behaviors, replacing them with more appropriate ways of acting. Contracts state the expected behavior, the consequences if unsuccssful, and rewards for achieving the goal. For example, "I will not hit anyone. If I hit someone, I will write an essay on why it is wrong to hit. If I do not hit anyone, I can select a reward from a list."

Behavior contracts encourage children to take responsibility for their behavior. Involving participants in the process increases ownership and cooperation. Chances for success rise if the contract focuses on one or two behaviors, so complex actions should be broken down. The different parts can be goals in future contracts, after previous behaviors are mastered.

---

**Behavior Contract**

Student's Name_____

Beginning Date_____ End Date_____

Goal

_____

Rewards

_____

Consequences

_____

Student's Signature_____

Teacher's Signature_____

Parent's Signature_____

Was the goal met?

|                    | Monday | Tuesday | Wednesday | Thursday | Friday |
|--------------------|--------|---------|-----------|----------|--------|
| Was the goal met?  |        |         |           |          |        |
| Teacher's initials |        |         |           |          |        |
| Parent's initials  |        |         |           |          |        |

*Figure 14.1* Behavior Contract

Rewards can be negotiated. Teachers should provide a list of items or activities they are willing to provide. Prizes should be inexpensive, easy to deliver, and appealing enough to stimulate behavioral change.

It is important to remember that the actions the contract is trying to replace brought some form of reward, are ingrained, and are probably automatic. As such, extinguishing the behavior and replacing it will not be instantaneous. It will take time and there will be setbacks. Praise the efforts as well as the successes. Use reminders to help the child, for example, "Count to 10."

- Connect those who aggress with children who display prosocial behavior. Students with well developed prosocial skills can serve as role models. These pupils are involved in positive activities, so those who bully would also be exposed. It also moves youngsters with poor behavior away from those who reinforce deviant conduct.

- Praise, praise, praise, and praise children even more. Praise little steps and big steps. Praise the efforts, the growth, the successes. Praise in front of the class and in private. Send notes to parents praising their children's progress.

  Praise can also be an effective and compassionate way to let children know their behavior is inappropriate and needs to change. For example, the teacher praises student "A" for following an anti-bullying rule. The praise indirectly tells student "B" that his or her misbehavior is noticed and needs to change. The message is delivered without reprimands or embarassment.

- Teachers can observe students' preferences and use their choices as reinforcers. For example, if a child enjoys free play and does not bully for one day, five extra minutes of this valued activity is awarded.

- Those who bully associate power with control and dominance. Guide these youngsters toward positive definitions of power, such as a leadership position on a team or leading others to correct an injustice. Give examples that demonstrate how power can be used to improve relationships and unsatisfactory conditions.

- Work on building the child's strengths. Take advantage of the student's abilities. Is the child intelligent and a good teacher? Let the youngster teach about bullying. Does the person display leadership ability? Let the pupil create an anti-bullying club or become a member of the safety squad. Does the child like helping others? He or she can become a tutor. Does the pupil enjoy the spotlight? Participating in a play can develop the child's acting and social skills while filling free time with positive projects. Closely supervise all activities.

- Recognize the feelings of those who bully. Ginott tells how one teacher stopped an angry, aggressive, and violent child from fighting. The teacher responded to an altercation by saying, "Juan, you seem angry. I can see by your face that you're very angry." "I sure am," he replied. "When you feel that angry, come to me and tell me about it" (1972, p. 162). The teacher taught Juan to use words instead of fists when angry, by recognizing and validating Juan's feelings instead of reprimanding him for having them.

- Include, rather than exclude. Often, children who misbehave are given time outs or detention, or are expelled for a period of time. This separation deprives them of opportunities to learn or practice appropriate behavior. Instead, consider inserting the child into a group setting that is closely supervised and surrounded with prosocial children. The adult can provide feedback and guidance while peers model healthier ways of socializing.
- Teach kindness with kindness. Another excerpt from Ginott's (1972) book illustrates a creative, concerned, non blaming, and non punitive approach to bullying. In this case, the teacher wanted to end the scapegoating of Andy, a student in her class. She sent a letter to Jay, the ringleader of the bullying:

> Dear Jay,
>
> Andy's mother has told me that her son has been made very unhappy this year. Name-calling and ostracizing have left him sad and lonely. I feel concerned about the situation. Your experience as a leader in your class makes you a likely person for me to turn to for advice. I value your ability to sympathize with those who suffer. Please write me your suggestions about how we can help Andy.
>
> Sincerely,
>
> Your Teacher.
>
> (pp. 167–168)

Jay did not respond but stopped bullying Andy.

- Keep records, for example keep and refer to Figure 7.2: Bullying Incident Report (page 93). If you do, those who aggress will know you take misbehavior seriously. Records can reveal trends in bullying and show successful and unsuccessful interventions. Documentation can also be used as evidence when confronting the child or parents.
- Let those who bully know that school personnel will be told about their misbehavior and will keep a careful eye on them.
- Make referrals, if necessary. Students who continuously bully may require additional support. Mental health professionals can help with anxiety, ADHD, depression, suicidal thoughts, effects of abuse, conduct or personality disorders, and substance abuse. They can also focus on self-esteem, empathy, conflict resolution skills, impulse control, and healthier ways to meet needs.
- Follow up with the youngster. This lets the child know that someone cares. (Crothers & Kolbert, 2008; Garrity, Jens, Porter, Sager, & Short-Camilli,1997; Melissa Institute for Violence Prevention and Treatment, n.d.; Pepler & Craig, 2000; Storey & Slaby, 2008; Van Acker & Talbott, 1999.)

There are not enough hours in the school day to follow all the suggestions. When a bullying incident occurs, teachers should select recommendations that are most applicable and helpful to the individual(s) and situation.

# Chapter 15

# Adult Support

## Teacher Support

Teacher support can buffer some of the ill effects of bullying. Support is like medicine; it counteracts the harm inflicted by enemies, relieves pain, and promotes healing. According to S. Cohen and Wills (1985) there are four types of support:

- *Esteem support*—Letting people know they are valuable, worthy, and accepted despite any difficulties or shortcomings.
- *Informational support*—Assistance in understanding and coping with a problem.
- *Social support*—Spending time with the person. The contact can positively affect mood and provide a distraction from stressful situations.
- *Instrumental support*—Financial aid, material resources, and services.

Teachers can easily provide the four kinds of support. For example, esteem support can be given by helping students identify their strengths, giving genuine praise, pointing out accomplishments, allowing them to vent, validating feelings, accepting them as they are, and letting them know they are not at fault for the bullying. Asking youngsters to help other students can also raise self-esteem. Informational and instrumental support can be given by educating those who are abused about bullying, equipping them with an assortment of strategies, and making referrals to mental health personnel, if required. Social support can be given by spending time with targeted children. It could be a substantial commitment or an extra minute or two while greeting pupils in the morning, walking the child to class, or having lunch together.

Research shows that caring adults can help at risk children overcome adversity. In one study, bullied students "who felt that they had one or more adults to turn to tended to do well, even during the worst bullying" (Seeley et al., 2011, p. 8). That is the motivation behind the "Bully Free: It Starts With Me" campaign by the National

Education Association (NEA). The NEA asks teachers to be that one adult who can make a difference in a bullied child's life. Educators can show their commitment by taking an online pledge (www.nea.org/home/Bullyfree-Take-the-Pledge.html).

## Mentors

Mentors are individuals who develop positive one-on-one relationships with youngsters or at risk children. The mentor can be an adult, young adult, older student, or teen who gives a time and energy commitment to talk, share activities, and be a friend. Children's lives have been changed because of mentoring. Mentored students' academic performance, social skills, and attendance improved as well as behavior and relationships with peers and adults. Their alcohol or drug use and physical abuse diminished.

Can mentoring have an effect on bullying? "The single best predictor for the absence of bullying behavior was having positive adult role models" (Espelage, Bosworth, & Simon, 2000, p. 331).

In one study, high risk children's aggressive behavior declined after three semesters of twice a week lunch dates with mentors. "Lunch Buddy" was a stand-alone program that used untrained college age mentors (Hughes, Cavell, Meehan, Zhang, & Collie, 2005).

Teachers can mentor students if they have the time or inclination. If not, educators can still carve out a few minutes during each day to make connections. For example, they can talk to children before or after class or school, during homeroom, lunch, class meetings, free periods, or advisement times, or during school clubs run by the educator. Teachers can also make arrangements for a child to be mentored by a colleague, adult in the community, senior citizen, or college or older student.

## Parents

Some angrily point their fingers at parents, blaming them for raising youngsters who bully. It is true that parents are children's first teachers and role models and have influence over their offspring's growth and development. However, the actions or inactions of parents are not the only contributory factors in bullying:

> Individual characteristics . . . the actions of peers, teachers and other adults at school, physical characteristics of the school grounds, family factors, cultural characteristics (e.g., race, ethnicity), and even community factors are implicated in the development and maintenance of bullying.
>
> (Espelage & Swearer, 2003, pp. 372–373)

That does not let all parents off the hook because parenting styles and behaviors are imitated by children. Youngsters raised in families that use and endorse violence and model antisocial acts are more likely to display aggressive behavior. Overly permissive parents who provide little supervision and no boundaries can also play a role in bullying. Children who do not receive emotional support from their parents are 7% more likely to bully (Barboza et al., 2009). At the other end of the spectrum, boys who are overprotected and have very close relationships with their mothers or whose fathers are distant have an increased risk of being abused. Girls who have hostile relationships with their mothers also have higher odds of being bullied.

Parents can be key players in social architecture because they are their children's teachers, mentors, and role models. Their words, gestures, actions, and inactions are observed by their children. Offspring repeat the kind, respectful, empathic, and inclusive acts displayed by their parents. Likewise, youngsters also imitate cruel, hurtful, and intimidating behavior.

## Parents as Partners

Parents should be partners in the march against bullying. They should be contacted early in the school year, before bullying occurs, and seen as collaborators who work toward their children's best interests.

Parents should tell their youngsters bullying is not acceptable and ask about bullying activities at school. If their children are bullied, parents should encourage friendship making and find social outlets, improve deficient skills, build self-esteem, keep lines of communication open, and provide non judgmental support. If offspring bully, parents have to let them know it is wrong, assure them that it will not be tolerated, issue effective consequences, and increase supervision. If children are bystanders, parents should explain the responsibility of bystanders and encourage upstander behavior. It is important for parents to be aware of the classroom anti-bullying rules (even better, if they participate in its formulation) and receive timely updates concerning their children's behavior, whether it be positive or negative.

One way teachers can prompt parent–child bullying discussions is by assigning interviews about bullying experiences. Students can ask parents what happened, the role(s) they played, their age, how they felt, and would they act differently now. Bystanders may hear a parent's regret for not intervening or be introduced to new ways of taking action. Those who bully can be sensitized to the harmful effects of bullying. It lets bullied children know they are not the only ones who are picked on and that their parents can be understanding allies.

In addition, parents can be encouraged to become actively involved in anti-bullying efforts by joining committees and modeling appropriate behavior in the classroom and home. Parental ideas and recommendations should be solicited.

Adults can learn about bullying online or in books but busy people have little time to research. The easier it is to obtain information, the more likely parents will become educated. Teachers should talk about bullying during parent–teacher conferences and host informational sessions. Unfortunately, less than one third of parents attend school meetings (Melissa Institute for Violence Prevention and Treatment, n.d.), so anti-bullying brochures, newsletters, and other resources would be helpful adjuncts to in school strategies.

Parents can also be first alert systems because children are more likely to report bullying to their caretakers than to teachers. In one study, 28% of targeted students told a family member; 27% told a friend; 19% told a friend and a family member; 12% told a friend, family member, and teacher; 6% told a family member and a teacher; 5% told a friend and teacher; and 4% only told a teacher (Hunter, Boyle, & Warden, 2004). Keeping lines of communication open helps in the timely disclosure of classroom bullying activity.

Apathy is the biggest hurdle to involvement. Bullying does not usually become an issue until it happens to someone's child. This obstacle may be overcome by sharing prevalence statistics because just about every child is tapped on the back by bullying. If parents do not want their youngster to become a statistic they have to proactively advocate and become involved.

## Anti-bullying Guidelines that Teachers Can Share With Parents

Adults need to be educated before they become an anti-bullying force because present day mothers and fathers are part of the generation that grew up believing bullying myths were as real as apple pie. Many adults want to help but do not know what to say or do. They can be guided through the bullying maze with the outline below. Each point can be supplemented by information contained throughout this book.

*Examine your parenting skills and home life.* Parents are role models for children. What you do, they do. How do you act? Do you hit your children? Are power and violence used in your home to discipline or solve problems? Are siblings allowed to bully each other? Do you put people down because of their looks, culture, race, religion, or sexual orientation? Do you make cruel jokes? Do you criticize or insult family, friends, or strangers? Do you silently watch bullying? Are your children unsupervised? Are you permissive? Are you overprotective? Do you let your children exclude others? If you answered "yes" to any of these questions you may inadvertently contribute to bullying.

*Form strong relationships with your children.* Parents should spend as much time as possible with their children. Relationships develop when people are together. Youngsters will talk about problems, including bullying, if warm and supportive relationships exist.

Play games, attend events (e.g., ballgames, concerts, plays), shop, plan and take vacations together, have outings (e.g., picnics, amusement parks, beach), and do joint projects (e.g., cooking, building) together. Plan interactive activities. Children will be more likely to participate if the pastimes are ones they are interested in and enjoy.

Discussions help parents learn what happens on the trips to and from school, in classrooms and hallways, at lunch, during recess, and at after school activities. Mothers and fathers should also be familiar with their offspring's friends, where they hang out, and if there is supervision.

*Find out about bullying in your child's life.* Keep your eyes and ears open, ask questions, and listen between the lines. Take the initiative. Don't wait for your child to bring up bullying because it might not happen.

Create opportunities for conversations if your youngster finds it difficult to discuss peer on peer abuse. Talk during drives in the car, at meals, and during walks and activities.

If you think your son or daughter is not picked on, think again. Almost 80% of children are bullied sometime during their school careers.

The U.S. Department of Health and Human Services, Substance Abuse and Mental Health Services Administration (SAMHSA) created the "15+ Make Time to Listen . . . Take Time to Talk . . . About Bullying" initiative to help parents begin discussions with their children (http://store.samhsa.gov/shin/content/SMA08-4321/SMA08-4321.pdf).

*Learn the signs of bullying.* Parents can find out if their children are bullied by learning the signs of bullying. The knowledge can lead to early detection and intervention:

- Does your child refuse to go or fear going to school or make up excuses so he or she can stay home? Your child may be trying to elude bullying.
- Does your child have an increasing number of headaches, stomach aches, and illnesses? The stress of bullying can compromise immune systems.
- Does your child complain of feeling sick right before school? Your child may be trying to avoid abuse.
- Does your child appear tired, more so than normal? The stress or injuries associated with bullying may tire out or keep your child up at night.
- Does your child refuse to take the school bus? Your child may fear bullying.
- Does your child want to be driven to and from school? Your child may want to steer clear of bullying.
- Does your child take an unusual route when walking to school? Your child may be trying to bypass high risk areas.
- Does your child come home from school hungry? Lunch or lunch money may have been stolen.
- Does your child come home with torn clothes or damaged possessions, or with possessions missing? The damage or loss may be caused by bullying.
- Does your child have more injuries than normal? He or she could be bullied.
- Does your child run to the bathroom immediately after arriving home? Your child may be afraid to use the school restroom because it is a bullying zone.
- Does your child play indoors after school? Your child may be hiding from neighborhood children who aggress.

- Does your child have friends? Youngsters are often afraid to befriend bullied children because associating with abused peers can make them potential bullying candidates.
- Does your child say "no one likes me" or make similar statements? Youngsters put down, demean, and ostracize the bullied population.
- Does your child cry a lot? Your child may be upset or depressed about bullying.
- Does your child refuse to talk about school or problems? Your child may be embarrassed, fear retaliation, or think telling will make the bullying worse.
- Does your child quickly minimize the page or turn off the computer when you enter the room? Your child may be trying to cover up cyberbullying.
- Does your child appear to be unusually sad? Bullying can lead to depression.
- Does your child appear to be quieter than normal? Your child may be sad or depressed because of bullying.
- Does your child have difficulty sleeping? Injuries or fears of bullying can interfere with sleep.
- Does your child wet the bed? Your child may be regressing to an earlier behavior because he or she is extremely upset or anxious about bullying.
- Does your child display a change in eating habits? An increase or decrease in eating can signal a bullying problem.
- Have your child's grades declined? The drop can be because your son or daughter is skipping classes or has difficulty concentrating.
- Does your child ask for extra money or steal money? Your child may be trying to replace stolen money or possessions.
- Does your child use alcohol or drugs? Your child may be self-medicating his or her pain. Or your child may be trying to get into the "cool" clique thinking that using illegal substances will win entrance into the group.
- Does your child have new friends that you disapprove of? Friendless children may think having any friend is better than having none, even those with antisocial behaviors.

*Educate your children about bullying.* Talk about bullying. Share bullying information from books, the internet, media, newsletters, and presentations. Some valuable discussion topics include the definition of bullying, different types, the dangers of bullying, myths, why people bully, where abuse takes place, differences between normal conflict and bullying, the different roles children take, how to protect oneself, ways to increase empathy, how to include others, ways to deflect peer pressure, the responsibility of bystanders, how onlookers can help, and ways peers can support those who are bullied. Reinforce the school's anti-bullying curriculum.

*Take precautions to prevent cyberbullying:*

- Learn about the internet. Know how to go online and what the internet offers.
- Find out the meaning of acronyms, slang words, and abbreviations youngsters use online and in text messages. Go to:

- www.safesurfingkids.com/chat_room_internet_acronyms.htm
- www.teenchatdecoder.com

- Keep the computer in a common area in your home so usage is monitored by adults.
- Set time limits for online use.
- Check instant message buddy lists and emails. Ask about these cyber friends. Who are they? How do your children know them?
- Familiarize yourself with the websites, blogs, and chat rooms your child visits. Ban potentially dangerous sites.
- Warn against disclosing personal information—names, addresses, phone numbers, schools, and passwords.
- Check your children's online profiles.
- Instruct your children to behave online as they would offline—use proper "netiquette."
- Let children know that annonymity on the internet is not assured. Identities can be traced.
- Give yourself a cyberbullying education.
- Talk to your children about cyberbullying. Were they ever cyberbullied? Do they see cyberbullying going on?
- Contact the internet service provider (ISP) if someone violates their "terms and conditions." (Learn the ISP's rules, regulations, and recommendations.)
- Give your children and their friends the following advice if they are cyberbullied:

  - Do not respond to cyberbullying.
  - Block people who cyberbully.
  - Log off.
  - Set up new email accounts and nicknames, and do not make them common knowledge.
  - Cyberbullying texts, emails, and conversations should be saved as proof.
  - Police should be contacted if safety is threatened.

- Bystanders should speak out against cyberbullying, just as in traditional bullying.
- Create an "I Will Not Cyberbully" contract with your children and have them sign it.

*Report bullying to teachers.* Parents should explain the difference between telling, which helps someone get *out* of trouble or prevents a person from being hurt, and tattling, which gets someone *into* trouble and can hurt him or her. Advocate reporting and follow your own advice. Adults should inform their child's teacher if they learn about a bullying incident. Always ask for your child's permission.

*Encourage children to become upstanders.* Parents should stress each person's responsibility to help others and encourage prosocial behavior. Discuss the different roles children take, how they promote or discourage bullying, and safe ways to help. Being an upstander is not "taking sides." It is the right thing to do.

*Know your child's friends and activities.* Which youngsters do your children associate with? Are they into academics? Sports? Drugs? Bullying? Do they play violent video games? What sites do they visit on the computer? What do they read? Where is their time spent? Are they positive or negative influences on your child?

Parents can learn about their children's peers by supervising, volunteering, observing, listening, questioning, and keeping in touch with their friends' parents. Mothers are often grapevines of useful information.

*Volunteer.* Parents who volunteer at lunch, at recess, in class, on sports teams, and at scouting observe how their children interact with other youngsters, the roles they play, and their friends, strengths, and deficits. Parents can also deter or stop bullying and serve as role models.

*Teach empathy.* Parents can ask children to put themselves into the shoes of others. "How would you feel if . . .?"

Teaching empathy can also be done indirectly. Ask offspring how they think characters on television shows and in the movies feel. How would the child feel in a similar situation? Do the same with current events from newspapers, books, the radio, and the internet. The questions can be impromptu; for example, if someone falls in a store while you are shopping point out the people who watch, laugh, and help. How would your child feel if he or she were the person who fell? What would he or she want bystanders to do?

Parents can role play with their children, too. Set up mock bullying situations with children taking turns playing the person who was bullied, the person who does the bullying, and the bystander. Afterwards, ask how they felt in the different roles.

*Establish household rules that discourage bullying.* These guidelines should be jointly created, discussed, and reinforced:

- Treat everyone with respect and kindness—siblings, family members, friends, visitors, and neighbors.
- Think before you speak or act.
- Put yourself in other people's shoes. Treat others as you want to be treated.
- Include everyone in activities.
- Assist those who are bullied or need help.
- Comfort those who are hurt.
- Tell adults if you cannot stop bullying or see a dangerous situation.

*Develop consequences for breaking rules.* Do not punish. Punishment is punitive and does not teach or change behavior. Instead, use formative consequences. They hold children

## Box 15.1: McGruff SafeGuard

The National Crime Prevention Council offers McGruff SafeGuard, a downloadable computer program that helps parents monitor their child's online activities (www.gomcgruff.com/m/index.asp). Parents are alerted (via email, cell phone, or online) when certain terms (e.g., bullying, swearing, loneliness, violent, sexual, alcohol, drug, dangerous acronyms) come up in emails, chat, instant messages, website visits, or social networks, or when the protected youngster is befriended by unknown people. Once detected, SafeGuard reports suspected internet predators to law enforcement officials and prevents the person in question from communicating with the youngster. The program also eyes search engine phrases, translates "kidspeak" abbreviations and acronyms, allows parents to block specific people from talking to their child, and keeps tabs on the total hours spent online.

In addition, there is a Parental-Control Browser Internet Filter for the iPhone, iPad, and iPod Touch (www.gomcgruff.com/browser/).

Both services are free of charge (National Crime Prevention Council, 2008–2010).

accountable, provide insight, help youngsters realize the impact of their behavior, and teach the correct way to act.

*Convey your love.* You love your child. It is the behavior that you may not like.

## If Your Child is Bullied

Children who are bullied struggle because they are at the short end of a power imbalance. If they were able to handle aggression they would not have been targeted in the first place. Their disadvantaged position is the very reason these youngsters need their parents' help and advocacy.

DO remain calm. Your child is upset and needs your comfort.
DO NOT ignore your child's feelings or minimize the pain.

DO say "I am here for you. You are not alone."
DO NOT let your personal history or issues prevent you from being a supportive partner.

DO commend your child if he or she tells you about a bullying episode. It takes a lot of courage to talk about being bullied.
DO NOT interrogate. Ask "What happened?" and let your son or daughter talk freely.

DO listen and take all accounts of bullying seriously. Youngsters will not seek parents' help unless it is needed.

DO NOT ignore or minimize any reports of bullying. If you do, your youngster will lose an important source of support.

DO validate your children's feelings. They come to you because you are seen as an understanding and compassionate ally.

DO NOT say "They were just fooling around," "Kids will be kids," "Ignore them," "Stay out of his way," "Try to be his friend," "Don't be a wimp," or use similar phrases. It justifies abuse.

DO identify the cause of bullying. Did it occur because extra supervision is needed or school rules are not in place? Is there some way your child contributed?

DO NOT go into attack mode. Yes, someone hurt your child and you want that person to "pay," but emotional reactions will not keep your youngster safe. Objectively assess the situation.

DO assure your child that bullying happens because the people who bully have issues. There is nothing wrong with your youngster.

DO NOT blame your child for the bullying. Blaming revictimizes and you will no longer be seen as a safe person.

DO explore whether your child's actions perpetuate bullying. Is he or she blushing, crying, running away, or handing over valuable possessions? These actions thrill those who aggress and encourage further bullying.

DO NOT eliminate the possibility that your child sustains the abuse. This statement does *not* blame your offspring. Those who aggress have free will and *choose* to bully. This suggestion is given to help parents explore ways to prevent and end the pain.

DO ask "How did you try to stop the bullying?"

DO NOT criticize your child for any strategies that did not work. Every failure is a learning experience. Your child was successful because he or she tried.

DO praise your child's efforts.

DO NOT immediately jump in with solutions if your child is having trouble thinking of effective ways to counter bullying. You do not want to convey the notion that your son or daughter is helpless. If help is needed, brainstorm ideas together and ask your child to select the best solution.

DO make sure all plans are safe.

DO NOT tell your child to "beat up the bully." Aggression raises your youngster's risk of injury.

DO role play strategies. There is a difference between cognition and action. Role play helps with transference.

DO NOT expect children to flawlessly perform new skills without practice.

DO emphasize the importance of assertive body language.

DO NOT let non verbal communication undermine your child's efforts.

DO tell the teacher about bullying, with your child's permission. It is the educator's job to safeguard all students.

DO NOT keep bullying a secret. That is what those who aggress want. Telling stops bullying.

DO make sure your child will be safe in school. Identify a safe adult or place your youngster can go to for help.

DO NOT "velcro" yourself to your offspring. Overprotectiveness can be harmful.

DO help your child develop friendships. Having even one friend can deter bullying.

DO NOT assume your child will naturally develop friendships. If so, he or she would already have friends.

DO teach your youngster to be positive. People are attracted to others who make them feel good. Build a repertoire of one liners (e.g., "Good job." "Great try." "I like your . . .").

DO NOT buy solitary games. Purchase and encourage interactive activities.

DO point out strengths and abilities. When children are beaten up (mentally or physically) their self-esteem takes a hit. Try to build it up.

DO NOT put down your child for any weaknesses.

DO find activities that your child enjoys, is able to do, and can perform successfully.

DO NOT push pastimes you enjoy, if it is not your child's preference. Respect your youngster's personality and individuality.

DO share experiences of being bullied (or a sibling's, friend's, or relative's).

DO NOT let your child think he or she is the only one who is bullied.

DO let your child know he or she has control. Your youngster cannot control the person who aggresses but can control how he or she reacts to mistreatment.

DO NOT say that nothing can be done to stop bullying. If one strategy does not work, try another. If that does not work, take a different approach, and keep trying until the abuse stops.

DO talk to other parents about bullying. If your child is bullied, so are others. Share strategies.

DO NOT confront the parents of those who aggress. They will probably be in denial and can become defensive. In many cases, it makes the situation worse.

DO let your child know your love is unconditional, you will work on this problem together, and you are always available for advice and support.

DO NOT abandon your child because bullying is a difficult or embarrassing topic for you.

DO contact professionals, if needed. This could include enrollment in an assertiveness, social skills, or anti-bullying training class; or visiting a social worker or psychologist to learn skills, express feelings, cope with depression or anxiety, or build self-esteem.

DO NOT think there is something "wrong" with your child, if assistance is needed. There isn't! Do not think there is anything wrong with you, either. The fact that you are reading this means you are a caring, loving parent interested in your child's welfare.

DO realize that the abuse will stop.

DO NOT think bullying will last forever. It is a terrible and trying time but your child *will* get through it. A parent's help and support can make this period a little easier to bear and minimize damage.

## *If Your Child Bullies*

It is critical to remember that bullying is a learned behavior. If bullying is learned, it can be unlearned. Those who aggress should not be seen as "terrible." It is their actions that are inappropriate. Many do not realize the harm they are doing. Others do not know appropriate ways to handle feelings or get their needs met. Some give in to peer pressure, think bullying is fun, abuse out of boredom or habit, believe participation helps them gain acceptance, or copy behavior they see. Determining the cause of bullying can be the starting point for ending it.

Those who bully will profit from their parents' guidance and support.

DO admit your son or daughter is involved in bullying.

DO NOT deny or minimize your child's participation.

DO evaluate your role. You may not realize that you are modeling or encouraging abusive behavior.

DO NOT excuse yourself, without carefully and honestly examining your parenting.

DO increase your children's supervision at home and in the community. Monitor all activities, including television, video games, and computer use.

DO NOT relax your vigilance. Bullying is usually done when supervision is minimal or non existant.

DO create household rules against bullying. Give examples of appropriate and inappropriate behavior.

DO NOT ignore rules or let offenses slide. Doing so condones mistreatment.

DO listen to your child's version of the bullying episode.

DO NOT accept excuses or rationalizations for bullying. There is *never* any acceptable reason for hurting another person. Non aggressive strategies solve problems.

DO ask your child what motived the bullying. Search for reasons behind the behavior.

DO NOT put a bandaid over the problem. It will be a temporary fix.

DO hold your children accountable for their actions.

DO NOT turn a blind eye or try to get your children out of disciplinary measures. You will be enabling antisocial behavior.

DO impose formative consequences that provide insight and teach prosocial behavior.

DO NOT punish.

DO explain the harm done by bullying.

DO NOT say "Kids will be kids." The statement justifies abuse.

DO help children develop empathy. Tell them to think before acting and ask "Will my actions or words hurt someone? If so, is there a better way to achieve my goal?" Ask how they would feel, if bullied.

DO NOT think empathy cannot be taught. It can.

DO explain that there are differences between people. We do not have to like or agree with everyone but should treat all people with respect and kindness.

DO NOT model disrespectful, exclusionary, or hateful behavior.

DO teach prosocial alternatives to antisocial behavior.

DO NOT assume your child knows appropriate ways to act. If that were the case, your youngster would not be bullying.

DO tell your child to avoid bullying situations and ignore comments that can be tempting.

DO NOT forget to teach your offspring how to resist peer pressure.

DO cooperate with your child's teacher and the school.

DO NOT exonerate your youngster or blame misbehavior on the teacher, school, or another student. You will be hurting your child.

DO role play new strategies.

DO NOT assume your child will transfer new skills without practice.

DO re-channel your child's aggression into positive avenues (e.g., sports).

DO NOT let your youngster's poor behavior go unchecked. It needs to be stopped at the earliest possible moment or it can potentially lead to a troublesome future.

DO investigate your child's friends and activities.

DO NOT think that outside influences have no effect on your youngster's behavior. They do.

DO praise and reward good behavior.

DO NOT stereotype your child as a "bad kid" who is beyond help. Misbehavior is the culprit and can change with support and a lot of hard work.

DO reinforce your love.

DO NOT withhold love because your child acts inappropriately.

## When Teachers Need to Talk to the Parents of Children Who Bully

Talking to the parents of those who aggress will not be on a teacher's top 10 list of favorite things to do. The news that their child has bullied is often met with denial, defensiveness, or myths, especially if the behavior was learned at home. However, there are steps teachers can take to make the task a bit easier.

Begin the meeting by talking about the child's strengths, progress, and positive contributions in class. Then, introduce the bullying. Share logs, written reports, and investigations documenting the child's involvement in bullying. It is hard to argue with evidence. Frame the bullying as a concern you have for their youngster. Explain the potential negative consequences of antisocial behavior and the damage that can be done to recipients.

Do not get pulled into a verbal duel if the parents argue about their child's participation in bullying because you will never win. Remain calm and repeat the facts. State the class and school anti-bullying rules and policies. Clearly share expectations and the consequences for current and future infractions. Stress that everyone is on the same team: You all have the common goal of helping their son or daughter. Ask for suggestions because you want to involve parents in the process and because they are the experts on their children.

Unfortunately, some parents are resistant. Teachers must deal with bullying with or without parental assistance.

## When Teachers Need to Talk to the Parents of Children Who Are Bullied

Parents of students who are bullied may be dealing with their child's mental or physical injuries and fears when they meet teachers. They can be angry and want answers or present as secondary victims who feel the pain as if it was inflicted upon them. Parents might be struggling with shame or worry about their child's future. They may question their parenting and inability to protect their youngster. Listen, empathize, and validate the parents' concerns.

Point out the child's strengths and positive qualities. Tell the parents that bullying is not allowed in your clasroom, there are rules and consequences in place, anti-bullying is taught throughout the year (e.g., in the curriculum, circle time), and any misbehavior is stopped immediately. In spite of all these efforts, bullying occurred and is being addressed. Outline classroom and school policies and consequences for bullying and provide whatever information you can without breaking confidentiality.

Right now, you want to brainstorm ways to help their child. Request suggestions. Depending on the particular child, he or she might need to improve or learn assertiveness, socialization, anger and frustration management, friendship, relaxation, anxiety management, communication, self-esteem, or conflict resolution skills. Anti-bullying strategies such as ignoring, avoiding, self-talk, comebacks, body language, and visualization may help. The child might need reassurance, someone to talk to, or a list of safe people and places in the school.

Jointly create a plan, implement it, and keep parents informed.

# Chapter 16

# Closing Comments

## Broken Windows

Social scientist James Q. Wilson and criminologist George Kelling introduced the "Broken Windows" theory in 1982. If a broken window is not fixed more windows will be damaged, the theory contends, because an object left in disrepair sends a signal that no one cares and no one is watching. Fix it and vandalism and other crimes will stop.

The theory was tested in the mid 1980s when the New York City Transit Authority hired Kelling as a consultant. They started by targeting petty crimes such as graffiti and fare beating. All defaced trains were taken off the tracks and not returned to service until they were spotless. When the seemingly innocuous fare beaters were apprehended, police found one in 20 carried weapons and one in seven had an outstanding warrant for crimes (Newman, 2009). In the end, subway crime dropped dramatically.

The "Broken Windows" theory can be applied to bullying. If acts such as pushing, hitting, name calling, exclusion, or disrespect are not immediately condemned, the message sent to children is that no one cares if they hurt students. It says the school is poorly run and children will not be protected. Unchallenged bullying, which essentially sanctions antisocial behavior, spreads like a contagious disease. It leads to more bullying and more dangerous activities. Bullying then becomes socially acceptable.

In contrast, if bullying is arrested when it takes its first breath youngsters loudly hear "We care about you and our school. We will not allow bullying." Schools will then cease to be bullying breeding grounds.

## Box 16.1: Fixing Broken Windows

| Broken windows in the classroom | Fixing broken windows in the classroom |
| --- | --- |
| Teachers disrespect or bully students | Teachers model prosocial behavior |
| No rules against bullying | Clear anti-bullying rules |
| No or ineffective consequences for bullying | Effective consequences for bullying |
| Students have free reign | Teachers vigilantly supervise students |
| Teachers allow or ignore bullying | Teachers immediately stop bullying |
| There are no expectations for behavior | Clear expectations for appropriate behavior |
| Bullying is seen as a rite of passage | Strong "Bullying is wrong" messages |
| Teachers do not commend upstander behavior | Teachers praise anti-bullying behavior |
| No anti-bullying presence | Anti-bullying in curriculum and events |
| Teachers focus on academic performance | Teachers include social emotional learning |
| "Whatever will be, will be" attitude | Teachers build community and connections |
| Teachers allow students to exclude classmates | Teachers promote inclusion |
| Teachers leave friendless children on the sidelines | Teachers encourage participation |
| Teachers let pupils ignore classmates | Peer support and friendship building is encouraged |
| Students are not motivated or challenged to achieve | Teachers expect high achievement |
| Competitive environment | Teachers foster cooperation |
| No collaboration | Whole school, parent, and community involvement |

## Making a Difference

Surgeon General, Dr. Regina Benjamin, concluded her speech at the U.S. Education Department's first Bullying Summit with the following story:

> A young lady was jogging along the beach . . . This older gentleman was tossing a starfish in the water and as she ran she saw him tossing one starfish at a time and by the time she finished her run she said . . . "I can't take it anymore, I need to know." So, she walked up to him and she said "Why are you bothering to toss the starfish into the water? There are hundreds and hundreds of starfish along the beach. As soon as the sun comes up they're all gonna burn out and die . . .

It's not going to make a difference so why do you bother?" So he looked at her, reached down, picked up a starfish and said "because it will make a difference to this starfish," and he tossed it into the water.

We can make a difference by finding our own starfish one at a time. There's so much we can do to help our children live in communities with dignity and without fear.

(Benjamin, 2010)

# References

Aftab, P. (n.d.). *Statistics and a snapshot of cyberbullying trends.* Retrieved January 12, 2012 from http://aftab.com/index.php?page=cyberbullying-statistics.

Alberti, J. (2008). *3 steps to end school violence.* Retrieved June 4, 2011 from http://gse.buffalo.edu/gsefiles/documents/alumni/Fall08_3_Steps_to_End_School_Violence.pdf.

American Psychiatric Association. (2000). *Diagnostic and statistical manual of mental disorders, DSM-IV-TR* (4th ed.). Washington, DC: American Psychiatric Association.

Anti-Bullying Alliance. (2006). *50 ideas for anti-bullying week.* Retrieved May 9, 2012 from http://peacefulschoolsinternational.org/wp-content/uploads/50_ideas_for_anti_bullying_week.pdf.

Anti-Bullying Alliance. (2008). *Tackling bullying in schools: A mapping of approaches.* London, UK: National Children's Bureau. Retrieved November 9, 2011 from www.antibullyingalliance.org.uk/pdf/aba_tackling_bullying_in_schools2.pdf.

Arnold, J. (n.d.,a). *Who is Jaylen?* Retrieved January 12, 2012 from www.jaylenschallenge.org/whois-jaylen.

Arnold, J. (n.d.,b). *Our story.* Retrieved June 4, 2011 from www.jaylenschallenge.org/index.php?option=com_content&view=article&id=54& Itemid=82.

Aronson, E. (2000). *Nobody left to hate: Teaching compassion after Columbine.* New York, NY: W.H. Freeman.

Aronson, E. (2004). How the Columbine High School tragedy could have been prevented. *Journal of Individual Psychology, 60*(4), 355–360.

Arseneault, L., Milne, B.J., Taylor, A., Adams, F., Delgado, K., Caspi, A., et al. (2008). Being bullied as an environmentally mediated contributing factor to children's internalizing problems: A study of twins discordant for victimization. *Archives of Pediatrics & Adolescent Medicine, 162*(2), 145–150, doi: 10.1001/archpediatrics.2007.53.

Arseneault, L., Walsh, E., Trzesniewski, K., Newcombe, R., Caspi, A., & Moffitt, T.E. (2006). Bullying victimization uniquely contributes to adjustment problems in young children: A nationally representative cohort study. *Pediatrics, 118*(1), 130–138, doi: 10.1542/peds.2005-2388.

Associated Press-MTV. (2011). *Executive summary: 2011 AP-MTV digital abuse study.* Retrieved February 2, 2011 from www.athinline.org/pdfs/MTV-AP_2011_Research_Study- Exec_ Summary.pdf.

Atlas, R.S., & Pepler, D. J. (1998). Observations of bullying in the classroom. *The Journal of Educational Research,* 92(2), 86–99, doi: 10.1080/00220679809597580.

Atria, M., Strohmeier, D., & Spiel, C. (2007). The relevance of the school class as social unit for the prevalence of bullying and victimization. *European Journal of Developmental Psychology,* 4(4), 372–387, doi: 10.1080/17405620701554560.

Bacchini, D., Affuso, G., & Trotta, T. (2008). Temperament, ADHD and peer relations among schoolchildren: The mediating role of school bullying. *Aggressive Behavior,* 34(5), 447–459, doi: 10.1002/ab.20271.

Barbetta, P.M., Norona, K.L., & Bicard, D.F. (2005). Classroom behavior management: A dozen common mistakes and what to do instead. *Preventing School Failure,* 49(3), 11–19.

Barboza, G.E., Schiamberg, L.B., Oehmke, J., Korzeniewski, S.J., Post, L.A., & Heraux, C.G. (2009). Individual characteristics and the multiple contexts of adolescent bullying: An ecological perspective. *Journal of Youth and Adolescence,* 38(1), 101–121, doi: 10.1007/s10964-008-9271-1.

Barratt, P., Joy, H., Potter, M., Thomas, G., & Whitaker, P. (n.d.). *Circle of friends.* Retrieved September 7, 2010 from www.leics.gov.uk/autism_circle_of_friends.pdf.

Bauer, N.S., Herrenkohl, T.I., Lozano, P., Rivara, F.P., Hill, K.G., & Hawkins, J.D. (2006). Childhood bullying involvement and exposure to intimate partner violence. *Pediatrics,* 118(2), e235–e242, doi: 10.1542/peds.2005-2509.

BeatBullying. (2010). Bullying accounts for up to 44% of child suicides. Retrieved July 6, 2010 from www.beatbullying.org/dox/media-centre/press-releases/June%202010/bullying-accounts-44percent-suicides.html.

Behaviour4Learning. (2005). *Quality Circles.* Retrieved September 8, 2007 from www. behaviour4learning.ac.uk/viewArticle2.aspx?contentId=10607. (No longer available.)

Benjamin, R. (2010). *Impact of bullying in schools.* Speech at U.S. Education Department Bullying Summit, Washington, DC, August 11. Retrieved September 10, 2010 from www. c-spanvideo.org/program/295011-5.

Beran, T., & Qing, L. (2007). The relationship between cyberbullying and school bullying. *Journal of Student Wellbeing,* 1(2), 15–33.

Berger, K.S. (2007). Update on bullying at school: Science forgotten. *Developmental Review,* 27(1), 90–126, doi: 10.1016/j.dr.2006.08.002.

Berkowitz, R., & Benbenishty, R. (2012). Perceptions of teachers' support, safety, and absence from school because of fear among victims, bullies, and bully-victims. *American Journal of Orthopsychiatry,* 82(1), 67–74, doi: 10.1111/j.1939-0025.2011.01132.x.

Bisenius, J.P. (2005). *Bully-proofing youth.* Presentation, Grove City, OH, August 10.

Bisignano, P., Lockard, K., & Randel, J. (2009). *Classroom meetings: Building relationships and community.* Retrieved April 10, 2010 from www.k12connections.iptv.org/documents/ AntiBully_ClassroomMtgMay09.ppt.

Blanco, J. (2008). *Please stop laughing at us.* Dallas, TX: Benbella Books.

Blum, R.W. (2005). *School connectedness: Improving students' lives.* Baltimore, MD: Johns Hopkins Bloomberg School of Public Health. Retrieved June 6, 2010 from http://cecp.air.org/ download/MCMonographFINAL.pdf.

Bollmer, J.M., Milich, R., Harris, M.J., & Maras, M.A. (2005). A friend in need: The role of friendship quality as a protective factor in peer victimization and bullying. *Journal of Interpersonal Violence,* 20(6), 701–712, doi: 10.1177/0886260504272897.

Borba, M. (2012). *19 signs your child is being bullied and what to do about it.* Retrieved March 30, 2012 from www.character.org/blog/2012/03/19-signs-your-child-is-being-bullied-and-what-to-do-about-it.

Bosworth, K., Espelage, D.L., & Simon, T.R. (1999). Factors associated with bullying behavior in middle school students. *Journal of Early Adolescence*, 19(3), 344–362, doi: 10.1177/0272431699019003003.

Bott, C.J. (2004). *The bully in the book and in the classroom.* Lanham, MD: Scarecrow Press.

Bott, C.J. (2009). *More bullies in more books.* Lanham, MD: Scarecrow Press.

Boulton, M.J. (1993a). Children's abilities to distinguish between playful and aggressive fighting: A developmental perspective. *British Journal of Developmental Psychology*, 11(3), 249–263, doi: 10.1111/j.2044-835X.1993.tb00601.x.

Boulton, M.J. (1993b). A comparison of adults' and children's abilities to distinguish between aggressive and playful fighting in middle school pupils: Implications for playground supervision and behavior management. *Educational Studies*, 19(2), 193–203. In M. Schafer, & P.K. Smith. (1996). Teachers' perceptions of play fighting and real fighting in primary school. *Educational Research*, 38(2), 173–181, doi: 10.1080/0013188960380205.

Bowles, S. (1998). Armed, alienated and adolescent. *USA Today*, March 26. News section, page 9A.

Bradshaw, C.P., Sawyer, A.L., & O'Brennan, L.M. (2007). Bullying and peer victimization at school: Perceptual differences between students and school staff. *School Psychology Review*, 36(3), 361–382.

Bradshaw, C.P., Waasdorp, T.E., O'Brennan, L.M., & Gulemetova, M. (2011). *Findings from the National Education Association's Nationwide Study on Bullying: Teachers' and education support professionals' perspectives.* Washington, DC: National Education Association. Retrieved December 13, 2012 from www.nea.org/assets/img/content/Findings_from_NEAs_Nationwide_Study_of_Bullying.pdf.

Brown, S., & Taylor, K. (2008). Bullying, education and earnings: Evidence from the National Child Development Study. *Economics of Education Review*, 27(4), 387–401, doi: 10.1016/j.econedurev.2007.03.003.

Brown, W.H., Odom, S.L., & Conroy, M.A. (2001). An intervention hierarchy for promoting young children's peer interactions in natural environments. *Topics in Early Childhood Special Education*, 21(3), 162–175, doi: 10.1177/027112140102100304.

Browning, L., Davis, B., & Resta, V. (2000). What do you mean "Think before I act?" Conflict resolution with choices. *Journal of Research in Childhood Education*, 14(2), 232–238.

Bruce, M.A., & Shade, R.A. (1996). Classroom-tested guidance activities for promoting inclusion. *School Counselor*, 43(3), 224–231.

Buhs, E.S., & de Guzman, M. (2007). *Bullying and victimization: What adults can do to help.* Retrieved September 10, 2011 from www.extension.unl.edu/c/document_library/get_file?folderId=221677&name=DLFE-3202.pdf.

Bully Police U.S.A. (n.d.). The School Rules the Bullies Award. Retrieved July 18, 2012 from www.bullypolice.org/schoolRULES.html.

Bystanders: Passive or active? (2009). *The Ouch Files*, 1(2). Retrieved January 4, 2011 from www.ouchthatstereotypehurts.com/OUCH_Files/Archives/OUCH_Vol1No2.html.

Card, N.A., & Hodges, E.V.E. (2008). Peer victimization among schoolchildren: Correlations, causes, consequences, and considerations in assessment and intervention. *School Psychology Quarterly*, 23(4), 451–461, doi: 10.1037/a0012769.

Carns, A.W. (1996). School bus safety: A peer helper program with a career development focus. *Elementary School Guidance and Counseling*, 30(3), 213.

Caruso, K. (n.d.). *Suicide warning signs.* Retrieved March 13, 2012 from www.suicide.org/suicide-warning-signs.html.

Castle, K., & Rogers, K. (1993). Rule-creating in a constructivist classroom community. *Childhood Education,* 70(2), 77–80.

CBC News Online. (2005). Sticks, stones and bullies. *CBC News,* March 23. Retrieved from www.cbc.ca/news/background/bullying.

CBC News Online. (2007). Bullied student tickled pink by schoolmates' t-shirt campaign. *CBC News,* September 19. Retrieved August 4, 2009 from www.cbc.ca/news/canada/nova-scotia/story/2007/09/18/pink-tshirts-students.html.

Centers for Disease Control and Prevention. (2010). *Youth risk behavior surveillance United States, 2009.* Morbidity and Mortality Weekly Report, 2010; 59(SS-5). Retrieved December 12, 2011 from www.cdc.gov/mmwr/pdf/ss/ss5905.pdf.

Centre for Justice & Reconciliation. (2008). *What is restorative justice?* Retrieved January 10, 2010 from www.pfi.org/cjr/restorative-justice/introduction-to-restorative-justice-practice-and-outcomes/briefings/what-is-restorative-justice.

Chang, L. (2003). Variable effects of children's aggression, social withdrawal, and prosocial leadership as functions of teacher beliefs and behaviors. *Child Development,* 74(2), 535–548, doi: 10.1111/1467-8624.7402014.

Chapell, M.S., Hasselman, S.L., Kitchin, T., Lomon, S.N., MacIver, K.W., & Sarullo, P.L. (2006). Bullying in elementary school, high school, and college. *Adolescence,* 41(164), 633–648.

Cillessen, A.H.N., & Mayeux, L. (2004). From censure to reinforcement: Developmental changes in the association between aggression and social status. *Child Development,* 75(1), 147–163, doi: 10.1111/j.1467-8624.2004.00660.x.

Cohen, E.G., & Lotan, R.A. (1995). Producing equal-status interaction in the heterogeneous classroom. *American Educational Research Journal,* (32)1, 99–120.

Cohen, M.A., & Piquero, A.R. (2009). New evidence on the monetary value of saving a high risk youth. *Journal of Quantitative Criminology,* 25(1), 25–49, doi: 10.1007/s10940-008-9057-3.

Cohen, S., & Wills, T.A. (1985). Stress, social support, and the buffering hypothesis. *Psychological Bulletin,* 98(2), 310–357, doi: 10.1037/0033-2909.98.2.310.

Coloroso, B. (2003). *The bully, the bullied, and the bystander.* New York, NY: Harper Resource.

Colvin, G., Sugai, G., Good, R.H., & Lee, Y. (1997). Using active supervision and precorrection to improve transition behaviors in an elementary school. *School Psychology Quarterly,* 12(4), 344–363.

Cook, C.R., Williams, K.R., Guerra, N.G., & Kim, T.E. (2010). Variability in the prevalence of bullying and victimization: A cross-national and methodological analysis. In S.R. Jimerson, S.M. Swearer, & D.L. Espelage (Eds.), *Handbook of bullying in schools: An international perspective* (pp. 347–362). New York, NY: Routledge.

Council on Scientific Affairs. (2002). Report 1 of the Council on Scientific Affairs (A-02), *Bullying behaviors among children and adolescents.* (Reference Committee D). Retrieved October 23, 2007 from www.ama-assn.org/ama/pub/category/14312.html. (No longer available.)

Cowie, H., & Hutson, N. (2005). Peer support: A strategy to help bystanders challenge school bullying. *Pastoral Care in Education,* 23(2), 40–44, doi: http://dx.doi.org/10.1111/j.0264-3944.2005.00331.x.

Cowie, H., & Sharp, S. (1994). How to tackle bullying through the curriculum. In S. Sharp, & P.K. Smith (Eds.), *Tackling bullying in your schools* (pp. 41–78). London, UK: Routledge.

Craig, W.M., & Pepler, D.J. (1997). Observations of bullying and victimization in the school yard. *Canadian Journal of School Psychology*, 13(2), 41–60, doi: 10.1177/082957359801300205.

Craig, W.M., & Pepler, D.J. (2003). Identifying and targeting risk for involvement in bullying and victimization. *Canadian Journal of Psychiatry*, (48)9, 577–582.

Craig, W.M., Pepler, D.J., & Atlas, R. (2000). Observations of bullying in the playground and in the classroom. *School Psychology International*, 12(1), 22–36, doi: 10.1177/014303 4300211002.

Crick, N.R., & Dodge, K.A. (1999). Superiority is in the eye of the beholder: A comment on Sutton, Smith, and Swettenham. *Social Development*, 8(1), 128–131, doi: 10.1111/1467-9507.00084.

Crothers, L.M., & Kolbert, J.B. (2008). Tackling a problematic behavior management issue: Teachers' intervention in childhood bullying problems. *Intervention in School and Clinic*, 43(3), 132–139, doi: 10.1177/1053451207311606.

Curtis, D. (2003). *10 tips for creating a caring school*. The George Lucas Educational Foundation. Retrieved May 9, 2009 from njbullying.org/documents/10TipsforCreatingaCaringSchool. doc.

Curwen, T., McNichol, J.S., & Sharpe, G.W. (2011). The progression of bullying from elementary school to university. *International Journal of Humanities and Social Science*, 1(13), 47–54.

David-Ferdon, C., & Hertz, M.F. (2009). *Electronic media and youth violence: A CDC issue brief for researchers*. Atlanta, GA: Centers for Disease Control. Retrieved September 19, 2010 from www.cdc.gov/violenceprevention/pdf/Electronic_Aggression_Researcher_Brief-a.pdf.

Davis, S. (with Davis, J.). (2007). *Empowering bystanders in bullying prevention*. Champaign, IL: Research Press.

Davis, S., & Nixon, C. (2010a). *The Youth Voice Project*. Retrieved November 6, 2011 from www.youthvoiceproject.com/YVPMarch2010.pdf.

Davis, S., & Nixon, C. (2010b). *Youth Voice Project national data set*. Retrieved November 6, 2011 from www.youthvoiceproject.com/YVPNationalData%20.pdf.

Dell'Angela, T. (2001). Teaching the buddy system. *Chicago Tribune*, April 11. Retrieved February 4, 2009 from http://articles.chicagotribune.com/2001-04-11/news/0104110228_ 1_kids-academic-achievement-4th-and-5th-graders.

Delpit, L. (1995). *Other people's children*. New York, NY: The New Press.

Demaray, M.K., & Malecki, C.K. (2003). Perceptions of the frequency and importance of social support by students classified as victims, bullies, and bully/victims in an urban middle school. *School Psychology Review*, 32(3), 471–489.

Dewar, G. (2009). *Teaching empathy: Evidence-based tips for fostering empathy in children*. Retrieved September 6, 2011 from www.parentingscience.com/teaching-empathy-tips.html.

Dinkes, R., Kemp, J., Baum, K., & Synder, T.D. (2009). *Indicators of school crime and safety: 2009* (NCES 2010–012/NCJ 228478). Retrieved June 4, 2010 from http://bjs.ojp.usdoj.gov/ content/pub/pdf/iscs09.pdf.

Dishion, T.J., McCord, J., & Poulin, P. (1999). When interventions harm. Peer groups and problem behavior. *American Psychologist*, 54(9), 755–764, doi: 10.1037/0003-066X.54.9.755.

Doll, B., Song, S., & Siemers, E. (2004). Classroom ecologies that support or discourage bullying. In D.L. Espelage, & S.M. Swearer (Eds.), *Bullying in American schools: A social-ecological perspective on prevention and intervention* (pp. 161–183). Mahwah, NJ: Lawrence Erlbaum.

Doll, B., Zucker, S., & Brehm, K. (1999). Reliability and validity of Class Maps. A poster presentation at the annual convention of the National Association of School Psychologists, Las Vegas, NV, April. In B. Doll, S. Song, & E. Siemers. (2004). Classroom ecologies that support or discourage bullying. In D.L. Espelage, & S.M. Swearer (Eds.), *Bullying in American schools: A social-ecological perspective on prevention and intervention* (pp. 161–183). Mahwah, NJ: Lawrence Erlbaum.

Due, P., Holstein, B.E., Lynch, J., Diderichsen, F., Gabhain, S.N., Scheidt, P. et al. (2005). Bullying and symptoms among school-aged children: International comparative cross sectional study in 28 countries. *European Journal of Public Health*, 15(2), 128–132, doi: 10.1093/eurpub/cki105.

Duncan, A. (2010). *Education secretary remarks on anti-bullying efforts*. Speech at U.S. Education Department Bullying Summit, Washington, DC, August 11. Retrieved September 4, 2010 from www.c-spanvideo.org/program/295011-1.

Duncan, R.D. (2011). Family relationships of bullies and victims. In D.L. Espelage, & S.M. Swearer (Eds.), *Bullying in North American schools*, 2nd ed. (pp. 191–204). New York, NY: Routledge.

Elliott, M. (2002). *Bullying pays! A survey of young offenders*. Retrieved April 15, 2009 from www.kidscape.org.uk/assets/downloads/ksyoungoffenders.pdf.

Ellis, L.A., Marsh, H.W., Craven, R.G., & Richards, G.E. (2003). *Peers helping peers: The effectiveness of a peer support program in enhancing self concept and other desirable outcomes*. Paper presented at the New Zealand Association for Research in Education and the Association for Active Educational Researchers (NZARE AARE), Auckland, NZ, November. Retrieved May 4, 2009 from www.aare.edu.au/03pap/ell03779.pdf.

Emmett, J.D., & Monsour, F. (1996). Open classroom meetings: Promoting peaceful schools. *Elementary School Guidance & Counseling*, 31(1), 3–10.

Espelage, D.L. (2010). Remark made during *Education secretary remarks on anti-bullying efforts*. Speech at the U.S. Education Department Bullying Summit, Washington, DC, August 11. Retrieved September 5, 2010 from www.c-spanvideo.org/program/295011-1.

Espelage, D.L., Bosworth, K., & Simon, T.R. (2000). Examining the social context of bullying behaviors in early adolescence. *Journal of Counseling and Development*, 78(3), 326–333, doi: 10.1002/j.1556-6676.2000.tb01914.x.

Espelage, D.L., Green Jr., H.D., & Wasserman, S. (2008). *Statistical estimation of friendship patterns and bullying behaviors among youth* (Technical Report 08-02). Bloomington, IN: Indiana State University. Retrieved July 9, 2009 from www.stat.indiana.edu/files/TR/TR-08-02.pdf.

Espelage, D.L., & Swearer, S.M. (2003). Research on school bullying and victimization: What have we learned and where do we go from here? *School Psychology Review*, 32(3), 365–383.

Faherty, C. (n.d.). *Understanding friends: A program to educate children about differences, and to foster empathy*. Retrieved October 28, 2011 from www.aspergersyndrome.org/Articles/Understanding-Friends-A-program-to- educate-childre.aspx.

Faris, R., & Felmlee, D. (2011a). *Social networks and aggression at the Wheatley School*. Retrieved June 24, 2012 from http://i2.cdn.turner.com/cnn/2011/images/10/10/findings.from.the.wheatley.school.pdf.

Faris, R., & Felmlee, D. (2011b). Status struggles: Network centrality and gender segregation in same- and cross-gender aggression. *American Sociological Review*, 76(1)48–73, doi: 10.1177/0003122410396196.

Farmer, T.W., Goforth, J.B., Hives, J., Aaron, A., Jackson, F., & Sgammato, A. (2006). Competence enhancement behavior management. *Preventing School Failure*, 50(3), 39–44, doi: 10.3200/PSFL.50.3.39-44.

Farmer, T.W., Petrin, R.A., Robertson, D.L., Fraser, M.W., Hall, C.M., Day, S.H. et al. (2010). Peer relations of bullies, bully-victims, and victims: The two social worlds of bullying in second-grade classrooms. *Elementary School Journal*, 110(3), 364–392, doi: 10.1086/648983.

Farrington, D.P., & Ttofi, M.M. (2011). Bullying as a predictor of offending, violence and later life outcomes. *Criminal Behaviour*, 21(2), 90–98, doi: 10.1002/cbm.801.

Fekkes, M., Pijpers, F.I.M., Fredriks, A.M., Vogels, T., & Verloove-Vanhorick, S.P. (2006). Do bullied children get ill or do ill children get bullied? A prospective cohort study on the relationship between bullying and health-related symptoms. *Pediatrics*, 117(5), 1568–1574, doi: 10.1542/peds.2005-0187.

Fekkes, M., Pijpers, F.I.M., & Verloove-Vanhorick, S.P. (2004). Bullying behavior and associations with psychosomatic complaints and depression in victims. *Journal of Pediatrics*, 144(1), 17–22, doi: 10.1016/j.jpeds.2003.09.025.

Feshbach, N.D. (1983). Learning to care: A positive approach to child training and discipline. *Journal of Clinical Child Psychology*, 12(3), 266–271, doi: 10.1080/15374418309533142.

Festinger, L., Pepitone A., & Newcomb, T. (1952). Some consequences of deindividuation in a group. *Journal of Abnormal and Social Psychology*, 47(2, Suppl), 382–389.

Findlay, L.C., Girardi, A., & Coplan, R.J. (2006). Links between empathy, social behavior, and social understanding in early childhood. *Early Childhood Research Quarterly*, 21(3), 347–359, doi: 10.1016/j.ecresq.2006.07.009.

Fiscella, K., & Franks, P. (2004). Should years of schooling be used to guide treatment of coronary risk factors? *Annals of Family Medicine*, 2(5), 469–473.

Fleming, L.C., & Jacobsen, K.H. (2009). Bullying and symptoms of depression in Chilean middle school students. *Journal of School Health*, 79(3), 130–137, doi 10.1111/j.1746-1561.2008.0397.x.

Floyd, N.M. (1987). Terrorism in the schools. *School Safety*, 22–25.

Fosse, G.K. (2006). *Mental health of psychiatric outpatients bullied in childhood*. Doctoral thesis, Department of Neuroscience, Faculty of Medicine, Norwegian University of Science and Technology, Trondheim.

Freedman, J.S. (2002). *Easing the teasing*. New York, NY: Contemporary Books.

Friendly Schools and Families. (n.d.). *I know bullying is going on*. Retrieved December 14, 2011 from www.friendlyschools.com.au/students/bystander.php.

Froschl, M., & Gropper, N. (1999). Fostering friendships, curbing bullying. *Educational Leadership*, 56(8), 72–75.

Fuller, D. (2008). The school bully: Does it run in the family? *University of Cincinnati News*, August 4. Retrieved September 5, 2008 from www.uc.edu/News/NR.aspx?ID=8699.

Garrett, N. (2009). SCHS students form club to combat bullying. *San Clemente Times*, (4)3, June 3. Retrieved October 9, 2011 from http://sanclementetimes.com/view/full_story/6697866/article-SCHS-Students-Form-Club-to-Combat-Bullying.

Garrity, C., Jens, K., Porter, W.W., Sager, N., & Short-Camilli, C. (1997). Bully proofing your school: Creating a positive climate. *Intervention in School & Clinic*, 32(4), 235–243, doi: 10.1177/105345129703200407.

Gay, Lesbian & Straight Education Network. (2009). *The experiences of lesbian, gay, bisexual and transgender middle school students* (GLSEN Research Brief). New York, NY: Gay, Lesbian & Straight Education Network.

Gibbs, N., Roche, T., Goldstein, A., Harrington, M., & Woodbury, R. (1999). The Columbine tapes. *Time Magazine*, December 20, 154(25), 40–52.

Gini, G., Albiero, P., Benelli, B., & Altoe, G. (2007). Does empathy predict adolescents' bullying and defending behavior? *Aggressive Behavior*, 33(5), 467–476, doi: 10.1002/ab.20204.

Gini, G., & Pozzoli, T. (2009). Association between bullying and psychosomatic problems: A meta-analysis. *Pediatrics*, 123(3), 1059–1065, doi: 10.1542/peds.2008-1215.

Ginott, H.G. (1972). *Teacher and child*. New York, NY: Macmillan.

Gladstone, G.L., Parker, G.B., & Malhi, G.S. (2006). Do bullied children become anxious and depressed adults? A cross-sectional investigation of the correlates of bullying and anxious depression. *Journal of Nervous and Mental Disease*, 194(3), 201–208, doi: 10.1097/01.nmd.0000202491.99719.c3.

Goldbaum, S., Craig, W.M., Pepler, D., & Connolly, J. (2003). Developmental trajectories of victimization: Identifying risk and protective factors. *Journal of Applied School Psychology*, 19(2), 139–156.

Goleman, D. (1993). Scientist at work: Ervin Staub; studying the pivotal role of bystanders. *The New York Times*, June 22. Retrieved June 3, 2007 from www.nytimes.com/1993/06/22/science/scientist-at-work-ervin-staub-studying-the- pivotal-role-of-bystanders.html?pagewanted=all.

Gonzalez, L., Brown, M.S., & Slate, J.R. (2008). Teachers who left the teaching profession: A qualitative understanding. *The Qualitative Report*, 13(1), 1–11.

Goodstein, P.K. (2008). *200+ ready-to-use reproducible activity sheets that help educators take a bite out of bullying*. Warminster, PA: Marco Products.

Goodstein, P.K., & Verdick, E. (2012). *Bystander power: Now with anti-bullying action*. Minneapolis, MN: Free Spirit.

Govender, P. (2008). Our kids are being bullied to death. *Times Live*, April 6. Retrieved August 21, 2011 from http://ramonthomas.com/2008/04/our-kids-are-being-bullied-to-death.

Greenbaum, S. (with Turner, B., & Stephens, R.D.). (1988). *Set straight on bullies*. Malibu, CA: National School Safety Center. Retrieved July 6, 2010 from www.eric.ed.gov/PDFS/ED312744.pdf.

Greene, B. (2001). "Why weren't you his friends?" *Jewish World Review*, March 19. Retrieved September 19, 2011 from www.jewishworldreview.com/bob/greene031901.asp.

Gronlund, N.E. (1959). *Sociometry in the classroom*. New York, NY: Harper & Brothers.

Gundlach, M. (2009). *What is it like to have a disability?* Retrieved June 14, 2012 from www.brighthub.com/education/k-12/articles/14783.aspx.

Haber, J.D. (2006). Successful bully prevention and management isn't rocket science. *Camping Magazine*, 79(2).

Haff, S. (2009). The bully play: Using the arts to engage students in bully prevention. *School Climate Matters*, 3(3), 1–2.

Haffner, C., McDougall, P., & Vaillancourt, T. (2007). What factors are associated with early adolescents' willingness to intervene in bullying episodes? Poster presented at the biennial meeting of the Society for Research in Child Development in Boston, MA. In P. McDougall (2007), Bullying in context: Why do they stand by and when will they stand up? *Education Letter* (Fall/Winter). Retrieved December 14, 2011 from http://educ.queensu.ca/alumni/letter/issues/QueensEducationLetterFallWinter07.pdf.

Hamarus, P., & Kaikkonen, P. (2008). School bullying as a creator of pupil peer pressure. *Educational Research*, 50(4), 333–345, doi: 10.1080/00131880802499779.

Hawker, D.S.J., & Boulton, M.J. (2000). Twenty years' research on peer victimization and psychosocial maladjustment: A meta-analytic review of cross-sectional studies. *Journal of Child Psychology and Psychiatry*, 41(4), 441–455, doi: 10.1111/1469-7610.00629.

Hawkins, D.L., Pepler, D.J., & Craig, W.M. (2001). Naturalistic observations of peer interventions in bullying. *Social Development*, 10(4), 512–527, doi: 10.1111/1467- 9507.00178.

Haynie, D.L., Nansel, T., Eitel, P., Crump, A.D., Saylor, K., Yu, K. et al. (2001). Bullies, victims, and bully/victims: Distinct groups of at-risk youth. *The Journal of Early Adolescence*, 21(1), 29–49, doi: 10.1177/0272431601021001002.

Hazler, R.J. (2000). When victims turn aggressors: Factors in the development of deadly school violence. *Professional School Counseling*, (4)2, 105–112.

Hazler, R.J., & Carney, J.V. (2002). Empowering peers to prevent youth violence. *Journal of Humanistic Counseling, Education and Development*, 41(2), 129–149, doi: 10.1002/j.2164-490X.2002.tb00137.x.

Heirman, W., & Walrave, M. (2008). Assessing concerns and issues about the mediation of technology in cyberbullying. *Cyberpsychology: Journal of Psychosocial Research on Cyberspace*, 2(2), 1–12.

Henry, D., Guerra, N., Huesmann, R.L., Tolan, P., VanAcker, R., & Eron, L. (2000). Normative influences on aggression in urban elementary school classrooms. *American Journal of Community Psychology*, 28(1), 59–81, doi: 10.1023/A:1005142429725.

Hinduja, S., & Patchin, J.W. (2009). *Bullying beyond the schoolyard*. Thousand Oaks, CA: Corwin.

Hinduja, S., & Patchin, J.W. (2010). Bullying, cyberbullying, and suicide. *Archives of Suicide Research*, 14(3), 206–221. Retrieved July 5, 2012 from www.touro.edu/EDGRAD/EAC/docs/Hinduja_Article_2010.pdf.

Hirschstein, M.K., Van Schoiack Edstrom, L., Frey, K.S., Snell, J.L., & MacKenzie, E.P. (2007). Walking the talk in bullying prevention: Teacher implementation variables related to initial impact of the Steps to Respect program. *School Psychology Review*, 36(1), 3–21.

Hittie, M. (2000, June). *Building community in the classroom*. International Educational Summit. Detroit, MI. Retrieved from www.wholeschooling.net/WS/WSPress/CommBldgMH.pdf.

Hodges, E.V.E., Boivin, M., Vitaro, F., & Bukowski, W.M. (1999). The power of friendship: Protection against an escalating cycle of peer victimization. *Developmental Psychology*, 35(1), 94–101, doi: 10.1037//0012-1649.35.1.94.

Hodges, E.V.E., Malone, M.J., & Perry, D.G. (1997). Individual risk and social risk as interacting determinants of victimization in the peer group. *Developmental Psychology*, 33(6), 1032–1039, doi: 10.1037//0012-1649.33.6.1032.

Holt, M., Keyes, M., & Koenig, B. (2011). Teachers' attitudes toward bullying. In D. Espelage, & S.M. Swearer (Eds.), *Bullying in North American schools*, 2nd ed. (pp. 119–131). New York, NY: Routledge.

Hoover, J.H., Oliver, R., & Hazler, R.J. (1992). Bullying: Perceptions of adolescent victims in the midwestern USA. *School Psychology International*, 13(1), 5–16, doi: 10.1177/01430343 92131001.

Huesmann, L.R., Eron, L.D., Lefkowitz, M.M., & Walder, L. (1984). Stability of aggression over time and generations. *Developmental Psychology*, 20(6), 1120–1134, doi: 10.1037/0012-1649.20.6.1120.

Hughes, J.N., Cavell, T.A., Meehan, B.T., Zhang, D., & Collie, C. (2005). Adverse school context moderates the outcomes of selective interventions for aggressive children. *Journal of Consulting and Clinical Psychology*, 73(4), 731–736, doi: 10.1037/0022-006X.73.4.731.

Humphrey, J.L., Storch, E.A., & Geffken, G.R. (2007). Peer victimization in children with attention-deficit hyperactivity disorder. *Journal of Child Health Care*, 11(3), 248–260, doi: 10.1177/1367493507079571.

Hunter, S.C., Boyle, J.M.E., & Warden, D. (2004). Help seeking amongst child and adolescent victims of peer-aggression and bullying: The influence of school-stage, gender, victimisation, appraisal, and emotion. *British Journal of Educational Psychology*, 74(3), 375–390, doi: 10.1348/0007099041552378.

Hymel, S., Av-Gay, H., & Darwich, L. (2009). Schoolyard humour: Funny how it hurts. Personal communication with Mike Maxell, September 24, 2008. In W. Craig, D. Pepler, &

J. Cummings (Eds.), *Rise up for respectful relationships: Prevent bullying.* PREVNet Series, Volume 2 (pp. 19–36). Kingston, Canada: PREVNet.

Hymel, S., Rocke-Henderson, N., & Bonanno, R. (2005). Moral disengagement: A framework for understanding bullying among adolescents. In O. Aluede, A.G. McEachern, & M.C. Kenny (Eds.), *Journal of Social Sciences,* Special Issue (8), 1–11.

Jablon, S. (n.d.). *Ten ways to build community in your classroom.* Retrieved February 4, 2011 from www.lookstein.org/articles/ten_ways.htm.

Jamie Isaacs Foundation for Anti-Bullying. (2010). *About us.* Retrieved March 13, 2012 from www.jamieisaacsfoundation.org/about.html.

Janson, G.R., Carney, J.V., Hazler, R.J., & Oh, I. (2009). Bystanders' reactions to witnessing repetitive abuse experiences. *Journal of Counseling and Development,* (87) 3, 319–326, doi: 10.1002/j.1556-6678.2009.tb00113.x.

Jenkins, C. (2007). Bullying costs school $4m. *St. Petersburg Times,* October 23. Retrieved January 10, 2012 from www.sptimes.com/2007/10/23/news_pf/Hillsborough/Bullying_costs_school.shtml.

Jiang, D., Walsh, M., & Augimeri, L.K. (2011). The linkage between childhood bullying behaviour and future offending. *Criminal Behaviour,* 21(2), 128–135, doi: 10.1002/cbm.803.

Johnson, D.W., Johnson, R.T., & Holubec, E. (Eds.). (2008). Cooperative learning and preventing bullying. *The Cooperative Link,* 23(1), March.

Johnson, D.W., Johnson, R.T., & Stanne, M.B. (2000). *Cooperative learning methods: A meta-analysis.* Minneapolis, MN: University of Minnesota.

Johnson, R.T., & Johnson, D.W. (1994). *An overview of cooperative learning.* Retrieved October 14, 2011 from http://clearspecs.com/joomla15/downloads/ClearSpecs69V01_Overview%20of%20Coop erative%20Learning.pdf.

Josephson Institute. (2011). *Josephson Institute's 2010 report card on the ethics of American youth.* Retrieved July 17, 2012 from http://charactercounts.org/programs/reportcard.

Juvonen, J., Graham, S., & Schuster, M.A. (2003). Bullying among young adolescents: The strong, the weak, and the troubled. *Pediatrics,* 112(6), 1231–1237, doi: 10.1542/peds.112.6.1231.

Juvonen, J., Wang, Y., & Espinoza, G. (2011). Bullying experiences and compromised academic performance across middle school grades. *Journal of Early Adolescence,* 31(1), 152–173, doi: 10.1177/0272431610379415.

Kaltiala-Heino, R., Rimpela, M., Rantanen, P., & Rimpela, A. (2000). Bullying at school: An indicator of adolescents at risk for mental disorders. *Journal of Adolescence,* 23(6), 661–674, doi: 10.1006/jado.2000.0351.

Kamps, D.M., & Kay, P. (2002). Preventing problems through social skills instruction. In B. Algozzine, & P. Kay (Eds.), *Preventing problem behaviors: A handbook of successful prevention strategies* (pp. 31–84). Thousand Oaks, CA: Corwin.

Kelly, K. (2004). Students explore living with a disability. *The Catholic Key,* December 3.

Keltner, D., & Marsh, J. (2006–2007). We are all bystanders. *The Greater Good,* (Fall/Winter). Retrieved August 11, 2011 from http://greatergood.berkeley.edu/article/item/we_are_all_bystanders/#.

Kentucky Adult Education. (n.d.). *Building community in the classroom to support learner persistence: A summary of strategies.* Retrieved June 3, 2012 from www.kyae.ky.gov/NR/rdonlyres/4A209125-3C3A-4107-BAFB CAFA3887C56C/0/StrategiestoBuildCommunityintheClassroom.doc.

Kidscape. (2010). *Possible signs of bullying.* Retrieved March 24, 2012 from www.kidscape.org.uk/parents/signsof.shtml.

Kim, M.J., Catalano, R.F., Haggerty, K.P., & Abbott, R.D. (2011). Bullying at elementary school and problem behaviour in young adulthood: A study of bullying, violence and substance use from age 11 to age 21. *Criminal Behaviour*, 21(2), 136–144, doi: 10.1002/cbm.804.

Kim, Y.S., Leventhal, B.L., Koh, Y.J., & Boyce, W.T. (2009). Bullying increased suicide risk: Prospective study of Korean adolescents. *Archives of Suicide Research*, 13(1), 15–30, doi: 10.1080/13811110802572098.

Kim, Y.S., Leventhal, B.L., Koh, Y.J., Hubbard, A., & Boyce, W.T. (2006). School bullying and youth violence: Causes or consequences of psychopathologic behavior? *Archives of General Psychiatry*, 63(9), 1035–1041, doi: 10.1001/archpsyc.63.9.1035.

KindActs. (2000). An interview with . . .Tania Walker. (2000). *The Kindness Connection*. Retrieved February 17, 2012, from www.kindacts.net/media/January00schools.pdf.

Klomek, A.B., Marrocco, F., Kleinman, M., Schonfeld, I.S., & Gould, M.S. (2007). Bullying, depression, and suicidality in adolescents. *Journal of the American Academy of Child & Adolescent Psychiatry*, 46(1), 40–49, doi: 10.1097/01.chi.0000242237.84925.18.

Klomek, A.B., Sourander, A., & Gould, M. (2010). The association of suicide and bullying in childhood to young adulthood: A review of cross-sectional and longitudinal research findings. *Canadian Journal of Psychiatry*, 55(5), 282–288.

Klomek, A.B., Sourander, A., Kumpulainen, K., Piha, J., Tamminen, T., Moilanen et al. (2008). Childhood bullying as a risk for later depression and suicidal ideation among Finnish males. *Journal of Affective Disorders*, 109(1–2), 47–55, doi: 10.1016/j.jad.2007.12.226.

Kochenderfer, B.J., & Ladd, G.W. (1996). Peer victimization: Cause or consequence of school maladjustment. *Child Development*, 67(4), 1305–1317, doi: 10.1111/j.1467-8624.1996.tb01797.x.

Kochenderfer, B.J., & Ladd, G.W. (1997). Victimized children's responses to peers' aggression: Behaviors associated with reduced versus continued victimization. *Development and Psychopathology*, 9(1), 59–73.

Kochenderfer-Ladd, B., & Pelletier, M.E. (2008). Teachers' views and beliefs about bullying: Influences on classroom management strategies and students' coping with peer victimization. *Journal of School Psychology*, 46(4), 431–453, doi: 10.1016/j.jsp.2007.07.005.

Kohn, A. (1987). The case against competition. *Working Mother*. Retrieved June 17, 2012 from www.alfiekohn.org/parenting/tcac.htm.

Kowalski, R.M., & Limber, S.P. (2007). Electronic bullying among middle school students. *Journal of Adolescent Health*, 41(6), S22–S30.

Kowalski, R.M., Limber, S.P., & Agatston, P. (2008). *Cyber bullying: Bullying in the digital age*. Malden, MA: Blackwell.

Kridler, W. (n.d.). *Help for "They won't let me play with them!"* Retrieved April 9, 2012 from www2.scholastic.com/browse/article.jsp?id=4113.

Krznaric, R. (2010). *Five ways to expand your empathy*. Retrieved July 25, 2012 from www.romankrznaric.com/outrospection/2010/01/01/324.

Kumpulainen, K., Rasanen, E., & Puura, K. (2001). Psychiatric disorders and the use of mental health services among children involved in bullying. *Aggressive Behavior*, 27(2), 102–110, doi: 10.1002/ab.3.

Langland, C. (2003). Students' first lesson: Getting along in peace. *Philadelphia Inquirer*, October 28. Retrieved January 7, 2012 from www.bridges4kids.org/articles/2003/10-03/PhillyInq10-28-03.html.

Larke, I.D., & Beran, T.N. (2006). The relationship between bullying and social skills in primary school students. *Issues in Educational Research*, 16(1), 38–51.

Larkin, R.W. (2009). The Columbine legacy: Rampage shootings as political acts. *American Behavioral Scientist*, 52(9), 1309–1326, doi: 10.1177/0002764209332548.

Lavoie, R. (2007). *Helping the socially isolated child make friends*. Retrieved November 11, 2011 from www.ldonline.org/article/Helping_the_Socially_Isolated_Child_Make_Friends.

Leary, M.R., Kowalski, R.M., Smith, L., & Phillips, S. (2003). Teasing, rejection, and violence: Case studies of the school shootings. *Aggressive Behavior*, 29(3), 202–214, doi: 10.1002/ab.10061.

Lenhart, A. (2007). *Cyberbullying and online teens*. Data memo from Pew Internet and American Life Project, June 27. Retrieved August 21, 2011 from www.pewinternet.org/~/media/Files/Reports/2007/PIP%20Cyberbullying%20Memo.pdf.pdf.

Lenhart, A., Purcell, K., Smith, A., & Zickuhr, K. (2010). *Social media and mobile internet use among teens and young adults*. Retrieved February 28, 2012 from www.rab.com/public/millennials/PewMobileSocial.pdf.

Lewis, T.J., Sugai, G., & Colvin, G. (1998). Reducing a problem behavior through a school-wide system of effective behavioral support: Investigation of a school-wide social skills training program and contextual interventions. *School Psychology Review*, (27)3, 446–459.

Libbey, H.P. (2004). Measuring student relationships to school: Attachment, bonding, connectedness, and engagement. *Journal of School Health*, 74(7), 274–283, doi: 10.1111/j.1746-1561.2004.tb08284.x.

Lickona, T. (2000). Sticks and stones may break my bones AND names WILL hurt me. *Our Children*, 26(1), 12–14. Retrieved November 18, 2011 from www.character-education.info/Articles/Preventing_Peer_Cruelty.htm.

Lieberman, A. (2006). *If you touch it, you bought it*. Retrieved March 11, 2012 from www.aish.com/tp/b/ll/48956091.html.

Luiselli, J.K., Putnam, R.F., Handler, M.W., & Feinberg, A.B. (2005). Whole school positive behavior support: Effects on student discipline problems and academic performance. *Educational Psychology*, 25(2–3), 183–198, doi: 10.1080/0144341042000301265.

Luukkonen, A. (2010). *Bullying behaviour in relation to psychiatric disorders, suicidality and criminal offences*. Oulu, Finland: University of Oulu. Retrieved May 4, 2012 from http://herkules.oulu.fi/isbn9789514263019/isbn9789514263019.pdf.

Macklem, G.L. (2003). *Bullying and teasing*. New York, NY: Kluwer Academic/Plenum.

Marsden, P. (1998). Memetics and social contagion: Two sides of the same coin? *Journal of Memetics—Evolutionary Models of Information Transmission*, 2. Retrieved June 8, 2010 from http://cfpm.org/jom-emit/1998/vol2/marsden_p.html.

Martin Niemoller Quotes. (n.d.). Retrieved May 21, 2012 from http://thinkexist.com/quotes/martin_niem%C3%B6ller.

McLaughlin, C., Arnold, R., & Boyd, E. (2005). Bystanders in schools: What do they do and what do they think? Factors influencing the behavior of English students as bystanders. *Pastoral Care*, 23(2), 17–22, doi: 10.1111/j.0264-3944.2005.00327.x.

McVey, L.J., Davis, D.E., & Cohen, H.J. (1989). The "aging game." An approach to education in geriatrics. *Journal of the American Medical Association*, 262(11), 1507–1509, doi: 10.1001/jama.1989.03430110097036.

Melissa Institute for Violence Prevention and Treatment. (n.d.). *Reducing bullying: Meeting the challenge*. Retrieved May 14, 2012 from www.teachsafeschools.org/Bully.pdf.

Mendler, B.D., Curwin, R.L., & Mendler, A.N. (2007). *Strategies for successful classroom management*. Thousand Oaks, CA: Corwin.

Menesini, E., Codecasa, E., Benelli, B., & Cowie, H. (2003). Enhancing children's responsibility to take action against bullying: Evaluation of a befriending intervention in Italian middle schools. *Aggressive Behavior*, 29(1), 1–14, doi: 10.1002/ab.80012.

Merrell, K.W., Gueldner, B.A., Ross, S.W., & Isava, D.M. (2008). How effective are school bullying intervention programs? A meta-analysis of intervention research. *School Psychology Quarterly*, 23(1), 26–42, doi: 10.1037/1045-3830.23.1.26.

Mian, R. (2011). LI teen rallies against bullying in Farmingdale. *LongIslandPress.com*, December 2. Retrieved December 15, 2011 from www.longislandpress.com/2011/12/02/li-teen-rallies-against-bullying-at-in- farmingdale.

Munsil, L., & Jolly, V. (2009). Did bullying lead to student's suicide? *The Orange County Register*, June 4.

Mynard, H., Joseph, S., & Alexander, J. (2000). Peer-victimisation and posttraumatic stress in adolescents. *Personality and Individual Differences*, 29(5), 815–821, doi: 10.1016/S0191-8869(99)00234-2.

Nakamoto, J., & Schwartz, D. (2010). Is peer victimization associated with academic achievement? A meta-analytic review. *Social Development*, 19(2), 221–242, doi: 10.1111/j.1467-9507.2009.00539.x.

Nansel, T.R., Overpeck, M., Haynie, D.L., Ruan, W.J., & Scheidt, P.C. (2003). Relationships between bullying and violence among US youth. *Archives of Pediatrics and Adolescent Medicine*, 157(4), 348–353.

Nansel, T.R., Overpeck, M., Pilla, R.S., Ruan, W.J., Simons-Morton, B., & Scheidt, P. (2001). Bullying behaviors among US Youth. *Journal of the American Medical Association*, 285(16), 2094–2100, doi: 10.1001/jama.285.16.2094.

National Association of Attorneys General. (2000). *Bruised inside: What our children say about youth violence, what causes it, and what we need to do about it.* Retrieved March 21, 2011 from www.ct.gov/ag/lib/ag/children/bruised.pdf.

National Center for Mental Health Promotion and Youth Violence Prevention. (2009). *An introduction to restorative justice.* Retrieved November 7, 2011 from www.promoteprevent.org/publications/prevention-briefs/introduction-restorative- justice.

National Centre for Restorative Justice in Youth Settings. (n.d.). *Restorative justice in school.* Retrieved April 10, 2012 from www.transformingconflict.org/Restorative_Justice_in_School.htm.

National Children's Bureau. (2004). *Peer support: An overview.* Retrieved May 14, 2011 from www.citized.info/pdf/external/ncb/Final_Peer_support_aw.pdf.

National Crime Prevention Council. (2008–2010). *McGruff Safeguard.* Retrieved June 8, 2012 from www.gomcgruff.com/m/index.asp.

Naylor, P., & Cowie, H. (1999). The effectiveness of peer support systems in challenging school bullying: The perspectives and experiences of teachers and pupils. *Journal of Adolescence*, 22(4), 467–479, doi: 10.1006/jado.1999.0241.

Newman, D. (2009). The tipping point (Review of the book *The tipping point: How little things can make a difference* by M. Gladwell). Retrieved January 28, 2012 from www.grassrootinstitute.org/system/old/Book_DVD_Reviews/INFO_Tipping.shtml.

Newton Public Schools Elementary Library Teachers. (2006). *Bullying K-5 recommended resources.* Retrieved September 22, 2012 from www.newton.k12.ma.us/libraries/documents/bullyingk_5.pdf.

Ochoa, M. (n.d.). 8 ways to welcome students. *Scholastic.* Retrieved July 21, 2012 from www2.scholastic.com/browse/article.jsp?id=3747342.

O'Connell, P., Pepler, D., & Craig, W. (1999). Peer involvement in bullying: Insights and challenges for intervention. *Journal of Adolescence*, 22(4), 437–452, doi: 10.1006/jado.1999.0238.

Oden, S., & Asher, S.R. (1977). Coaching children in social skills for friendship making. *Child Development*, 48(2), 495–506, doi: 10.2307/1128645.

Oliver, R., & Oaks, N.I. (1994). Family issues and interventions in bully and victim relationships. *School Counselor*, 41(3), 199–203.

Olweus, D. (1993a). *Bullying at school: What we know and what we can do*. Oxford, UK: Blackwell.

Olweus, D. (1993b). Bully/victim problems among schoolchildren: Long-term consequences and an effective intervention program. In S. Hodgins (Ed.), *Mental disorder and crime* (pp. 317–349). Newburg Park, CA: Sage Publications.

Olweus, D. (2011). Bullying at school and later criminality: Findings from three Swedish community samples of males. *Criminal Behaviour*, 21(2), 151–156, doi: 10.1002/cbm.806.

O'Moore, M. (2000). Critical issues for teacher training to counter bullying and victimization in Ireland. *Aggressive Behavior*, 26(1), 99–111, doi: 10.1002/(SICI)1098-2337(2000)26:1<99::AID-AB8>3.0.CO;2-W.

Orpinas, P., Horne, A.M., & Staniszewski, D. (2003). School bullying: Changing the problem by changing the school. *School Psychology Review*, 32(3), 431–444.

Paley, V.G. (1992). *You can't say you can't play*. Cambridge, MA: Harvard University Press.

Peer Support Australia. (n.d.). *Peers helping peers—Research into the effectiveness of the peer support program: Study conducted in 2003*. Retrieved October 13, 2011 from http://peersupport.edu.au/program_results.html.

Pellegrini, A.D., Bartini, M., & Brooks, F. (1999). School bullies, victims, and aggressive victims: Factors relating to group affiliation and victimization in early adolescence. *Journal of Educational Psychology*, (91)2, 216–224.

Pellegrini, A.D., Long, J.D., Solberg, D., Roseth, C., Dupis, D., Bohn, C. et al. (2010). Bullying and social status during school transitions. In S.R. Jimerson, S.M. Swearer, & D.L. Espelage (Eds.), *Handbook of bullying in schools: An international perspective* (pp. 199–210). New York, NY: Routledge.

Pepler, D.J. (2006). Bullying interventions: A binocular perspective. *Journal of the Canadian Academy of Child and Adolescent Psychiatry*, (15)1, 16–20.

Pepler, D.J., & Craig, W. (2000). *Making a difference in bullying* (Report #60). Toronto, Canada: York University. Retrieved May 23, 2012 from www.melissainstitute.org/documents/MakingADifference.pdf.

Pepler, D.J., Craig, W., Connolly, J., & Henderson, K. (2002). Bullying, sexual harassment, dating violence, and substance use among adolescents. In C. Wekerle, & A.M. Wall (Eds.), *The violence and addiction equation: Theoretical and clinical issues in substance abuse and relationship violence* (pp. 153–168). Philadelphia, PA: Brunner/Mazel.

Petersen, K.S. (2008). *Safe & caring schools grades 3–5*. Minneapolis, MN: Free Spirit Publishing.

Petrosino, A., Guckenburg, S., DeVoe, J., & Hanson, T. (2010). *What characteristics of bullying, bullying victims, and schools are associated with increased reporting of bullying to school officials?* (Issues & Answers Report, REL 2010—No. 092). Washington, DC: U.S. Department of Education, Institute of Education Sciences, National Center for Education Evaluation and Regional Assistance, Regional Educational Laboratory Northeast and Islands. Retrieved February 27, 2012 from http://ies.ed.gov/ncee/edlabs/projects/project.asp?ProjectID=239.

Phillips, R., Linney, J., & Pack, C. (2008). *Safe school ambassadors*. San Francisco, CA: Jossey-Bass.

Porter, H.C. (2006). *The bully and me*. Kelowna, Canada: Northstone.

Powell, M.D., & Ladd, L.D. (2010). Bullying: A review of the literature and implications for family therapists. *American Journal of Family Therapy*, 38(3), 189–206, doi: 10.1080/01926180902961662.

Pranis, K. (n.d.). *Guide for implementing the balanced and restorative justice model* (NCJ 167887). Retrieved October 10, 2011 from www.ojjdp.gov/pubs/implementing/accountability.html.

Promoting Relationships and Eliminating Violence Network (PREVNet). (2007a). *Bullying in schools: Guidelines for intervention and prevention*. Retrieved March 20, 2012 from http://prevnet.ca/LinkClick.aspx?fileticket=12OoTroJx9Q%3d&tabid=391.

Promoting Relationships and Eliminating Violence Network (PREVNet). (2007b). *Making a difference in bullying: What teachers of elementary students need to know*. Retrieved March 20, 2012 from http://prevnet.ca/LinkClick.aspx?fileticket=%2fOcuHPgCMjI%3d&tabid=39.

Putallaz, M., & Gottman, J.M. (1981). An interactional model of children's entry into peer groups. *Child Development*, 52(3), 986–994, doi: 10.1111/1467-8624.ep8861532.

Putallaz, M., & Wasserman, A. (1989). Children's naturalistic entry behavior and sociometric status: A developmental perspective. *Developmental Psychology*, 25(2), 297–305, doi: 10.1037/0012-1649.25.2.297.

Quabbin Mediation. (n.d.). *Training active bystanders*. Retrieved March 31, 2009 from www.quabbinmediation.org/html/tab.html. (No longer available.)

Ragozzino, K., & O'Brien, M.U. (2009). *Social and emotional learning and bullying prevention*. Educational Development Center. Retrieved May 21, 2011 from www.promoteprevent.org/sites/default/files/root/materials/NCPublicationsTools/SE LBullying.pdf.

Ramsey *v.* State, No. A-7295. (2002). Retrieved April 22, 2012 from http://caselaw.lp.findlaw.com/data2/alaskastatecases/2002/ap-1832.pdf.

Renda, J., Vassallo, S., & Edwards, B. (2011). Bullying in early adolescence and its association with anti-social behaviour, criminality and violence 6 and 10 years later. *Behaviour*, 21(2), 117–127, doi: 10.1002/cbm.805.

Rigby, K. (1997). What children tell us about bullying in schools. *Children Australia*, 22(2), 28–34. Retrieved September 7, 2011 from www.education.unisa.edu.au/bullying/childtelus.htm.

Rigby, K. (2003). Consequences of bullying in school. *Canadian Journal of Psychiatry*, 48(9), 583–590.

Rigby, K., & Johnson, B. (2005). Student bystanders in Australian schools. *Pastoral Care*, 23(2), 10–16, doi: 10.1111/j.0264-3944.2005.00326.x.

Rigby, K., & Johnson, B. (2006). Expressed readiness of Australian schoolchildren to act as bystanders in support of children who are being bullied. *Educational Psychology*, 26(3), 425–440, doi: 10.1080/01443410500342047.

Ritter, J. (2002). AMA puts doctors on lookout for bullying. *Chicago Sun-Times*, June 20.

Rizzo, T.A. (1989). *Friendship development among children in school*. Norwood, NJ: Ablex Publishing Corporation.

Robers, S., Zhang, J., Truman, J., & Snyder, T.D. (2010). *Indicators of school crime and safety: 2010* (NCES 2011-002/NCJ 230812). Washington, DC: National Center for Education Statistics, U.S. Department of Education, and Bureau of Justice Statistics, Office of Justice Programs, U.S. Department of Justice. Retrieved August 21, 2011 from http://nces.ed.gov/pubs2011/2011002.pdf.

Roberts Jr., W.B. (2006). *Bullying from both sides*. Thousand Oaks, CA: Corwin.

Roberts Jr., W.B., & Coursol, D.H. (1996). Strategies for intervention with childhood and adolescent victims of bullying, teasing, and intimidation in school settings. *Elementary School Guidance & Counseling*, 30(3), 204–212.

Roou, D. (2004). Fighting the lunchroom bully. *Principal Leadership*, 4(5), 27–29.

Ross, D.M. (2003). *Childhood bullying, teasing, and violence: What school personnel, other professions, and parents can do* (2nd ed.). Alexandria, VA: American Counseling Association.

Salmivalli, C. (1999). Participant role approach to school bullying: Implications for interventions. *Journal of Adolescence*, 22(4), 453–459, doi: 10.1006/jado.1999.0239.

Salmivalli, C. (2010). Bullying and the peer group: A review. *Aggression and Violent Behavior*, 15(2), 112–120, doi: 10.1016/j.avb.2009.08.007.

Salmivalli, C., Huttunen, A., & Lagerspetz, K.M.J. (1997). Peer networks and bullying in schools. *Scandinavian Journal of Psychology*, 38(4), 305–312, doi: 10.1111/1467-9450.00040.

Salmivalli, C., Karna, A., & Poskiparta., E. (2010). From peer putdowns to peer support: A theoretical model and how it translated into a national anti-bullying program. In S.R. Jimerson, S.M. Swearer, & D.L. Espelage (Eds.), *Handbook of bullying in schools: An international perspective* (pp. 441–454). New York, NY: Routledge.

Salmivalli, C., Lagerspetz, K.M.J., Bjorkqvist, K., Osterman, K., & Kaukianen, A. (1996). Bullying as a group process: Participant roles and their relations to social status within the group. *Aggressive Behavior*, 22(1), 1–15, doi: 10.1002/(SICI)1098-2337(1996)22:1<1::AID-AB1>3.0.CO;2-T.

Salmivalli, C., Lappalainen, M., & Lagerspetz, K.M.J. (1998). Stability and change of behavior in connection with bullying in schools: A two-year follow-up. *Aggressive Behavior*, 24(3), 205–218, doi: 10.1002/(SICI)1098-2337(1998)24:3<205::AID-AB5>3.0.CO;2-J.

Sapon-Shevin, M. (2005). Ability differences in the classroom: Teaching and learning in inclusive classrooms. In D. Byrnes, & G. Kiger (Eds.), *Common bonds: Anti-bias teaching in a diverse society*, 3rd ed. (pp. 37–51). Olney, MD: Association for Childhood Education International. Retrieved April 12, 2012 from www.sig2.hawaii.edu/resources/briefings/topic7/downloads/articles/pdf/Article01.pdf.

Sapon-Shevin, M., Ayres, B.J., & Duncan, J. (1994) Cooperative learning and inclusion. In J. Thousand, R. Villa, & A. Nevins (Eds.), *Creativity and collaborative learning: A practical guide to empowering students and teachers* (pp. 45–58). Baltimore, MD: Brookes.

Saxon, R. (2005). Kindness curbs kids' name-calling. *Education Digest*, 70(6), 8–13.

Scaglione, J., & Scaglione, A.R. (2006). *Bully-proofing children: A practical, hands-on guide to stop bullying*. Lanham, MD: Rowman & Littlefield Education.

Schafer, M., & Smith, P.K. (1996). Teachers' perceptions of play fighting and real fighting in primary school. *Educational Research*, 38(2), 173–181, doi: 10.1080/0013188960380205.

Schwartz, D., Dodge, K.A., Pettit, G.S., & Bates, J.E. (1997). The early socialization of aggressive victims of bullying. *Child Development*, 68(4), 665–675, doi: 10.1111/1467- 8624.ep971002 1682.

Seeley, K., Tombari, M.L., Bennett, L.J., & Dunkle, J.B. (2011). *Bullying in schools: An overview*. Retrieved May 15, 2012 from www.ojjdp.gov/pubs/234205.pdf.

Sentse, M., Scholte, R., Salmivalli, C., & Voeten, M. (2007). Person–group dissimilarity in involvement in bullying and its relation with social status. *Journal of Abnormal Child Psychology*, 35(6), 1009–1019, doi: 10.1007/s10802-007-9150-3.

Servant, A. (2006). *Top ten strategies for a good classroom community*. Retrieved May 9, 2009 from www.associatedcontent.com/article/66282/top_ten_strategies_for_a_good_classroom.html?cat=4. (No longer available.)

Sharp, S. (2001). Peer-led approaches to care. *Pastoral Care*, 19(4), 21–24, doi: 10.1111/1468-0122.00208.

Sharp, S., & Cowie, H. (1998). *Counseling and supporting children in distress*. London, UK: Sage.

Shore, K.A. (2003). *Elementary teacher's discipline problem solver*. San Francisco, CA: Jossey-Bass.

Simon, S.B. (1973). *I am lovable and capable: A modern allegory of the classical put-down.* Niles, IL: Argus Communications. Retrieved June 14, 2009 from www.eric.ed.gov/PDFS/ED086582.pdf.

Simpson, M.D. (2011). *Rights watch: Confronting the bullies.* Retrieved January 13, 2012 from www.nea.org/home/43496.htm.

Singleton, M. (1997). *Dare to care: An innovative program teaching elementary school students the importance of caring.* Retrieved June 21, 2009 from www.eric.ed.gov/PDFS/ED415975.pdf.

Skapinakis, P., Bellos, S., Gkatsa, T., Magklara, K., Lewis, G., Araya, R. et al. (2011). The association between bullying and early stages of suicidal ideation in late adolescents in Greece. *BMC Psychiatry*, 11(1), 22–30, doi: 10.1186/1471-244X-11-22.

Slavin, R.E. (1991). Synthesis of research on cooperative learning. *Educational Leadership*, 48(5), 71–82.

Smith, D.L., & Smith, B.J. (2006). Perceptions of violence: The views of teachers who left urban schools. *The High School Journal*, 89(3), 34–42.

Smith, K. (2010). *"We don't do that here": Lincoln Olbrycht's story* (Web log post, September 22), Developmental Studies Center. Retrieved July 12, 2012 from www.devstu.org/blogs/2010/09/22/we-dont-do-that-here-lincoln-olbrychts-story.

Smith, P.K. (2011). Why interventions to reduce bullying and violence in schools may (or may not) succeed: Comments on this special issue. *International Journal of Behavioral Development*, 35(5), 419–423, doi: 10.1177/0165025411407459.

Smith, P.K., & Slonje, R. (2010). Cyberbullying: The nature and extent of a new kind of bullying, in and out of school. In S.R. Jimerson, S.M. Swearer, & D.L. Espelage. *Handbook of bullying in schools: An international perspective* (pp. 249–262). New York, NY: Routledge.

Sourander, A., Helstela, L., Helenius, H., & Piha, J. (2000). Persistence of bullying from childhood to adolescence: A longitudinal 8-year follow-up study. *Child Abuse & Neglect*, 24(7), 873–881, doi: /10.1016/S0145-2134(00)00146-0.

Srabstein, J. (2008). Deaths linked to bullying and hazing. *International Journal of Adolescent Medicine and Health*, 20(2), 235–239. Abstract retrieved July 19, 2011 from www.safetylit.org/citations/index.php?fuseaction=citations.viewdetails&citationIds[]=citjournalarticle_89653_24.

Starr, L. (2004). *Bullying and diversity lesson: What's your name?* Retrieved January 21, 2012 from www.educationworld.com/a_lesson/00-2/lp2061.shtml.

Starr, L. (2009). *Names can hurt you: De-myth-tifying the classroom bully.* Retrieved November 9, 2012 from www.educationworld.com/a_issues/issues102.shtml.

Storch, E.A., & Esposito, L.E. (2003). Peer victimization and posttraumatic stress among children. *Child Study Journal*, 33(2), 91–98.

Storey, K., & Slaby, R. (2008). *Eyes on bullying: What can you do?* Newton, MA: Education Development Center. Retrieved May 4, 2012 from www.eyesonbullying.org/pdfs/toolkit.pdf.

Strauss, V. (2010). New data on bullying: 17% report regular abuse. *The Washington Post*, October 20. Retrieved October 26, 2010 from http://voices.washingtonpost.com/answer-sheet/bullying/2010bullyvictimdata.html.

Sullivan, K., Cleary, M., & Sullivan, G. (2004). *Bullying in secondary schools: What it looks like and how to manage it.* London, UK: Paul Chapman.

Sutton, J., Smith, P.K., & Swettenham, J. (1999). Bullying and "theory of mind": A critique of the "social skills deficit" view of anti-social behavior. *Social Development*, 8(1), 117–127, doi: 10.1111/1467-9507.00083.

Tokunaga, R.S. (2010). Following you home from school: A critical review and synthesis of research on cyberbullying victimization. *Computers in Human Behavior*, 26(3), 277–287, doi: 10.1016/j.chb.2009.11.014.

Ttofi, M.M., Farrington, D.P., Losel, F., & Loeber, R. (2011). The predictive efficiency of school bullying versus later offending: A systematic/meta-analytic review of longitudinal studies. *Criminal Behaviour and Mental Health*, 21(2), 80–89, doi: 10.1002/cbm.808.

Twemlow, S.W., Fonagy, P., & Sacco, F.C. (2001). An innovative psychodynamically influenced approach to reduce school violence. *Journal of the American Academy of Child & Adolescent Psychiatry*, 40(3), 377–379, doi: 10.1097/00004583-200103000-00019.

Twemlow, S.W., Fonagy, P., Sacco, F.C., & Brethour Jr., J.R. (2006). Teachers who bully students: A hidden trauma. *International Journal of Social Psychiatry*, 52(3), 187–198, doi: 10.1177/0020764006067234.

Unnever, J.D. (2005). Bullies, aggressive victims, and victims: Are they distinct groups? *Aggressive Behavior*, 31(2), 153–171, doi: 10.1002/ab.20083.

U.S. Department of Commerce. (2010). *Back to school: 2010–2011* (CB10-FF.14). Retrieved November 20, 2011 from www.census.gov/newsroom/releases/pdf/cb10ff-14_school.pdf.

U.S. Department of Health and Human Services. (n.d.). *Recognizing the warning signs*. Retrieved January 9, 2012 from www.stopbullying.gov/topics/warning_signs.

U.S. Department of Health and Human Services, Health Resources and Services Administration (HRSA). (n.d.). *How to intervene to stop bullying: Tips for on-the-spot intervention at school*. Retrieved April 12, 2012 from http://safeschools.state.co.us/docs/SBN_Tip_4%20How%20to%20 Intervene.pdf.

U.S. Department of Health and Human Services, Substance Abuse and Mental Health Services Administration (SAMHSA). (n.d.). *Suicide: Some answers*. Retrieved May 4, 2010 from www.samhsa.gov/prevention/suicide.aspx.

U.S. Department of Labor, Bureau of Labor Statistics. (2010). *Education pays*. Retrieved February 11, 2012 from www.bls.gov/emp/ep_chart_001.htm.

Vaillancourt, T., Brittain, H., Bennett, L., Arnocky, S., McDougall, P., Hymel, S. et al. (2010). Places to avoid: Population-based study of student reports of unsafe and high bullying areas at school. *Canadian Journal of School Psychology*, 25(1), 40–54, doi: 10.1177/0829573509358686.

Vaillancourt, T., Hymel, S., & McDougall, P. (2007). Bullying is power: Implications for school-based intervention strategies. In J.E. Zins, M.J. Elias, & C.A. Maher (Eds.), *Bullying, victimization, and peer harassment* (pp. 317–337). New York, NY: Haworth.

Van Acker, R., & Talbott, E. (1999). The school context and risk for aggression: Implications for school-based prevention and intervention efforts. *Preventing School Failure*, 44(1), 12–20.

Van der Wal, M.F., de Wit, C.A.M., & Hirasing, R.A. (2003). Psychosocial health among young victims and offenders of direct and indirect bullying. *Pediatrics*, 111(6), 1312–1317.

Vaughan, K., & Clarke, N. (1999). Note blames the victims. *Rocky Mountain News*, April 24. Retrieved May 8, 2010, from www.rockymountainnews.com/news/1999/apr/24/note-blames-victims.

Veenstra, R., Lindenberg, S., Munniksma, A., & Dijkstra, J.K. (2010). The complex relation between bullying, victimization, acceptance, and rejection: Giving special attention to status, affection, and sex differences. *Child Development*, 81(2), 480–486, doi: 10.1111/j.1467-8624.2009.01411.x.

Vieno, A., Gini, G., & Santinello, M. (2011). Different forms of bullying and their association to smoking and drinking behavior in Italian adolescents. *Journal of School Health*, 81(7), 393–399, doi: 10.1111/j.1746-1561.2011.00607.x.

Vossekuil, B., Fein, R.A., Reddy, M., Borum, R., & Modzeleski, W. (2002). *The final report and findings of the safe school initiative: Implications for the prevention of school attacks in the United States*. U.S. Department of Education, Office of Elementary and Secondary Education,

Safe and Drug-Free Schools Programs and U.S. Secret Service, National Threat Assessment Center, Washington, DC. Retrieved December 4, 2011 from www.ed.gov/admins/lead/safety/preventingattacksreport.pdf.

Wang, J., Nansel, T.R., & Iannotti, R.J. (2011). Cyber and traditional bullying: Differential association with depression. *Journal of Adolescent Health*, 48(4), 415–417, doi: 10.1016/j.jadohealth.2010.07.012.

Wessler, S.L. (2003). It's hard to learn when you're scared. *Educational Leadership*, 61(1), 40–43.

Whitaker, P., Barratt, P., Joy, H., Potter, M., & Thomas, G. (1998). Children with autism and peer group support: Using "circles of friends." *British Journal of Special Education*, 25(2), 60–64, doi: 10.1111/1467-8527.t01-1-00058.

Wilde, M. (n.d.). *The bully and the bystander*. Retrieved May 12, 2012 from www.greatschools.org/parenting/bullying/the-bully-and-the bystander.gs?content=593&page=1.

Willard, N. (2007). *An educator's guide to cyberbullying and cyberthreats*. Retrieved December 1, 2009 from http://csriu.org/cyberbully/documents/educatorsguide.pdf.

Williams, K., Chambers, M., Logan, S., & Robinson, D. (1996) Association of common health symptoms with bullying in primary school children. *British Medical Journal*, 313(7048), 17–19.

Wilton, M.M.M., Craig, W.M., & Pepler, D.J. (2000). Emotional regulation and display in classroom victims of bullying: Characteristic expressions of affect, coping styles and relevant contextual factors. *Social Development*, 9(2), 226–245, doi: 10.1111/1467- 9507.00121.

WiredSafety.org. (2012). What are Teenangels? We are pleased that you asked! Retrieved June 27, 2012 from www.teenangels.org.

Yale University. (2008). Bullying and being bullied linked to suicide in children, review of studies suggests. *ScienceDaily*, July 19. Retrieved August 21, 2011 from www.sciencedaily.com/releases/2008/07/080717170428.

Ybarra, M.L., Diener-West, M., & Leaf, P.J. (2007). Examining the overlap in internet harassment and school bullying: Implications for school intervention. *Journal of Adolescent Health*, 41(6, Suppl 1), S42–S50, doi: 10.1016/j.jadohealth.2007.09.004.

Yenne, L. (n.d.). *Special needs awareness week*. Retrieved July 16, 2011 from www.kinf.org/bestprac/misc/special.pdf.

Yoneyama, S., & Naito, A. (2003). Problems with the paradigm: The school as a factor in understanding bullying (with special reference to Japan). *British Journal of Sociology of Education*, 24(3), 315–330, doi: 10.1080/01425690301894.

Zehr, H. (2002). *The little book of restorative justice*. Intercourse, PA: Good Books.

# Index

Note: Page numbers in **bold** indicate boxes.